AESTHETICS

Key Concepts in Philosophy

Continuum *Key Concepts in Philosophy*

Key Concepts in Philosophy is a series of concise, accessible and engaging introductions to the core ideas and subjects encountered in the study of philosophy. Specially written to meet the needs of students and those with an interest in, but little prior knowledge of, philosophy, these books open up fascinating, yet sometimes difficult ideas. The series builds to give a solid grounding in philosophy and each book is also ideal as a companion to further study.

Key Concepts in Philosophy available from Continuum:

Aesthetics

Key Concepts in Philosophy

Daniel Herwitz

continuum

Continuum International Publishing Group
The Tower Building
11 York Road
London SE1 7NX

80 Maiden Lane
Suite 704
New York
NY 10038

www.continuumbooks.com

British Library Cataloguing-in-Publication Data
A catalogue record for this book is available from the British Library.

ISBN-10: HB: 0-8264-8918-4
PB: 0-8264-8919-2
ISBN-13: HB: 978-0-8264-8918-0
PB: 978-0-8264-8919-7

Library of Congress Cataloging-in-Publication Data

Herwitz, Daniel Alan, 1955–
    Aesthetics : key concepts in philosophy / Daniel Herwitz.
        p. cm.
    Includes bibliographical references.
    ISBN-13: 978-0-8264-8918-0 (HB)
    ISBN-10: 0-8264-8918-4 (HB)
    ISBN-13: 978-0-8264-8919-7 (pbk.)
    ISBN-10: 0-8264-8919-2 (pbk.)
    1. Aesthetics. I. Title.
    BH39.H474 2008
    111'.85—dc22

2007039680

Typeset by Servis Filmsetting Ltd, Manchester
Printed and bound in Great Britain by
Cromwell Press Ltd, Trowbridge, Wiltshire

TABLE OF CONTENTS

ACKNOWLEDGEMENTS

This book is the result of conversations with Ted Cohen, Lydia Goehr, Michael Kelly, and Kendall Walton, and of a half-life of teaching, with contributions from a generation of students. I wish to thank the University of Michigan Aesthetics Seminar for sharp discussion of the section on film.

Selections from this book have made earlier, similar appearance in *Modern Painters*, the *Journal of Aesthetics* and *Art Criticism*, *Action, Art, History: Engagements with Arthur Danto* (edited by Daniel Herwitz and Michael Kelly, copyright Columbia University Press, 2007, reprinted with permission of the publisher) and *Blank: Art, Apartheid and After*.

I wish to thank the Lille P. Bliss Bequest and the Museum of Modern Art for the rights to a reproduction of Picasso's *Les Demoiselles d'Avignon*, and the Andy Warhol Foundation for rights to a reproduction of Warhol's *Brillo Box*.

This book is dedicated to the memory of Richard Wollheim, dazzling philosopher and wonderful friend, whose writings have always been for me exemplary.

CHAPTER 1

INTRODUCTION

This is a book of openings, not of conclusions. It aims to introduce students to key concepts, or better, questions in aesthetics. The book is meant to stimulate questioning, to make the reader want to think more and read more, rather than attempting to supply the reader with an end of story, or set of answers. The approach is also to limn something of the vastness of aesthetics, something not always done in books of this kind. What distinguishes this book is the wide approach it takes, while remaining focused on philosophy. Aesthetics has suffered because of the institutional divide in Anglo-American humanities departments which have bifurcated it into philosophy on the one hand and reflection on art and beauty from within the rest of what is called Arts and Letters. This bifurcation is a product of the eighteenth century, which set aesthetics as a distinct branch of philosophy, a 'science' as it was then called, and of the nineteenth century with its formation of the disciplines and forms of disciplinary knowledge (Foucault), each to its own end. Ours is the legacy of those centuries.

Aesthetics is in the first instance a branch of philosophy, just as, within the current system of the disciplines, ethics is. If you are a student of public policy you will in all likelihood be told to take a philosophy course if you want to do ethics. And yet questions of the right, the good, of human rights and institutional justice are in this global world of humanitarianism, political science and public policy important domains of ethics done outside of philosophy, in alliance with its concepts, relying on them, yes, but equally, inventing new ones for philosophy. Philosophers have themselves branched out; some work for the United Nations, in healthcare, and in government; some continue to do philosophy in transformed form, in a new register of thought. Similarly while the central focus of aesthetics has been the legacy of its birth as a 'science' in the eighteenth century and its institutionalization as part of the discipline of philosophy in the nineteenth, it has wide scope, and this scope is central to demonstrating its importance for human life. Avant-garde and modern art has devoted itself to, for example, abstract reflection on what art is – a reflection as refined, audacious or experimental as the art objects these movements have produced. This kind of reflection is often called Art Theory, but is a cousin to the enterprise of philosophical aesthetics and in a broad sense part of it. This is particularly true because its thoughts, say associated with art critic Clement Greenberg or Michael Fried, have returned to philosophy and become the subject of intense debate there. Central to modern theatre has been writing about what theatre is which has similarly returned to philosophy through the writings of Stanislavski, Brecht and Beckett. From the moment film was invented at the end of the nineteenth century a furious reflection has taken place among critics, intellectuals, free thinking modernists and filmmakers – in the medium of essay but also film image and screenplay – about what film is. The richness of aesthetics consists in the many cultural positions from which reflection on art, beauty, sublimity, nature, emotion, intuition and experience has taken shape. And so two things are true: first, one fails to understand what aesthetics is without understanding its primary association with philosophy (in the eighteenth and nineteenth centuries and their legacy today); second, one fails to appreciate the cross-currents of thought that comprise the subject if one does not appreciate that it is also a property of Arts and Letters generally and that it loops back from the broad quarters of Arts and Letters to philosophy. The bifurcation of philosophy from Arts and Letters is an institutional issue (pertinent to the ideologies and social organization of the university, of publishing and so on). It is not an accurate representation of how thought about art and beauty has taken shape since the eighteenth century.

This book is a book in philosophy and for philosophy students, but also a book for students of literature, art, music, film, television and architecture because it seeks to reveal the central focus of aesthetics within philosophy, and also the wide scope of thinking about art and beauty in modern times. The book is partly about cross-currents between these forms of reflection across the humanities and arts (Arts and Letters).

The best of philosophical aesthetics has almost always aimed at producing a dialogue between art, the broad intellectual currents of the time and the history and practice of philosophy. Between system and culture, aesthetics has lived for David Hume, G. W. F. Hegel, R. G. Collingwood, Clive Bell, Roger Fry, Richard Wollheim and Arthur Danto, to name a few key players in this particular trade. These writer/philosophers have all relied deeply upon the certainties and uncertainties of their experience of art and beauty, staking their own self-trust and confusion in relation to public dialogue about the arts, and assimilating these into larger philosophical issues which have exercised them, about knowledge, science, history, truth, human identity, morals and so on. Such thinkers have always relied on companion critics, historians, writers of all kinds, in thinking through their subjects. Hume was himself a critic and historian of note who earned a living by writing to order about these topics and worked in public life (Hume was never able to get a position in a university on account of his religious scepticism). John Dewey, the great American philosophical liberal and pragmatist thinker, wrote *Art as Experience* in dialogue with Albert Barnes, collector of the new modernism in painting, in constant, stunning view of Matisse, Picasso and the ebullience of Parisian modernism. These works of art blew the man away and his views about the chaotic depths of aesthetic experience derive from that fact. And so Collingwood, writing about art as expression (in *The Principles of Art*) assimilated (in the 1930s) work of Sigmund Freud and his then revolutionary views of the unconscious, and of Marcel Proust and his literature of recollection, along with general concepts of history and human expression upon which he was working in his philosophy of history. Roger Fry articulated his theories of significant form in direct response to cubism: Fry was himself a cubist painter. Hegel articulated his theses about the historical role of art as cultural expression as part of his vast historical synopsis. His theory of the end of art in the light of his highly optimistic belief that history had come to completion in his generation, indeed finished up in his very lap. One could go on to speak of the importance of early film critics and early films, and of Shakespearian comedy for Stanley Cavell. Or of the importance of post-war British figurative painting with its chaotic globules of human flesh and physiognomy, psychoanalysis, the art criticism of Adrian Stokes, and the experience of being a novelist for Richard Wollheim. Hume believes he is capable of explaining taste and judgement only because he is a master of both, and aims in his masterpiece 'Of the Standard of Taste' to rhetorically convince the reader of those qualities. Philosophy lives because of the philosophy which came before it, because of the philosophy which is happening all around it as it writes about aesthetics and art; but philosophical aesthetics also arises out of the experience of art and beauty and through intense dialogue with Arts and Letters, not to mention the historical urgencies of morals, society and self which have made it impossible for such thinkers not to think, for such writers not to write. There are exceptions, Kant being the most celebrated. But these are exceptions, not the rule. Even Kant is influenced by the politics and silence of his times if not the art.

If philosophers have often relied on broad currents of intellectual thought – not to mention intense engagement with the art of their time – in formulating their thoughts, those outside of philosophy have often approached it in writing as they write. Clement Greenberg relies on Kant (as he understands Kant anyway) in formulating his analysis of the avant-gardes. Erwin Panofsky is Hegelian to the core in approaching the aesthetics of art history. These thinkers appropriate philosophy in formulating their thoughts on style, medium, expression. It was a central focus of Hegel's aesthetics to argue that even art itself (great art anyway) is implicitly philosophical, a form of 'absolute spirit', a form of self-reflective thinking in paint or tone rather than word or paragraph, in story rather than argument, in gesture and implicature rather than proof and demonstration. Hegel will be taken up in Chapter 4. Art becomes philosophy proper when the philosopher brings out its inner voice (which is the voice of the thinker) through a process of clarification/translation. It is like supplying the words for a man who is stumbling upon a great idea without quite being able to articulate it, in whose genius the idea appears intuitively, in the form of a radiant image which needs to be analytically unpacked. This is simply a change in form, not a change in its line of work. For the trade of art has always been the same trade, according to Hegel, as the philosopher's: the knowledge trade, knowledge about self, identity, society, truth with a capital T.

This idea that art is aesthetics because it is in the knowledge business in some obscurely philosophical way is as old as Aristotle, who claimed that poetry is more philosophical than history because it reveals the inner workings of human action and the human soul (according to the laws of probability and necessity) rather than simply telling us what happened (which is what Aristotle believed history does). The claim that art is in the knowledge trade is a long-standing one in philosophy. Either art is worthwhile because it more or less delivers knowledge (in implicit form, through narrative, whatever) or it lacks integrity because it is willful, obscurantist, seductive, champagne fizzing before the mind, clouding its every capacity, dulling its every portal.

The final chapter (Chapter 6) of this book will consider the complex question of art and truth, a question about the ways the arts have of meditating on their own media and identities, and the kind of translation at stake in re-describing this as philosophical in gel. The point here is that there is a real question about what is at stake in thinking of art as doing philosophical aesthetics or some adjunct enterprise on occasion, if not always, and conversely there is a real problem with the philosophical measurement which requires it (like some staff sergeant) to measure up (chin in, chest out) in this regard or be consigned to the ranks of French perfume.

Of course a French perfume is a thing of beauty, the object (like wine) of international competitions and judgements of experts and whizzes. Which shows that matters of taste (in wine, food, perfume, clothes, houses, furniture, pure bred dogs, hair colour and abs – aerobicized or not) are not the same as matters of art within the ranks of some philosophy. The question of how taste and art relate will be a key question in Chapter 3. More broadly the concern now is between various ways the game of aesthetics are played – inside and outside of philosophy, inside and outside of art. And by inside art can also be meant an artist's turning to 'theory' in the course of articulating a position about what art is, that would open a space for his or her new creation, and seek to influence its understanding, shape its experience. El Lizzitsky does this, and John Cage, and Pierre Boulez by writing volumes; Andy Warhol does it by writing diaries about what's on sale in Bloomingdales and who the Velvet Underground slept with on a particular night. What is the relation between reflection on art (or life or consumerism or celebrity) by an artist in the throes of staking himself or herself into the domain of the art of the future (be it the new revolutionary society or the expanded mini-mall), and reflection on it by a philosopher writing out of the discipline he or she inherited from the eighteenth and nineteenth centuries? Arthur Danto goes so far as to call Warhol a philosopher in dark glasses, a genius avant-la-lettre. Perhaps he too is a philosopher of the Hegelian kind: implicit, waiting for a Hegel, that is, Danto to come along and clarify/translate his achievement, thus substantiating its truth and bringing it to fruition (see Chapter 5).

This attempt to focus widely on aesthetics may be found in the *Encyclopedia of Aesthetics* edited by my colleague Michael Kelly (of which I was a sub-editor).[1] This book is allied to that encyclopedia project. Much of its discussion is about 'philosophers': Hume, Kant, Hegel, Dewey, Danto, Wollheim, Derrida and others. But it is also about filmmakers, art critics, historians and others across the arts and humanities. Its point is partly to understand how the various ways these persons approach aesthetics are similar and different – and how they depend upon one another. Aesthetics might be thought of as an enterprise in the spirit of what twentieth century philosopher Ludwig Wittgenstein called a 'language game'. Wittgenstein thinks of language generally as a set of games, and has this to say about what a game is:

> Consider . . . the proceedings that we call 'games'. I mean board-games, card-games, ball-games, Olympic games, and so on. What is common to them all? . . . you will not see something that is common to *all*, but . . . we see a complicated network of similarities overlapping and criss-crossing: sometimes overall similarities, sometimes similarities of detail.
>
> I can think of no better expression to characterize these similarities than 'family resemblances'.[2]

There is no essential definition to a language game, no single set of features which make all the things we want to call 'games' into games. Rather, there are strands of similarity and difference, and the interesting question becomes: how are these games related? Aesthetics is a widely practised game; important for human thought. But it is practised in a number of different ways. This book will be about those ways, but also about the history of the subject, how it came to be constituted in philosophy as a distinct enterprise. This happened in the eighteenth century, which the following two chapters are about. It is a moment when philosophy applied its particular span of methods to the task of understanding, and defining, the beautiful. It is a moment when these methods trumped kinds of writing offered by the humanities generally, and in doing so, seemed to divorce the subject of aesthetics from its rightful place in the larger sphere of Arts and Letters.

This book is about the immense contribution of philosophy to thinking about art and beauty since the eighteenth century. But also about how this self-proclaimed divorce between philosophical methods and those of the humanities generally put aesthetics, ironically, in a corner, one unappreciated by the wider humanities which it is in fact so central to. By understanding the genealogy of this divorce, both the philosophical contribution and the artificial separation may be absorbed. That is the key concept here.

Central to the philosophical method applied in the eighteenth century (although not, as we shall see, uniformly; Hume for one resisted it) is the method of 'essential definition'. The goal of essentialist definitions is to explain exactly what makes a thing a thing, what is necessary to its composition, and what is sufficient to make it what it is. With a list of necessary and sufficient conditions in hand we can say exactly what makes music music and not another thing (mere noise for example), beauty beauty (and not mere attractiveness for example), art art (and not nature or mere language or drawing for example), and so forth. This goal of essential definition has been a central tendency within the history of philosophy. And with good reason: the world is like Descartes' wax, constantly fickle in its changes of shape, chaotic and inscrutable to perception, something we must gradually make our way through as knowers and actors. There is a reason why philosophy has aimed for clarity and control over what William James called the blooming buzzing confusions of human experience. Without an established order to perception, the world, the structure of beliefs, there could be neither knowledge nor any other kind of human interaction that would prove sustainable. Just as the human sense organs, the human mind, language and society provide order to the world, in category and concept, domain and range, so it is a worthy goal to heighten these forms of knowing and arranging, which has been a central tendency of philosophy. Where there is order and definition, there is conceptual control over the vagaries of matter.

The eighteenth century was about defining beauty and the sublime, the nineteenth about defining art. We have, in the present, inherited both. The project of philosophical definition and all that goes with it has been so central to the subject, and advanced it so far, that there would be no subject at all called aesthetics apart from this game.

There have always been counter-tendencies within philosophy which believe that the philosophical goal of Platonic or other definition, of parcelling the world into clear and distinct concepts, a lucid catalogue of things, has been more destructive than creative, the victory Pyrrhic. And there have been every gradation between that counter-tendency, which is called scepticism, and positive philosophy aiming for essential definitions. Scepticism and more recently post-structuralism have argued that the very obsession with finding exact clarity to the world in all of its parts and dispensing with those which fail the test of exactitude (like art) is itself the problem. The philosopher is, so suggest Sixtus Empiricus, Voltaire, Nietzsche, Wittgenstein, Rorty, Derrida, his or her own worst enemy. The project of knowledge is unachievable and productive of anxiety, the goal of control over the world is a form of human grandiosity or hubris with tragic, cruel consequences. Where there is the aim of conceptual control over a subject (art, beauty) which does not admit of it, violence is done to that subject. If the subject is human beings (colonial peoples, women, minorities) then the claim to completely categorize them is an adjunct to the game of colonial control, or the modern state (Foucault). Philosophical scepticism aims first to demonstrate by some kind of argument, that such subjects do not admit of essential definition. It then aims to show that human beings (the philosopher in particular) will be a lot better off if they renounce this game (at least when played over these particular subjects).

These counter-tendencies within philosophy have allied philosophy with Arts and Letters. Michel de Montaigne's essayistic/philosophical technique was to appropriate the 'wisdom of the ancients', to draw on what was said and thought in the past as a way of understanding this or that moment in life, and to do so in a way that tests that wisdom for its relevance today. This game of the appropriation of ideas to this or that purpose, without pretence of universality, has most recently been found in postmodern aesthetics and criticism, in for example the essays on art written by Arthur Danto for the *Nation Magazine* when he is not writing as a philosophical theorist but a genius trying to understand this or that moment of the art and culture being (over) produced in New York. The essay, that centrepiece of Arts and Letters, seeks assimilation of past thought in the light of a particular urgency of the present. It is a far cry from the project of a universal definition of art or beauty to be found in other pages of philosophy. Montaigne does not aim for universal truths of a trans-historical nature that would demonstrate the essences to things. He aims to make sense of the world in the best way he can, the most fair, integral, tolerant, humane. And so philosophy, including the philosophy of art, taken more broadly to include scepticism, has been a lot closer in its approach to art and beauty to modes of thought happening across the arts and humanities. His philosophical practice is close to that of the aesthetically minded art critic, or even artist.

Philosophy has sometimes turned towards *art* when it has taken the sceptical turn. Voltaire wrote *Candide* as a novel because he wanted to lambast philosophical optimism by running it up against the realities (suitably exaggerated) of life. To do this he needed to invent a story, to write fiction. Kierkegaard turns to a melange of essay, criticism and fictional memoir in *Either/Or* Part 1 in order to expose the emptiness, as he sees it, of the aesthetic position, the position of repetitively accumulated pleasures, compulsively acquired. Philosophy is rather a matter of revelation, of showing the reader this emptiness by showing what kind of character inhabits it. This again requires the invention of characters, of fiction. When philosophy aims for self-exposé it cannot remain expository: rather the goal must be to place the philosophy as a certain kind of character within the stream of life and show how badly he comes off on account of his disciplinary compulsions.

Philosophy turns to as story-telling and fiction when it believes itself in need of instruction from the best of art about how it, as a form of inquiry, should better be living its life, when it aims to get off its high horse and return to the flux of life entirely. The goal is life conceived as an aesthetic, a kind of experience enhancing pleasure through self-recognition and openness to the frissons of sense, the varieties of people and experience. Philosophy, never entirely free of the literary spirit, actively embraces that spirit in the name of another kind of truth than the one usually supposed by it. In turning to literature it is speaking to philosophy, as a character in a story which reveals the character to be hopeless, deluded, out of step with its own potential rhythm of embodiment in life, with its own aesthetics and politics. This raises the question of what truth in art is, such that philosophy would want it almost above and beyond its own, a question for the final chapter (Art and Truth).

What then does the student learn about beauty and art in studying the subject of aesthetics *broadly*? A set of definitions, a picture of its history, a repertoire of ways of grasping art, a feel for the importance of ideas in their context, a sense that as art and culture change, so also do the terms of understanding, a grasp of the importance of debating philosophical ideas about art and beauty abstractly while also needing to locate them in context, and finally a sense of the aesthetic turn within philosophy as a corrective or style of philosophizing in its own right. Also the history of a philosophical method which has since the eighteenth century been critical to defining the subject as a philosophical one, made great strides, and sadly, separated aesthetics from the broader humanities. Where the student takes the study of art and beauty, given the motley history of the subject – as motley as the histories of human life and art it is of: this is beyond the book to answer.

CHAPTER 2

THE BIRTH OF AESTHETICS

The discipline of philosophical aesthetics arises in the eighteenth century. But note, that is not the first time philosophers wrote about art or beauty. Plato wrote extensively – and negatively – about the poets of his day, and would have banished them from his ideal republic. For he believed poetry to be a form of seduction, an issuance of language which sent smoke rings before the mind rather than argument or proof, insinuating its influence over the passions in the heat of performance (poetry was recited rather than read), generating cult rather than rational civility. For Plato (see his dialogue, *Ion*) the poet was a hypocrite, claiming to elevate the mind with knowledge while sending it reeling into hypnotic trances. Plato reserves a place for beauty in his philosophy: it is the beauty of ideal forms, mathematical proofs and rational deductions. Knowledge is the beautiful and the good because it is knowledge of those ideal truths which comprise the true reality of things. Our world, being a mere appearance or approximation of ideal forms (our justice a weak copy of the real thing, our state a poor replica of the ideal), art is all the worse. For if poetry is a performative drug, then painting and sculpture are mere copies of copies, attempts to simulate the world in a way indecipherable from it. It would take centuries before Hegel would reinterpret Greek sculpture (if not painting) as an incarnation of idealized harmony (between the gods and the world of men), elevating it to the status of awesome representation rather than inadequate and fraudulent simulation.

Plato would have found it insane to think that beauty, much less art, was a genuine philosophical subject (in the manner of justice, rhetoric, the good, even love). Aristotle, already more attuned to the varieties of life than his teacher, differed. Writing about tragic drama (his companion treatise on comedy is sadly lost) Aristotle argued that poetry (by which he meant the rhythmic incantation of tragic drama) does indeed approximate philosophy, is more philosophical than history anyway. For history merely relates the world as it has happened: just the facts, as the detective used to say on the American TV programme *Dragnet*; whereas poetry (tragic drama) narrates the world according to the laws of probability or necessity. Treating drama like any other subject (the soul for example), Aristotle outlines its essential features in a hierarchy of importance. Plot and character are most essential, since drama is a story unfolding through character, the tragic element being that downfall happens through a combination of human failing (hubris, jealousy, excessive passion) and fate. It might not have happened that way, even with the main characters being as they are. But fate also played its hand, to tragic results. Tragic drama highlights the laws of human life which lead us (or can do) to ruin. Oedipus suffered the defect of hubris (arrogant self-assurance, a contempt for the uncertainties of the world), but it also takes the invisible hand of fate to have him kill his father and marry his own mother! Nor must Prometheus' fury have led to his being chained to a rock for the birds to peck at his eyes and tear at his flesh. That took a particular circumstance.

When the circumstance is shattering but unrelated to a flaw in human character, the drama is not tragic but simply horrifying, pathetic, a story of victimization, of a good man's being struck by lightning. The moral element in tragedy has to do with the way personal flaws spin themselves out into devastating results, results which, one wants to say, have gone beyond any kind of just reward for the protagonist involved. The moral element (that person's failure of character) has placed them in the spider's web of fate, so that without knowing it they were spinning the web of their own demise: fate became theirs. This particular kind of story, Aristotle writes, is what makes tragic drama the thing that it is, the thing which plays a profound role in the conduct of human life (the social life of his place and time). For Aristotle also understands that life and theatre are not the same, and that when such tragic events are represented in the public theatre nothing has actually happened, except a play. No real person has died, only the character, who is there to be endlessly played, endlessly destroyed.

This experience of art in the form of fiction is critical, Aristotle says, to its power over us, and its social benefit. Because we know, watching the stage, that what is happening is happening in the domain of fiction (not really happening in life, not actual), we are free to exercise our capacities for fear and trembling, pity and terror, in a way that brings them to public acknowledgement and allows us relief from the terror of life. Yes, that might happen to us! We too might lose a beloved child, kill our own fathers without realizing it, end up tied to the earth, pecked at by birds! We know ourselves to be also imperfect, also jealous, wild, unwilling, frozen, filled with hubris. We know, that is, intuit, that fate could also wallop us, we could end its victims. A tragic drama tells a story, Aristotle believes, of more important persons (kings, queens) and in a more concentrated way that life would offer, because that allows the audience (of his time) powerful admiration and identification with the theatrical protagonist. We sit in awe of the power of fate over such great and powerful individuals, filled with terror at such immense vagary.

The point of the drama consists exactly in this. To purge us, Aristotle says, of our inner fear and trembling, our pity and terror. Knowing that we live with the possibility of disaster, knowing we too could end up tragic victims of our own actions, the point of drama is not merely moral instruction (try to be a better person!) but relief. By purging our ever-present anxiety, we are brought to communal empowerment and returned to life better able to live it. Theatre provides a unique experience because what is happening is fictional, not actual. It is a form of recognition, and a form of collective purgation.

Nowadays we have lost this communal experience of theatre, so close in ritual value to religion, and the question of where the aesthetics of recognition and purgation simultaneously occur is a problematic question. The gym, the spa, the couch, the talk show: these don't do it. Perhaps we find a similar collective experience in the cinema, although in the cinema, everyone is alone in a dark place in a way they were not in the open theatre on the hill above the Greek city.[1] Most probably history has changed experience, and we as a society are no longer able to find such creative rituals available. Where fate seemed a matter of terror and awe, it is now a consumer item, something to be controlled by consumerism: medical technologies, pharmacopeia, botox, confession, therapy. Or so the system advertises, and so many Americans at least, fall into the complacent delusion of believing. Possibly we displace the underlying terror onto terror elsewhere, call this the Guantanamo effect.

Both Plato and Aristotle share what aesthetician Michael Kelly calls an iconoclastic position vis-à-vis the poetry of their day.[2] Both believe its integrity or lack thereof depends on whether poetry measures up to the philosophical demand that it offer philosophical knowledge. Iconoclasm is on Kelly's view the assimilation of a subject to one's own, the claim that the subject has value only if its value is the same kind as one's own. And so Plato lambasts the performance artist/poet of his day as a fraud, someone claiming to deliver knowledge when this poet is a drug dealer. This may or may not have been true of such poets: there have been after all plenty of frauds, hucksters, seducers, charlatans, snake oil salesmen, and worse in the history of the arts. The point is the only way for poetry to have any value on Plato's view is if it offers knowledge (if it is like philosophy). Aristotle praises poetry (tragic drama) on account of its depth of recognition, its being 'more philosophical than history'.[3] Aristotle has far more to say than that: tragedy occasions a profound and unique experience, which is central to its value for life. Nevertheless it is critical for Aristotle that poetry deliver knowledge – and philosophical knowledge at that.

The one philosopher would banish his poet, the other offer his poet pride of place within the state. Both measure art from the perspective of its capacity to yield knowledge. This is the iconoclasm. Plato considers poetry fraudulent because it mesmerizes the rational knower and stimulates his descent into the lower form of the soul, the 'appetitive', under the illusion that something is being learned. For Aristotle the knowledge is a kind of recognition (of the probable or necessary laws of what will happen to certain kinds of characters with certain flaws).

Amazingly neither of these philosophers considers beauty a worthy subject pertaining to art. One may generalize (at a certain risk, but with a certain merit) and baldly say that until the mediaeval age beauty is associated with seduction and manipulation, not aesthetic value – unless it is the philosopher's beauty of ideal form, mathematical organization, virtue. The unity of the good, the true and the beautiful is a philosopher's unity, which the poet, unless a quasi-philosopher, fails to achieve in his work. Rather his beauty is a form of seduction by the senses, of manipulation by mellifluous voice. It will be the mediaevals (Saint Augustine, Saint Thomas Aquinas) with their desire to aestheticize God's world, who will turn to beauty in a way that associates it with design rather than knowledge, and their discussions will almost entirely be theological (about God as divine architect). Only in the eighteenth century will beauty be celebrated as a distinct experience of the senses, and celebrated apart from some necessary link with knowledge or even design.

The Greek discussion about art is instead about the *social role* of the art of the time, about the public virtue of such forms of representation. For good or bad, the poet exists among the Greek citizens of his day, and the question is: does he do good or not, and why? Plato's poet engenders an obfuscating, cult-yielding spectacle. The emphasis is on cult as well as obfuscation. For Aristotle's poet the experience is one of community-driven, collective purgation (through identification and recognition). Both acknowledge that the arts have critical social roles and they are interested in understanding the public value of these roles (positive or negative).

These philosophers write first and foremost about particular arts. Plato never asks 'What is art?' or 'What is beauty?' in the way he asks 'What is justice?' or 'What is the ideal state?' His consideration is focused on those arts of his day which he believes degenerate, because falsely cloaked in the mantle of knowledge, when they are nothing but seduction and manipulation. Whatever generality he makes about representations of this kind is negative. These representations are degenerate. They are mere copies of copies, not integral forms which may be known philosophically, in the way justice or mathematics may be known. Art is a less than proper object of philosophical study. Aristotle, more tied to particular things, does not dismiss tragic drama in the way Plato dismisses poetry. He writes about tragic drama in the way he writes about politics or the soul: as a species of thing to be understood like any other. But neither rises at the end of the day from a discussion of particular arts to a categorical definition of art: each for his own reasons. This will happen only in the nineteenth century, after the eighteenth century has revisited aesthetic experience, redefined its terms, and then found it worthy of categorical definition. Definition can be the bugaboo, the obsession of philosophy. However, aesthetics may only be freed from the grip of definition after it has been dignified as a subject with a categorical shape. This has historically happened by gifting aesthetics the power of definition. Once so established, the task can now (and only now) be to free aesthetics from the grip of definition.

As we shall see (Chapter 4) the overriding concern with particular things found in Greek writing on the arts is a virtue which will return in the nineteenth century when the modern system of the arts focuses philosophical attention on particular media – literature, painting, tragic drama, poetry, architecture. At that point the Aristotelian approaches to tragedy will prove templates for the study of individual media. However there will always also be in nineteenth century writing the aim of categorical definition. Hegel will want to say something about art as a category of thing, but also about individual media and their distinct shapes. The Greek way of thinking about art will be combined with the eighteenth century's aim of aesthetic definition.

This will be one of a number of ways in which the Greek way of approaching the arts will return as a philosophical legacy. There are others. Hegel will return to Plato's and Aristotle's focus on public value of the arts, against the individual notion of the eighteenth century. And will return to Greek iconoclasm: to the claim that art has value because it generates knowledge, or recognition.

This return to classicism is also a hallmark of Romanticism in the arts. Romantic art of the nineteenth century wished to recapture the collective experience of Greek drama for modern life. It went so far as to build itself a temple in Bayreuth to the gods of music, where European peoples could assemble for the experience of a nationalizing self-renewal through the recognition of the world's shattering tragedies of life, and in a way recast as German myth. Half a century later it happened again in Salzburg, where the simple mediaeval drama of *Everyman* became the centrepiece of a collective congregation of devotion. But note, these Wagnerian and Austrian extravaganzas were a corruption of the Greek ideal in a hundred ways, as Nietzsche raged on about in his essays against Wagner.[4] For what intervened between ancient Greece and nineteenth-century Europe was the history of Catholicism, which supplants the humility of the tragic stance before the gods into a world-conquering messianic zeal around the violence of the cross (so said Nietzsche anyway). Greek tragedy was not about nationalism, nor modernity in progress of expansion across continents through high class elites who would pay the big bucks to attend these black tie affairs and swoon to the brass filled basso rhetoric of a Bayreuth without air-conditioning (in those days). It was not about the conversion of tragedy into myths of power through lineage (the descent of the gods, the legacy of Everyman). Nor was it about the transposition of awe into devotion, and devotion into cult. Bayreuth crossed the line from Aristotle's poet to Plato's, becoming a world-seducing cult-forming craze whose ritual drama has since been played out in countless other mass cultural events, from Nazi Nuremberg to (dare one say it) the drama around Princess Diana (People's Princess, queen of the castle and the tabloid, herself benign, frazzled, desperate, her cult a longing for religion, monarchy and television soap opera in one fell swoop). Plato and Aristotle are powerful critics of art even if it may be too simple to think that the values of art, much less of beauty generally (insofar as beauty is connected to art) are those of epistemology: of the yielding of knowledge through represented form.

I list these features of Greek aesthetics because they change so dramatically in the eighteenth century. The eighteenth century is about beauty, not art. Art is of interest to it only insofar as it is part of the general experience of beauty. The eighteenth century rethinks aesthetic experience as sensuous, rather than knowledge-giving, and dignifies this vision of experience with categorical definition. For the first time the abstract question 'What is beauty?' is given room within philosophy to be born. Moreover the focus on aesthetic experience for the eighteenth century is on *individual experience*, not social value, although collective experience also becomes fundamental as a by-product which a philosopher like Kant takes seriously. This is in accord with the century's concern with the achievement of liberty, indeed with its individualistic, libertarian stance, which celebrates individuals as Robinson Crusoe like boats in the sea of life, each with his or her own desires and interests, each with his or her desire for capital gains and happiness, virtue and reward. This is the century of revolution in the name of representation by the people for the people, which means each and every person counts like any other. It is the century in which autonomy is proclaimed, at least in constitutional form and for white men of age (and class). It is the century of economic perspectives on human values.

Such a century also begins to liberate individual experience from containment by religion and monarchical control. This becomes in the domain of philosophical aesthetics the freeing of beauty from the burden of knowledge. The drive to identify knowledge with science and economy makes this perhaps inevitable.

We shall also see that nationalism, colonialism and the birth of the museum play critical roles in soliciting this new concept of aesthetic experience. Its point will be that finding something beautiful is not to be measured as knowing or learning something, but instead a kind of experience which has value because of its wondrous sensuality. The great insight of the eighteenth century is to free sensual experience (of roses, mountaintops, beautiful paintings) to have value in and for themselves. Aesthetics is born as a subject when beauty becomes the central focus. Beauty can only become the central focus because philosophy is ready to free its experience from knowledge, when it is ready to understand the value of the experience as having its own end. In order to do that, the individual and his or her life must come to be valued as having its own end, as an end in itself. Only when human lives, when the human subject, is freed from dependency upon God, Platonic forms or whatever, only when the subject is taken to be the ground of experience, of knowledge, of life, can aesthetic experience arise as a topic for philosophy, beyond what the Greeks had already done in writing about art.

Aesthetics is born as a modern discipline because it takes the work of modern philosophy to produce it, not only because it is born in modern times, times of capital growth, scientific accumulation of fact, nationalism and colonialism. This work of achieving modern philosophy depends upon the Renaissance, with its humanist stance to life. It depends upon René Descartes with his reversal of the terms of philosophy: the origin of all knowledge being in the *human subject* (the knowing mind), rather than the state, the forms, a capricious, transcendental God. The truths of science (for which Descartes is writing) are derived from reason rather than theology. Indeed God's existence is 'proved' by Descartes from the existence of the thinking being (himself), rather than the other way around. Aesthetics depends upon the British empiricist's rejection of Cartesian rationalism and its emphasis on the experience of the senses as the origin of all knowledge and virtue, upon Locke and his derivation of science from human perception. Sense is freed from negativity and valued as a basic source of empirical confirmation, hence, scientific gain. Sense is also understood by British thought as the ground of the liberal state. The liberal society of England is one in which natural right is articulated as the basis of the contract between citizen and state, something Socrates had already articulated in gel but without the concept of rights conferred by nature upon all subjects of a state alike. This collective dignity ascribed to individuals in virtue of their capacities as moral actors and knowers depends on the authority of individual experience and liberty rather than God-given, preordained rationality. Agents themselves may, on the basis of their own experience, reject the contract offered by the state. Their judgements, derived from their experiences, authorize them. All this depends on a revision of the senses as dignified, dignified for scientific confirmation and political justice.

The modern state also becomes formulated under the ideal constitutional claim that persons are an end in themselves, an object of respect in virtue of their being the beings that they are. This general idea of humanity (in actuality offered only to white males of the correct class), is found in the pages of Kant, himself writing out of influence of British liberalism and empiricism, if also in debate with that movement.

All these currents of thought and social change become the context for legitimation of the experience of beauty in and of itself, and apart from the iconoclastic demand that beauty offer knowledge. The senses are trusted differently, their autonomy becomes paramount in theory and sometimes in practice. Moreover the scientific standpoint begins to apply itself to the totality of the human subject, what Michel Foucault called the birth of the human sciences, an act of social control no doubt, but also self-facilitation.[5] A general interest is born in the human subject in all of his aspects and faculties (women were not yet part of the equation so I shall use the word 'his'). This also leads the eighteenth century to think differently about the experience of beauty from the Greeks or the mediaeval. For aesthetic experience is part of the vast armament of concepts deployed to capture the mechanisms and vicissitudes of the human being, considered as a subject of study. Each is legitimate because humans are creatures of liberty, also because they are increasingly becoming objects of disciplinary knowledge. This is a natural outgrowth of the scientific stance, also of the systems of control which those sciences do, in modern society, seek to articulate through their analytical powers. And so the interest in human *faculties* arose, those parts of mind and spirit, emotion and response, which science should detail, and which allow the human being to have the experiences and derive the results from those experiences, that he can. Faculties are what make humans free and autonomous, powerful players in market economy and joyful inhabitants of life; they are also conceptual attempts produced by the new sciences and philosophies to turn humans into objects of study and manipulation.

Aesthetics, with its emphasis on individual experience in and for itself, also arises out of the institutions of eighteenth-century life: it arises in concert with the concert hall, the museum and the institutions of the European nation state that abstract art from the site of its making and any further purpose associated with it. The modern museum displaces works of art from the sites of their making and the streams of life in which they are set and places them in ordered relations (chronological, regional, by media, etc.) with other artworks – some of which would seem quite unrelated to each other when viewed *in situ*. Having stolen artworks from the sites of their enmeshment and turned them into *sights* to be viewed in abstraction by the fascinated and absorbed art viewer; artworks are now relegated to the realm of autonomous enjoyment (read: enjoyment abstracted from and oblivious of context). As the accumulation of capital, a nation (France) may take pride in the Egyptian obelisks, Russian icons, Renaissance devotional paintings and mediaeval church facades it has collected and presented within its rarefied halls. There is a reason why a cult of worship arises around the booty of the museum (the cult of the dandy favoured by the brothers Goncourt). For these objects become a shrine in their own right, a shrine to experience in and for itself. Similarly the museum licenses the European gaze over its colonial produce, allowing Orientalism to arise as a form of interpretation which – having removed Indian, Middle Eastern, later Chinese, Japanese, African objects from their embroilment with devotion, magic, worship, the practice of religion, the guardianship of house and home, the celebration of war and whatever else, the object itself may be framed by the omnipotent gaze of the experiencing European mind, and become a correlate of his or her feelings. And so art, transduced into mere aesthetic object (the object of aesthetic experience in and for itself) is licensed to be reinterpreted along the lines of whatever fantasy takes hold of the European mind and is played out over the object. Innocent and monstrous, licentious and pure, the object becomes a mere sign for this experience.

The aesthetic attitudes formulated in the eighteenth century also respond to the art of the time, which with the rise of bourgeois classes bent on pursuing their interests and pleasures in marketplace and cultural museum, conjoin with painters like Watteau, Constable and Reynolds whose genius is in the celebration of scene, figure, child at the ball, and whatever else this rising class enjoys and cultivates for the pleasures of viewing. Aesthetics assimilates art to experience, and experience to something happening in relative abstraction from the larger social ambit of roles art has played in life (Greek tragic drama). Similarly the art of the time is made for this, just as the music of the time (rococo) for enjoyment at table and with an after-dinner digestif.

The eighteenth century also invented the distinction between useful and fine art, which was a distinction in *kind* and of *category* associated with the growth of museums and concert halls. Useful arts were things crafted for use in life; fine arts things worthy of appreciation in and of themselves. The distinction was never clear, neither in its abstract formulation (what is it for a thing to have, as opposed to not have, a use?) nor in its application to the highly ornamented useful things which seemed chronically to blur the distinction (as blurred as that between art and craft), things like gold leaf tables with their gilded legs (are they really useful, and for what apart from decorating the spaces of the rich?). However, the ideology behind this distinction was connected to the institutions which served it: museums were filled with things now deemed of their own occasion, in and for themselves, while houses were not. Later museums of useful art would arise (The Museum of Decorative Arts in Paris for example). The point here was to institutionally license a distinction in the way objects were to be treated, to codify in public space a new way of relating publicly to objects. In a sense a new mode of experience was created, according to which arts were merely looked at rather than present in church (for devotion through beauty), public theatre (for tragic purgation) or cladded onto the facades of churches to incite fear or authority. Aesthetics as a new movement in philosophy was motivated by this larger world it is of, and played its role in shaping this world, by turning philosophy towards (so-called) experiences in and for themselves.

It is through this distinction that beauty can be liberated as an experience of its own value, for its own sake, apart from all 'useful' ends.

The faculty articulated (and variously debated) by the eighteenth century which occasions in humans the experience of the beautiful is called 'taste'. Taste is the central concept of the eighteenth century in its thinking about aesthetics, indeed the very conceptual pin which undergirds the new concept of aesthetics. This faculty of taste is what allows for the invention of the term 'aesthetics'. This term is adopted from the Greek word 'aeskesis', a term coined by Alexander Gottlieb Baumgarten (1714–62) in his book *Aesthetica* (1750).

'Aeskesis' carries the meaning of 'sense perception'. Aesthetics was for Baumgarten the study of *sensibility* as a particular kind of cognition, the cognition of particular things rather than abstract concepts. Sensibility is sensation (the use of the five senses) but something more, a kind of intuition/cognition/formulation of the thing which judges it beautiful. A poem might carry a message behind it (the metaphysical poets always offered one) but what made the poem beautiful was its particular twist of language, its invocation of rhythm through enjambment, the pleasure offered by its strophes, punctuations of thought, its use of forms (sonnet, villanelle). Everything depends for the poem on its particularities of incarnation, on how it happens and the pleasure taken in its reading and recapitulation in memory. The term 'aeskesis' was adopted to capture the essential characteristic of sensuous experience for its own sake in the experience of the beautiful. And so the beautiful became understood as having its own realm, apart from general concepts, residing in particular things. The cognition of the poem as beautiful is a particular experience, sui generis (different from all others in kind).

In focusing on sensibility Baumgarten is not saying that concepts may not be present at the background of the experience of the beautiful. What he is saying is that they are not central to what makes this experience what it is. Cognition of the beautiful is cognition of sensuous particulars, be they embodiments of ideas or not. It is in and for itself, of its own value, sensuous, and wholly absorptive. This faculty operates indifferently as to whether the 'object of the beautiful' is a rose or a poem, a blue sky or a church. It is the faculty of taste, unique in kind, in order to make this unique kind of experience possible. Since the experience is unique, it can fall under philosophical definition. Finally philosophy may give a categorical answer to the question 'What is beauty?' since it has a concept of the kind of experience, and the mechanisms/faculties generating it, which can make this experience essentially distinct as a kind. The eighteenth century changes focus: from Greek drama to the individual encountering the rose. And it does this because of its interest in redefining the human subject as a creature of sense and liberty, and because of its interest in achieving a field of representation in which definition becomes possible. Aesthetics as a distinct kind of experience, and aesthetics as a philosophical subject, arise as one whole cloth. Only when the experience is understood as sensuous, in and for itself, and apart from all knowledge, can the goal of defining it become possible.

This faculty of cognition through which the sensuous experience of the beautiful is shaped is a faculty that is more than mere perception, since it is also a shaping faculty, an imaginative faculty, a faculty which takes overall cognizance of its object. But it is less than conceptual since it is not about knowing that object. Peter Kivy characterizes this faculty in his book on the eighteenth century as a *seventh sense* (the title of his book).[6] It is distinct from cognition per se (knowing), it goes beyond mere perception (the five senses) and it is also distinct from the moral sense (the sixth sense).

Where beauty is central art is less so. Aristotle might, had he wished to dwell on it, have focused on aspects of tragic drama which are beautiful: the rhythmic antiphony of individual and choral voices, the movement of figures on stage, the mellifluous language. Were one in a meditative cast of mind one might try to avoid focusing on anything else when watching a play by Sophocles. It is very difficult, because of the profound integration of sound, character and story. There is no experience of the beautiful aspects of Sophocles' play distinct from the richer experience of his art which Aristotle so brilliantly explores. Beauty is part of what holds the audience in their position of absorption. Antiphony is what allows the audience to shift perspective from identification with the main characters to a wider commentary on circumstance. The chorus also supplies back story (like the titles in a silent film). It eclipses time as well as encapsulates action. A rapt viewer of the play does not have two separate experiences: one of beauty and another of awe, identification and theme. Baumgarten's faculty is invented (or discovered) to dignify those cases of the experience of the beautiful which are sui generis: the tasting of wine and olive, the sight of rose or frangipani. It has nothing to say about the role of a tragic drama in public life. By identifying beauty as the exercise of a particular cognitive/perceptual faculty, whose end is in itself, Baumgarten opens the field of inquiry into beauty as a subject, while closing the book on its organic relations to the wider fact of art in social life.

It is sometimes also thought of as a theory of imagination. In a recent article[7] Kant scholar and historian of eighteenth-century philosophy Paul Guyer has argued that the main achievement of aesthetics in that century was the articulation of a theory of imagination, and one way to understand philosophy's approach to the faculty in question is that it is identical to, or deeply integrated with imagination. Addison writes in 1712 of the various pleasures of the imagination (in an essay of that title)[8] which include pleasures of grandeur and novelty as well as beauty. This wider scope of aesthetic experience will lead to later categories of the sublime and the picturesque, as well as to the fascination with collections, colonies and goods flowing into Europe from every corner of empire. Addison and Baumgarten will both emphasize the experience of beauty, moreover, as synthetic. It goes beyond perception insofar as it actively puts together elements into a special kind of uniform whole, and the recognition of that whole, along with the active process of synthesizing it in the imagination, is the experience of the beautiful. If one asks how beauty resides in the property of things while also going beyond their (ordinary) properties, the role of the imagination fused with that of the senses is brought in to explain the process.

These ideas will lead to Kant, who conceives of the aesthetic as the work of imagination, something we shall take up in the next chapter. The point here is that sense, imagination and judgement are brought together as one in the theory of aesthetics. This is another of the eighteenth century's innovations: to think of the experience of the beautiful as itself a kind of *judgement*, to conceive of the pleasure taken in a beautiful thing as the ground for judgement, indeed the judgement itself. *Pleasure is judgement.* Every June the Ann Arbor Arboretum is awash in hundreds of peonies of every white and red gradation. As their bunched flowers hang in the air, drooping slightly from the weight of the flower, they seem to resemble the tilted arc of a ballerina. Where there are peonies there is always the dewy scent of perfume, which floats in the air like opium from a silver pipe. Everyone knows peonies are beautiful, that they give pleasure if also allergy. When I judge the peonies beautiful, this judgement is grounded in, indeed constituted by the pleasure I take in these flowers.

That pleasure in judgement means that the faculty of cognition, or seventh sense, of whatever any particular philosopher writing in this genre calls it, is operating as an avowal, a form of assertion, without any further ground than the experience itself. How can one person's taste be trusted over another's? This becomes the central philosophical question of aesthetics, given that it is about individual experiences in which the pleasure taken is the *judgement itself*. Can one ever provide a convincing reason for finding something beautiful apart from appeal to one's own experience (which another seems not to share if they disagree about something's being beautiful)? Is the giving of a reason for finding something beautiful anything more than a personal report (I am feeling pain in my tooth and I am finding that flower beautiful)? Is beauty a property of the thing judged (the flower) or of the person judging (I feel pleasure here)? And if it is nothing more than an individual's experience of a thing, how could there ever be a standard of beauty? Is beauty therefore nothing more than that which happens in the eye of the beholder?

In raising this set of concerns the eighteenth century in effect returned to a central circularity attaching to values which Socrates had already understood in his dialogue, *Euthyphro*. (Always, one might say, the Greeks). Euthyphro is a priest whom Socrates meets at the court of Athens and engages in a long discussion about the virtue of piety. As luck would have it both are at court about charges of impiety. Euthyphro, a priest, has charged his own father with that; Socrates has been charged by a group of antagonists with the same thing, and will, soon, be put to death for that (and related charges) after his famous trial. The charge is serious, not to be taken lightly, and yet Euthyphro seems to treat his laying of charges against his own father (something a Greek would do only in dire circumstances) with all the seriousness of a child chasing butterflies. Once again Socrates finds he is speaking to a man who treats serious matters lightly, who does not know how ignorant he is about the very issue of piety, whose arrogance assures him that as a priest he knows all. Euthyphro, a perfect candidate for Socratic cross-examination ('elenchus') is quickly engaged in the question of what piety is, and whether he knows how to define it.

In the course of this tortuous discussion (which in no way raises the self-doubt or moral seriousness of Euthyphro who goes away convinced that Socrates is a fool ready to waste a person's valuable time) the circularity of virtues arises as a problem for any definition of a virtue (way of knowing what it is on Socratic/Platonic grounds). Is an action pious because we believe it to be pious? Or do we believe it to be pious because it is pious (independently of our attitude)? Does the origin of virtue reside in our perception or in the thing itself, objectively. Socrates will not use those words exactly, but that is what the tangle amounts to. He never extricates himself from it. And this tangle is rediscovered about beauty by the eighteenth century, leading to a problem of judgement and taste (whose opinion counts). Is beauty (or goodness) in the eye of the beholder or in the thing beheld? When we find a supermodel, 6'3" weighing 98 pounds sauntering down the catwalk (like some rare bird exhibited in a vitrine), wearing an outfit that is adopted from old Hollywood movies of American Indians in frayed leather thongs, we may wonder if beauty is in the eye of the beholder or a property of nature itself! For the nineteenth century favoured plump ballerinas, while the eighteenth the man of leisure with pipe, port and portly middle. Okay, this is fashion, a world invented by advertising, mass consumption and ideology, not to mention the history of sexuality and the state of medicine with its promise of infinite youth, a youth, that is, created by technologies and medications, diets and face lifts, which being fabricated from the start may therefore remain fabricated forever (for an 80 year old as well as a 13 year old). When we turn from ready-to-wear to field and flower however, it might strike us that nature really is beautiful in itself, since everyone everywhere seems to find it so. Well do they? I lived a decade in South Africa, in the 1990s, and it is the English, the Afrikaner, the European tourist or American on safari who loves the desert and the savannah. Africans do not, to them it is too real, too violent, too much a daily danger for the entrancement of the aesthetic stance. Are they wrong? What is the wrong or the right here? Again we come back to the problem of giving reasons: what reason could convince someone that the Sabie River, snaking its way to the Indian ocean through the Kruger Game Park, with its submerged rhinos and single bull elephant standing knee deep in its mud as the sky turns mauve in the dazzling twilight, is anything more than someone else's view of it than their own? When we discover beauty it is rather like we discover the Discovery Channel. On the other hand tell someone that, alright, you say beauty is entirely in the eye of the beholder, that it is in no way an objective thing. Here is something I find beautiful: a car crash by the road with the mangled bodies of children hanging from the broken front door. The person will call it a bad joke, then assume there is something wrong with you. There are apparently constraints on what the human imagination is willing to and as a norm able to find beautiful. Does that make beauty objective? Well one is first owed an account of objectivity, of what is meant by this abstract remark beyond the obvious: there are human norms about what we are willing to treat as beautiful, norms with moral/psychological consequences.

Is beauty merely an artefact of my pleasure, something created by me and about my attitude? Or is there some kind of objective norm to the matter, and if so, how shall it be argued, what reasons given for it, where is it to be found? Furthermore, if taste is purely subjective what does it mean to call the judgement that something is beautiful (the judgement of taste) the product of a faculty of cognition? Any time one attributes a faculty to a person, the implication is that it can go wrong, someone can mis-perceive, mis-identify, think badly, and so on. The very attribution of a faculty of taste suggests that like vision, hearing, or abstract thought, some people have it better than others (can see, hear, think better), some people have it go wrong (I didn't see properly, I didn't hear you, my hearing went loopy, I'm all in a muddle today, I can't think straight). This question of the objectivity of taste, and of the very nature of the judgement, is what the next chapter is about.

CHAPTER 3

TASTE AND AESTHETIC JUDGEMENT

TWO KEY QUESTIONS ABOUT TASTE

The eighteenth century was polarized around two questions about taste. First, whether there is any measure of objectivity to its judgements, whether a standard of taste exists or rather: *De gustibus non disputandum est*, about taste (quoth the old Roman adage) there is no disputing. One person likes opera, another jumps from the rafters when he finds himself in the opera house, believing it to be a highfalutin European pomposity meant for windbags and buffoons. Margaret Dumont, the classic American rich dame angling for the Eurocentric drippings of fine taste, sits raptly attentive in the film *A Night at the Opera*, as Asucena belts out her prophesies of doom in sub-bel canto; Groucho, sitting in the grand tier, puts his thumbs in his ears, wiggles his fingers at singer and stage and yells out: buggabuggabugga. No two experiences of a night at the opera are the same and especially not in the film of that name. Hermann Gottlieb, German impresario out for Dumont's pocketbook chases Chico and Harpo around backstage as they sail from the wings wreaking silent film havoc in this sound film filled with operatic sound. The film is a Marx Brothers battle of taste and passion, also a battle for the soul of America, since it concerns immigrants stowed away in the steerage of boats sailing straight for New York and the statutes of liberty, equality and freedom of taste.

Is taste purely a matter of what you like, with no disputing possible? To say there is a standard of taste is to say someone's taste is better than another's, either in the kind of thing you like (should one really like opera?) or in your particular choice of thing within a genre. Henry (Walter Matthau) takes Henrietta (Elaine May) out to dinner at a fancy New York restaurant (in *A New Leaf*, written and directed by May). Henry has run through all his inheritance and is on the brink of foreclosure. He has devised a plan to marry an heiress then do her in. Henrietta, filthy rich of the kind that never wears make-up and has to be dusted off three times a day, fits the bill perfectly. Henry is courting her with his smarmy upper-class style. He orders a bottle of Mouton-Rothschild 1952, saying to her, 'I think '52 is a good year, don't you?' She replies with a question. 'Have you ever tasted Mogaen-David extra heavy malaga wine with soda water and lime juice?' 'I can't say that I have', he sneers. 'It's just delicious, and every year is good' is what she replies. Taste is a matter of the *kind* of wine you prefer (within that category of item).

Given that the eighteenth century believes that the judgement of taste is nothing but the *pleasure taken in the experience itself*, the question becomes whose pleasure counts, and how on earth would it be justified.

This was a heady enough question to occupy the middle classes during an entire century. The question remains with us today as we try to fend our way through the heap of teenage date movies, big-time wrestling matches, spice girl recordings, Paris Hilton photos and other sputum of mass entertainment. A person could get lost in the 8,000 varieties of sitcom and sun-dried tomato which America chucks out into the arena of the market during any given season. The question is multiplied when the genre is opened up. Now it is no longer about which drink you prefer. 'You drink beer, how déclassé!' Or about kinds of music: 'How can you like rap music when opera is so highfalutin?' or travel: 'You really like to travel to Las Vegas for your holidays? The Costa Brava of Spain! Yeech!'

And even if tastes can be compared, ranked, argued, proved better or worse within genres, as the field diversifies, the ranking becomes less plausible. How does one compare, much less rank Italian opera against Japanese Noh theatre or Chinese opera? Abstract expressionist paintings to cave art and then to West African masks, Tlingit totem poles, American quilts made by Amish communities in the nineteenth century? Isn't this a ridiculous enterprise? Moreover, two Americans might compare their notes about preferred travel and how to travel (on a cruise vs backpacking), but Japanese tourism is known to operate along quite different cultural lines, particularly having to do with the desire to travel en masse and take photographs of ordinary things like the interior of the train station or the telephone pole next to the grand opera house. This is, one presumes, a cultural thing. Can one rank whole cultures (the Japanese vs the American) in their travel preferences or is this a continuation of colonialism by other means?

As eighteenth-century England and France expanded their wealth and range of market, with goods flooding in from the colonies and artisans making items for bigger markets, these questions became more pressing. They were also of philosophical concern, given the desire of philosophical theory to identify the judgement of taste with the pleasure itself, as I said earlier. How then to retain a place for qualitatively better or worse tastes? This seemed something few could do without. Even a known boor or bumpkin wants to ape the ways of the gentry and pass himself off in their finery, meaning he believes their ways are of higher value in some sense or another.

The second issue of concern for the eighteenth century's understanding of taste had to do with its distinctive place in the wider ambit of human interests. Someone has a love of painting, opera, wine and roses, a taste for them. How is this 'interest' and 'capacity for enjoyment' to be distinguished from other kinds of interests that a person might take in any of these things: a financial interest, or epistemic, moral, kinky, whatever. If taste is marked out as a special kind of experience, a special relation to its object, how shall this 'specialness' be defined? The great advance of the eighteenth century is meant to be a way of conceiving taste that sets it apart from all (other) interests. A biologist may study a rose; the biologist's regard for it will, it is assumed, be different from the person who swoons before its beauty. An impresario of opera of the Hermann Gottlieb kind will approach opera from the financial standpoint, wanting the power, glory and cash from a great performance. It is appealing to say that Gottlieb, or better, a schlock Hollywood producer, does not value opera, or film, in and for itself. This person wants something from it in the way I want something from an ATM cash machine. It is reasonable to think the biologist is not interested in the rose in and for itself but instead as a species in a larger pattern of botanical kinds (flowers, fruits, trees). This is reasonable but also problematical, since the biologist is fascinated by the botanical organization of *this* singular item in the plant kingdom as much as anyone else. Perhaps more, since the person of taste simply cognizes the rose as a sensual item whereas the biologist is interested in facts about *it*. Evidently it is not simply the valuing of a thing in and for itself that counts: it is *how* the thing is valued. And taste is a form of valuation for which pleasure is paramount (rather than botanical knowledge).

This too carries problems. Although decorum would have prevented discussion in public, the eighteenth century knew as well as anyone else that great sex is also valued in and for itself. The making of love is also, in spite of the moralizing (an act to reproduce the species, God's duty), one where pleasure is paramount. Ideally each partner treats the other in and for herself/himself. Taste in one's partner (or partners, if one runs that way) is part of what love is all about. The eighteenth century must therefore consider how taste values a thing/person in and for itself/themselves, but also the quality and kind of pleasure that defines the experience.

The divisions within philosophical aesthetics of the time pertain to how these questions are answered. On the one hand there is a strong concept of taste as disinterested, found in the pages of Addison and Kant (to whom we shall turn below). This concept defines taste sharply: has the purpose of separating the kind and character of the experience of taste and its judgement from all others. Then there is the other approach, identified with Hume. David Hume (1711–1756) treats taste as one among a great many other human interests. Where it collides with other kinds of interests is left happily vague. The Kantian sphere of taste is narrow, its division from other spheres of human life is sharp. Hume's sphere of taste is wide, the line between it and others is less than sharp. This debate about how sharply taste (and aesthetic experience generally) can be demarcated from other aspects of human activity is a template for later aesthetics. Later centuries will pose it about art. How sharply can art be distinguished from other items, how open a concept of art do we want? And so, we shall see, on the one hand John Dewey, who thinks of art as totally continuous with human experience in its widest sense; on the other hand Arthur Danto, who thinks of its sphere as sharply defined at any given point in time (although that sphere may be very broad in practice).

Both approaches to taste have their problems. The side which sharply defines taste as disinterestedness must explain how taste stands to one side from all other interests, which enter into its deployment only marginally. And by these are meant intellectual, financial, erotic, moral and psychological interests. And it must say something positive and believable about the character of a 'disinterested' regard for an object: about what the experience is like.

31

Baumgarten calls this experience the cognition of sensuous particulars; Addison points to its particular freedom of imagination and love of novelty. We shall turn to these approaches below in their deepest theorization: by Kant. Note here that the concept of disinterestedness arises with Addison not only in theory but in practice, through his experience of the theatre, so important an art form in this century. Here is his idea. When Desdemona is strangled on stage we are shocked, moved, possibly horrified. We might throw up. But we do not feel the need to rescue her, like the famous yokel who runs onto the stage and punches Othello out, then carries the damsel on his back, out of the theatre, and calls the police. We do not feel the need to rescue her because we know it is theatre, not life. This is what it is to know the difference between these things. How one comes to know this is a fascinating story, and very hard to tell. That it happens is indubitable. The upshot of this knowledge is what Addison thought of as the state of disinterestedness which we deploy in the theatre in ways we simply do not and cannot in actual life. We may be made uncomfortable by fiction, even shut the book (like the person who closes his eyes when Othello grasps Desdemona's neck). We do not seek to intervene in the story, rescue Anna Karenina before she jumps under the train, kidnap Iago before he does his dirty work.

If disinterestedness is meant to mark a difference in quality of perception between theatre (let's say, fiction) and actual life, it is an uncomfortable way of marking this difference. For I am nothing if not *interested* in Othello; I am wholly caught up in his movements on stage, invested in his point of view, and ready to debate the play at length afterwards, discussing motivation, plot, male violence, female solicitation, race, culture, whatever: as has literary scholarship for the past hundreds of years! If that is not evidence for an interest, then nothing is. Disinterestedness is the promise of a theory which never quite works in practice, for it turns out to be little more than a marker for what we already know, that our attitude towards theatre is unique; until the concept is connected to a theory of the faculty of disinterestedness, which, as we shall see, has its best shot in the work of Kant, but even there, doesn't quite come off.

The other side of this debate was taken up by David Hume, who argued taste is one among many kinds of interest. This is a theory by a man *interested* in the world, including but not uniquely the world of taste. A scion of impoverished Scottish gentry, Hume was everything from diplomat to essayist to historian of England. After his masterpiece, *Treatise of Human Nature*, published when he was 26 years old, fell, in his words, 'stillborn' from the press, he made his career writing public essays on everything from politics (he was a conservative liberalist) to literature, the most widely read history of England of its day, as secretary to British diplomats and finally, in a prominent position in the British ambassadorial community in Paris, where he was known as 'le bon David' on account of his irrepressible cheerfulness – an attribute of character which happily co-existed, he often remarked of himself, with his steely intelligence and tough account of the world.

Consider how his approach to the theatre differs from Addison's. Taste in art is a conundrum, Hume thinks, and one which he approaches in a way not entirely dissimilar from Addison, but with an interesting twist. In 'Of Tragedy' he asked the question so many have asked before and since: why does a story so evidently painful and sad cause, in the theatre, pleasure rather than pain? His answer is not one of disinterestedness (we are disinterested in consequence, or meaning, or whatever). On the contrary, theatre is a place where interests shift and that is the answer. Hume begins with the obvious: 'It is certain that the same object of distress, which pleases in a tragedy, were it really set before us, would give the most unfeigned uneasiness.'[1] That we believe/know the characters on stage to be fictional means we believe/know nothing is actually happening to anyone (any actual person) in our presence, in this play. This recognition means we know what theatre is (that it's fictional), and it allows an attitude to form towards the play profoundly different from what we might/would feel were the moment one of actual life rather than a play. But this is not an attitude of disinterestedness. It is a particular kind of interestedness, which is able – amazingly – to take pleasure in things that, were they happening in actual life, would shock.

Hume's question about tragic drama is then: what is it about the art form that allows this particular interest to form? At the backdrop of Hume's essay is of course Aristotle: his famous idea that we take pleasure in imitations. There is also, Hume says, a peculiar way in which the embroidery of art, the mantle of excellent form and beautiful harmonization of voices, offsets the difficulty of the story, lending its own kind of pleasure. This is a powerful and important notion: that in art pain can be acknowledged because it appears in the formal guise of something beautiful, because of the art in the art, the fluency of language, gorgeous mellifluousness of aria, the rhythmic counterpoint of protagonist and choral commentary. Fiction allows story to be embroidered with art. Or at minimum, the distance conveyed by representation (a painting of a public tragedy that happened five years past, in Lower Manhattan, displayed in a museum).

If one were telling something terrible directly to someone, letting them know their mother or best friend died, it would be out of place to embroider the telling in finely wrought form. Not even in the Marx Brothers' films do they convey this kind of news in their screwball comedy. Actual suffering generates a different interest, a different quality of engagement in us. Finery of ornament is precluded. In fiction the point is in the telling: in the embroidery of language wrought to perfection, the poetry of syllable and stanza, the gift of music in speech. There is pleasure in this which offsets the story.

Hume also agrees with Addison that we take pleasure in the novelty of a well wrought work of art or artefact. It is just that this is an interest!

Now Hume's particular vision of human interests illustrates his worldly toughness. It reserves a place for taste which is clearly, but only provisionally, distinguished from related moral 'passions', as Hume puts it. The emphasis on 'passions' of the mind is critical. Judgement depends on them. All moral judgement, he claimed, is rooted in human passions. Reason is their slave, he famously quipped. We never act purely on the basis of abstract thought. I may in the abstract think it would be a good thing to love all humanity but this thought will little lead to any action of mine – much less to a general system of rules called 'justice' set forth by my society – unless I am heated by actual feeling to achieve this goal. To realistically grasp what human beings hold as virtuous one must always, Hume tells us, find out what actually compels them. The study of human passions is the key, the only real key, to the study of human interests and what humanity believes – truly believes rather than deluding itself it believes – is virtuous. Virtues are objects of human passion.

Of these there are two, natural and artificial. Natural virtues are objects of motivation humans have in virtue of their 'nature' (their being born the kinds of beings they are). All have a motive to eat, sleep and so on. Some are naturally sympathetic towards others, and may be motivated to act in the interests of others in the light of this beneficent instinct. Hume was such a person, and cheerfully so. Artificial virtues, like justice, are the product of social agreements in which agents are passionately invested. In the tough, self-interested vision of the eighteenth-century man of markets, Hume believes an honest, cosmopolitan stance towards others will tell us this: of all the human passions, Hume wrote in the *Treatise*, '. . . avidity alone, of acquiring goods and possessions for ourselves and our nearest friends, is insatiable, perpetual, universal'.[2] Human beings are above all motivated by self-interest, although (with Hume as exemplary instance) they are also capable of limited generosity. Writing against the illusion of general human beneficence perpetrated by the fictions of religion Hume pictures the human being as above all a being who desires more for self. How then do morals arise for such a being at all, given that a virtue (moral good) will be truly believed/set forth by society/followed if and only if it is in accord with actual human passions? On Hume's explanation we are passionate about artificial virtues like justice because they allow our greed maximum valence by keeping our possessions legally safe and secure.

What kind of interest is taste? What kind of 'passion' compels it? Hume's answer is that taste is a combination of natural and artificial talents, inborn talents of perceptual refinement, and talents cultivated through training, like training in the violin or in archery. What compels it is the pleasure associated with the exercise of this passion, which he calls 'delicacy of taste'. We take pleasure in the things we consume for their own sakes, and in the things we own for reasons of pride, but also enjoyment. We desire community with such objects: we love our mock Tudor houses with their indoor swimming pools, the wide screen TVs with surround sound systems, the French wines, Japanese plunge baths, Vetiver soaps, Chinese porcelain, second homes in Jackson Hole Wyoming, tax shelters in the Caribbean, private jets and safaris, the endless supply of Ralph Lauren Safari, the memberships in gyms at the top of fancy apartment buildings, fresh cut flowers year round, top of the line hairdressers and interior decorators, and high quality accountants – this is an interest (Hume calls it avidity).

Before turning to these questions, note that Hume's notion of taste is a wide one, with the virtues and difficulties of that kind of view. When I like *Don Quixote* I like the book for its way of telling stories, for its picture of nobility as a kind of out of date fiction (now transposed into the new key of literary fiction). I like its intense sense of irony, its wide angled scope (life does not compute to any simple formula but its living and the wisdom gained during its living, remain an open adventure). When I enjoy my house I enjoy it because it makes the neighbours jealous, and gives me the illusion I'm King of the Castle. As I wander around its royal-mediaeval wood-panelled bathrooms I believe myself in an Ealing Studios movie, a Richard Burton playing John F. Kennedy playing Camelot. This does not mean I have good taste, it means, I have taste and exercise it, a capacity for pleasure taken in things for themselves. But taking pleasure in a thing for itself is taking pleasure in it in any number of ways. Another might be appalled by the nouveau riches decor, the childish egocentrism of sticking it to the neighbours, the tiny mentality of my enjoyment. Still another might find all that appealing, but dislike the house on formal grounds: it is too big for its lot and sited like a Beverly Hills Mansion (the prototype, rather than Camelot) in the manner of a grand hotel on a Monopoly board. Hume is a naturalist: values are rooted in facts about people, here, the kind of things, the variety of things, they like.

Whereas the tradition of disinterestedness (Addison, Kant) aims to carve out a sharply autonomous region of human capacity and pleasure called taste, and works hard to explain how taste differs from other kinds of interests, it is for Hume, and naturalists like him, an advantage of giving taste a wide scope that it is continuous with other interests (pride, avariciousness, narcissism, class status and the acquisition of property, the erotic). The flip side is that Hume must make clear how taste is even provisionally distinguished from moral sentiments and other related interests. Taste can't be the same as moral duty, or financial strategy (although one can have a taste for these activities). Hume's approach relinquishes the claim of essential definition of taste. But he must say something about the quality of experience (and the quality of pleasure associated) which marks it as distinctive: otherwise he has no subject at all. It is in his short essay 'Of the Delicacy of Taste and Passion' this topic is taken up. Hume speaks to the difference between taste and other sentiments. In particular delicacy of taste is distinguished from delicacy of passion, the first being a genuine human good, Hume thinks, the second a burden:

> delicacy of taste is as much to be desired and cultivated, as delicacy of passion is to be lamented, and to be remedied, if possible.

The good or ill accidents of life are very little at our disposal; but we are pretty much masters [of] what books we shall read, what diversions we shall partake of, and what company we shall keep.[3]

Delicacy of passion has to do with the fragility and intensity of our receptiveness to life and its shocks of fate. Delicacy of taste has to do with our choice in kind of person or object to be enjoyed. 'Some people are subject to a certain *delicacy of passion*', Hume begins the essay,

which makes them extremely sensible to all the accidents of life, and gives them a lively joy upon every prosperous event, as well as a piercing grief when they meet with misfortune and adversity. Favours and good offices easily engage their friendship, while the smallest injury provokes their resentment. Any honour or mark of distinction elevates them above measure, but they are sensibly touched with contempt. People of this character have, no doubt, more lively enjoyments, as well as more pungent sorrows, than men of cool and sedate tempers.[4]

Delicacy of taste produces 'the same sensibility to beauty and deformity of every kind', as '[delicacy of passion] does to prosperity and adversity'.[5] The sentiments are similar in kind, distinguished only by the circumstances to which they respond or which they engage. Taste engages beauty or deformity, passion prosperity or adversity. The feelings themselves seem, to all intents and purposes, the same.

Hume's point in the essay is to preach the one value over the other. A good life is one in which delicacy of passion is subdued and delicacy of taste triumphs. We live better if we can shift the one into the other. The more one cultivates this active sphere of choice, the more one is empowered to respond more calmly (as the beneficent and ever-cheerful Hume himself was able to do) to the flotsam and jetsam, ups and downs of (one's) life.

In turn, he thinks, moral passions carry the weight of pressure towards action in a way that taste does not, since the pleasure of taste is its own reward. Yes, art might also awaken our moral sentiments, serve as a call to arms, and this might be part of what makes it great. But insofar as it is an object of taste it is also that which gives pleasure as its own reward. Hume shares this view with the eighteenth century as a whole, even though in his case the line between taste and moral sentiments might be somewhat blurred (as perhaps it should be, given the ways art has served the politics of German cult formation, Italian nationalism, Indian struggle for independence from the British, American anti-slave politics, and even Hippie culture in the 1960s).

We now understand that taste provisionally differs from moral sentiments in the weight of pressure towards action (but only provisionally), and that its delicacy trumps (or should trump) delicacy of passion. We do not yet understand what delicacy is! What makes either taste or passion delicate?

HUME'S STANDARD OF TASTE

We shall turn to this question through another: what is a standard of taste? For Hume's real interest is in that question. His best remarks about delicacy appear in the course of a discussion of it. The *locus classicus* of this discussion is his essay, 'Of the Standard of Taste'.

'It is natural', Hume begins the essay, 'for us to seek a standard of taste; a rule by which the various sentiments of men may be reconciled; at least a decision confirming one sentiment and denying another.'[6] The problem has to do with the great variety of sentiments people have about the people and things of this world, and the fact that taste is a matter of sentiment. One man's Tudor castle is another's MacMansion, better blown up than left standing as the monument to travertine bathrooms and postmodern 'gentry' that it is. Some prefer the walkways of Disneyland, others the hairpin turns of Monaco. Some go for the novels of William Trevor and Margaret Atwood, others Harold Robbins and Barbara Cartland. For some Prince Charles is persona of excellence and virtue, for others he is buffoon, betrayer. For some the entire British monarchy can sink into some Balmoral Lake and never rise to murder another fox again (except on Fox TV where they would be welcomed). For others they are the last of the great traditions, a living icon or period piece to be adulated and adored. These are moral and political debates, but also matters of taste. Where taste ends and morals or politics begin, Hume would have said, can be less than clear. One thing one admires in Dickens is his social picture of impoverishment and cruelty in eighteenth-century England: this is literary praise but also moral and political praise. It was not for nothing that Karl Marx said one could learn more about money by reading the pages of Balzac than many a book in economics. Part of what we admire Balzac for is his astonishing understanding of how money resides at the source of so much of Parisian life, from matters of status to matters of love and betrayal. Hume is interested in the many tastes persons have, and whether and how they might be reconciled. Is taste purely one's own business, given that it is about pleasure taken in a thing? Or can a person's taste be established as better or worse?

Hume is marvellously subtle; he begins by acknowledging both sides of the issue. According to one species of philosophy and common sense well represented in Hume's time, there is no disputing at all between these various sentiments. They are after all, sentiments, and, '[a]ll sentiment is right; because sentiment has reference to nothing beyond itself'.[7] There is no way of arguing between pleasures, mine is mine, yours is yours and that, like our height or eye colour, is the end of the story. I have the right to decide not to spend time with you if you eat like a horse, or to reside in your house if I think it revolting, but that is simply my preference, there is no justification to my choice beyond it.

On the other hand, Hume tells us, look at our practices and you will find an opposing species of commonly held belief. We believe, our practices tell us, that tastes may be better or worse, and that this view is justifiable, indeed both reasonable and necessary. Our commitment is shown in the fact that the very people who proclaim that everyone's taste is his own business (no disputing possible) will lambast as moronic anyone who seriously claims 'Ogilvie is better than Milton' (a grand slammer of the eighteenth century although nobody has even heard of Ogilvie today), that Paris Hilton is a better speaker than Bill Clinton or Tony Blair, that Jackie Collins a finer writer than W. H. Auden, or I am a better dancer than Mikhail Baryshnikov. As soon as basic norms of taste are violated – by the person who shows up at the university cocktail party wearing a pink thong and platinum blonde wig with a bird's nest and live parrot settled into it – we all know this is either some postmodern joke (about gay rights?), that the individual is nuts, or that a new level of taste is being achieved of the negative variety. It takes a violation of norms to demonstrate that a norm is in fact there in our practices, in spite of what we believe or think we believe about ourselves.

Belief in a standard of taste is present in our practices, since we all hold to norms of taste, and a norm is a value, not simply a 'personal preference' about which no one would believe dispute is possible. Witness the fierceness of debates around literature or film and you will be convinced everybody believes there are such norms, however hard to fathom, and related, that reasons can be given why thing X (the films of Jean Renoir) is better than thing Y (the films of Arnold Schwartzenegger), even if they don't convince everybody, and we know this. Nothing follows about being barred from liking a good hunt for the bodies in a good Austrian accent. We all like many kinds of things.

What *does* follow is a commitment, within the practice, to some films over others, and hence, to some tastes being better than others. As Ted Cohen puts it, Hume's commitment to a standard of taste is in the first instance transcendental:

> I understand Hume's argument fundamentally to be this: if you wish to say that your taste is not simply different from what it once was, but that it has improved (or deteriorated), then you must suppose that there is, in Hume's sense, a 'standard of taste,' because except against the background of such a standard, there is no way to make sense of the idea of improved taste. Thus I understand Hume to have offered a 'transcendental' argument well before the argument of Kant's *Critique of Judgment*.[8]

Insofar as a person is committed to elevating their own taste they are heretofore committed to a standard. Since many of us are so committed (others not), this means we are committed to there being some kind of standard of taste.

The immediate problem arises when it is asked who sets this standard, whose taste is definitive or exemplary, since public opinion is wildly diverse in its answers. The burden of Hume's essay is dialectical: by showing us that we do know what makes an expert an expert in this field, he aims to convince us that our belief in there being a standard is not simply a commitment, but something justified. By showing who the true judges are, by showing we know how to recognize them, he justifies the commitment to there being a standard.

Now we have another headache: namely the fickleness of our trust in judges wherever they may be found. A person judges brilliantly about this and then ridiculously about that. He proves adeptness in understanding and appreciating avant-garde literature but cannot follow the point of a great deal of womens' writing. She is excellent on American literature some of the time but seems to go off for no reason. Sometimes (on a good day) she is perspicuous, other times totally quirky and frankly ungenerous.

This problem is a general one about judgement for an empiricist like Hume, not simply a problem pertaining to taste. A phenomenon occurring once, for one person, and judged so, is not yet 'established as fact'. It is when the sun rises every morning and many confirm it, that this becomes taken to be indisputable truth. Judgements of taste may never have this degree of indisputability (extreme probability) but they are established in the same way: by the confirmation of expert witnesses over time, the experts being the true judges. Similarly, it is through confirmation of repeated judgement that the expert status of a judge is established.

This may seem an enormous circle. We take the judge to be an expert because we trust his or her judgements over time, not simply once, which might be a fluke. But this means we already know what is right for this judge to believe, since we are, in effect, testing him or her! It seems like membership in the club of the true judges is judged by us, which means we already have good taste and are in no need of these judges to stand as exemplary for us. This defeats the whole purpose of the enterprise, which is supposed to be about learning to recognize who a true judge is so we can, through the standard set, endeavour to raise our own taste.

Hume has two answers to this problem. First, Hume's innovation is to argue that the standard of taste and the test of time are the same thing: that as in all forms of knowledge or belief, it is the conservation of meaning over time through the confirmation of many judgements which gradually sets the standard, against which new judges are judged. Without a build-up over time of a shared standard, there could be no way of speaking of a standard at all – any more than, for an empiricist like Hume, there could be a point of reference for truths in science apart from the gradual build up of fact and information through testimony and confirmation of experiment over time. One way to grasp the expert status of a putative judge of taste is by measuring his or her judgements against the existing standard. Hume is a conservative.

But this is not enough. Standards of truth in science are built up over time because we trust the judgements of perceivers and experimenters, whose results can be confirmed in a way that is unproblematical. This is exactly what is at issue about judgers of taste. Whose eyes count and why? Whose ears tell us more about good sound than others and where do we find this person? The whole standard might be thought a fraud by some brash upstart challenging the dumb complacency of the bourgeoisie, and their clubs of membership claiming authority and truth about taste. You say this canon of judgements about Milton and Shakespeare constitutes the rule of the court of taste, do you? Well a pox on you, you self-important buffoons. You deliver the Emperor's New Clothes and claim they are the world's greatest fashion statement. I'm for the new, for what the people want, for steamy literature, Las Vegas mansions that glitter in the night and films composed entirely of special effects. Your confirmations over time mean nothing to me except that a lot of old stuffy upper-class men have had their idiocies confirmed by a lot of other stuffy, upper-class men. This is a class thing.

There must be a way for individuals to recognize who the true judge is apart from reference to the standard and its canonical judgements about canonical works. So second, we return to the central question: who then is this expert witness, this true judge? It is here that the best remarks about delicacy of taste are made by this philosopher, remarks which also tell us something about how taste differs from other kinds of experiences, being an act of delicacy.

There are five criteria, Hume tells us, which allow us to recognize a true judge:

> Strong sense, united to delicate sentiment, improved by practice, perfected by comparison, and cleared of all prejudice, can alone entitle critics to this valuable character; and the joint verdict of such, wherever they are to be found, is the true standard of taste and beauty.[9]

Some are, I have said, natural virtues, others artificial (matters of social training and convention). I will go over them in turn. First, the quality of strong sense: the true arbiter of taste must be sharply moved by the sensuous qualities of art, place, whatever. He is the one who weeps over the beauty of a sunset, cannot speak after a fine performance of a string quartet, is loath to return down the mountain because he is overwhelmed by the view. He is the one so taken with the purple of the stamen, the scent of rosemary in the chicken casserole, the touch of wind in the felt green hat of an elderly woman strolling in the art deco neighbourhoods of Los Angeles, that he must go home and immediately record his impressions in diary or poem, essay or blog.

Strong sense, however, may lead to misperception if not qualified by delicate sentiment, which is, Hume tells us, the ability to notice the subtle parts of a thing. I shall return to this, for Hume introduces it by a fascinating, and controversial example. Delicacy of taste (sentiment) is at the core of the discussion, and I shall turn to it last.

The other characteristics are clearer: the true judge must have practised, since taste, like athletics or mental gymnastics, falls away when not exercised and pushed to expansion. Jascha Heifetz once remarked: If I don't practise one day, I know it; two days, the critics know it; three days, the public knows it. It is the same with critics of film, or painting, or food, wine, cities, travel. I myself lost touch with painting for a number of years and it took some mental effort to get back into it. We all have such experiences of being 'out of touch, out of it, out of practice'. It is the same with comparison. Someone whose entire experience of the big city is Ann Arbor will fail to know a city, and be able to speak of the virtues and vices of cities with authority, until he or she knows New York, San Francisco, London, Tokyo, Berlin, San Paolo, Johannesburg, Shanghai, Dubai, Warsaw, Istanbul, Jerusalem, Cairo. As no one knows all these places well, just as no one can have a synoptic memory of the entirety of the world's painting, or sculpture, or even the music of the western operatic form (from Italian masterpieces in the 1600s to the present), no one can be a true judge in and of himself or herself. We make choices about what we can compare with what, what we remain most practised in, and so on. Hence the need for a jury of such, a test of time in which different judges form a corrective to the limits of each and a better judgement 'of humanity' emerges.

Of course this is highly optimistic, this common judgement of humanity. It all points to Hume's elitist preference for the few great masterpieces of art, city life, wine about which there is such a common vision (since everyone, with minor exceptions, is awed). There is more to life than Shakespeare, even if nothing better. And for most objects of taste history does not compute, I think, to a common judgement which corrects for individual exaggerations, but instead evidences sharp and incontestable differences of opinion which give vent to lack of reconciliation between the interests, and prejudices, of distinct ages. The joint verdict of humanity is a verdict exposing depth of argument between judges, as well as depth of agreement. The verdict is, as in the case of morals, inevitably partial, inevitably an expression of basic human differences, socially constituted.

This is especially true of the fifth criterion, that the judge be 'cleared of all prejudice'. Fat chance of that, which Hume himself not only knows, but illustrates about himself by ending the essay with an inappropriately placed and textually bizarre rant against the Catholic church. The subtext is that Hume's elegance of style, subtlety of example, deep knowledge of taste, and portfolio as a significant critic of his day, sets him up as among the true judges. If he is clearly uncleared of his own hatreds, then who else would be? Critics are qualified by their Eurocentrism (which condemned modern art outside of Europe and America to second-class status for generations), their condescension towards women (which required a woman to have a room of her own in order to write), their hatred of their neighbours, pre-judgements about human experience, practice, judgement, quality of mind and sensibility. Indeed Hume has underestimated this problem in spite of so brilliantly raising it about himself. For the depth of pre-judgement according to which, as E. H. Gombrich puts it, the artist paints out of his or her stereotypes of the world and the beholder constructs meaning and value thought their own, is ineradicable, making it unclear that understanding, much less proper evaluation, is possible apart from prejudice. Hume's point is that when prejudice gets too extreme, judgement goes down. We can do better; this he knows. More recent points like those made by Gombrich are that at the deepest level of human experience, representation (in painting, literature and so on) is conditioned by stereotypes, which must be unearthed in order for the meaning and value of a work to be unfolded. This is the hermeneutical problem of interpretation per se, the problem Gadamer calls that of 'pre-judgement'. It is because pre-judgements through which the world is understood and filtered condition meaning that consensus may well not be achieved over time (through the test of time). For many works, each generation views it differently, and the task of returning to original meanings, or recovering them, or appropriating them, becomes a vast, perhaps impossible one.

We may now take up Hume's remarks about delicacy: delicacy of sentiment or taste. Hume introduces this second criterion of the true judge through the story told by Sancho Panza about his kinsmen (misremembered by Hume, a fact irrelevant here) in *Don Quixote*. It is critical to the making of a true judge. Anyone can (given time, money and a good teacher) practise, even make comparisons (take the Grand Tour, visit all the right museums). Delicacy of sentiment is a natural born property of the few. Sancho Panza's kinsmen are among the lucky ones:

> It is with good reason, says SANCHO to the squire with the great nose, that I pretend to have a judgment in wine; this is a quality hereditary in our family. Two of my kinsmen were once called to give their opinion of a hogshead, which was supposed to be excellent, being old and of a good vintage. One of them tastes it, considers it; and, after mature reflection, pronounces the wine to be good, were it not for a small taste of leather which he perceives in it. The other, after using the same precautions, gives also his verdict in favour of the wine; but with the reserve of a taste of iron . . . You cannot imagine how much they were both ridiculed for their judgment. But who laughed in the end? On emptying the hogshead, there was found at the bottom an old key with a leathern thong tied to it.[10]

Panza's kinsmen have delicacy of taste in that they have the ability to discriminate – in this case literally taste – the subtlest portions of a thing and relate its composition from those parts. Their judgements are made on the basis of such fine discriminations. They can taste the faintest ingredient, and also sense its role in the overall shape of the wine (which is a discordant one). Presumably they can similarly taste (and note) ingredients which give the grape concord (a faint hint of raspberry, with overlay of strawberry and heaps of vanilla, a strange, grassy taste, from the hint of peat in this California soil, a feel for the oak in the cask – you know the language as well as I). Young conductors are sometimes tested on their musical chops by dyed in the wool orchestras who play a game with them of wrong notes: a piccolo player will play something different from what is in the score, then a cellist, to see if the conductor can pick up their faint failures or discords. Composition students of the French teacher Nadia Boulanger were trained to play Bach pieces leaving out one or another of the inner voices: this was a matter of practice makes better, but also delicacy is the starting point. Practice accomplishes little for a person lacking in natural talent, even in the case of a critic or 'virtuoso listener'! Natural talent involves strong sense of course, but also delicacy of sentiment. The artist has it, the conductor, wine maker, critic, and qualified enthusiast.

Neither of Panza's kinsmen got everything right, it took the 'joint verdict' of both to capture what was in the wine. Crucially they did taste what was *in the wine*, among its (objective) properties, and this was demonstrated by the finding of the relevant cause. Hume means to show us that a true judge is a 'true' judge because what he tastes is what is there in the object. Taste is not an imaginative invention but a limning of what a thing really is in its subtlest sense. This is crucial to Hume's belief that taste is on the same footing with morals, and also science (even if less demonstrable, more controversial). Each of these activities is about establishing (to the best of human ability) what is there, and doing it through perception, training, expertise which must in turn be corroborated and qualified by others over time. It is classic empiricism: one person will not get very far, over time humanity will leap ahead in understanding the world, articulating better moral values to correspond to human passions and motives, refining its tastes and truing its judgements. This is what the eighteenth century calls human progress. It has achieved, Hume thinks, good principles of justice (liberal, about property, with freedom of choice), science is improving, and taste is already canonical. Hume would rant against religion, still a negative force perpetrating itself in university, Parliament, philosophical thought, even taste. He is brave in this way.

PROBLEMS WITH THE STANDARD

That the kinsmen's judgements are corroborated by the finding of the leathern key is critical for the essay. Not only does it show that the man of taste judges objectively (if his judgement be 'true'), it also shows the reader that we have independent ways of proving the validity of a judge's claims. We can (if luck be with us) recognize the true judge from among the many drinking from this hogshead by finding an independent cause of his judgement. Lovely when it happens, but in general we are not so lucky. This is not because as often as not the leathern thong has disappeared, the causal evidence vanished (it sat in the wine cask for long enough to tarnish the wine but was then removed, leaving the judgements of these kinsmen unproven). It is because such judgements, contra the spirit of this essay, go beyond anything that can be corroborated by independent fact. Yes, the young conductor may stop the orchestra and demand that the piccolo player play the right notes. This will prove his chops because the orchestra know the piccolo player really did play wrong notes. But a brilliant ear does not equal brilliant taste, and much of the shaping of music which the conductor does is a matter of *imaginative vision*, not subtle conformity to the musical score. Ability to hear subtle wrong notes or instinctively feel micro-variations in tempi is a gift (improved by practice). But there is far more to making music than conformity to the score. We have all heard performances of Mozart that immediately put us to sleep, or make us feel someone is clod-hopping through the tulips with a bayonet for a baton. I once heard a Los Angeles Philharmonic performance of Mahler's *Fifth Symphony* described as Mahler on valium. It felt like that to me too. It would be easy to say the conductor and orchestra failed to conform to what is in the score, but they (as far as I can tell) played all the notes right, followed metronome markings as much as everyone else does (meaning not entirely but enough), paid attention to instructions about loudness, acceleration and even mood. Everything was there except, one wants to say, the musical spirit, which was spilled out by a man (the conductor) whose taste would do better in light opera or white man's cocktail hour jazz at some New York upper east side hotel. Disastrous! The point being, the failure of taste here was not, I think, about what is in the object, if the score may be counted as the object here. It was a failure to make music of it, to imaginatively make the music live. There is nothing, apart from comparison (look how much better this or that conductor/orchestra does it!) and the dictates of one's own ears, which would prove the judgement. No magic bullet may be found which would demonstrate a failure of taste here (or a vast human difference about what counts as 'live action music'!). For most judgements of taste, I think, there is no leathern thong to be found, since those judgements are not about any property of the object of taste (what is clearly marked in the score, clearly a property of the wine) but about ability to animate that object, perceive and imagine it in a certain way. This is what Wittgenstein called 'seeing-as', a way of taking the world in a certain mood or register, of feeling it through as such, making music of it. Taste is not, pace Hume, objective beyond a certain point: the point being the ability to detect subtle parts of composition. A cook may find a tomato sour to the palette and we shall be thrilled if it is later established that this humble fruit was placed on a towel which had touched the top of a bottle of balsamic vinegar. But the cook's taste is also for combination, texture, presentation, overall rhythm of foods, and these things are matters of taste in the sense that the only proof is in the pudding: in whether we like it.

This old and venerable notion of taste puts the true judge in a different category from Hume's. Hume's is meant to be a guardian of truth, since he is the man who can detect what is truly there in the object beyond our capacity to do so when helped by his peers on the jury (towards a joint verdict). We learn from him and endeavour to be like him, thus truing ourselves to the world and bettering (it is expected) our pleasures. However, there is nothing in nature which guarantees that the Los Angeles performance of Mahler is truly, by any standard, tasteless. I found it so, but there is a community of listeners who I can respect I think, who admire this man and his work. Nothing can arbitrate between André Previn and Georg Solti playing Mahler except critical preference, and there are fine judges I think in both camps. If we overall prefer Solti (which I think sociologically is the case) that is our preference for a certain reading of depth and power. We want to say the depth and power is there in the object, but this language is a metaphor if by there in the object you mean there in a way that independent evidence could corroborate (with a leathern thong or by proof of the score). Mahler becomes Mahler through what Lydia Goehr, writing against the view that the work is contained in the score (writing about fidelity to the score as itself a particular musical practice), calls a musical practice of his performance and life in culture.[11] Our taste for certain ways of performing him is a matter of how we fit into this practice and hear in the light of it. Since the practice is not objective but freestanding, which camp we are in within it, and related, which critics we admire, is a matter of how we sit within communities of taste, and how we freely move onto our own ground.

Most debates of any real subtlety are not resolvable through reference to some decisive fact about the object in question. Judgements are *exemplary*, not truth-giving. We follow them because they establish, and heighten our preferences. Different judgements are therefore not wrong or right, not necessarily even better or worse: they appeal to specific communities of taste. Where the weather is nice all the time and everyone walks around in tennis shorts Previn might have been just right, even if I personally couldn't stand almost anything he did that wasn't French, jazzy or from a Hollywood film. For those in more searing worlds Mahler's depths of love, generosity, forgiveness, comedy, transcendence, loss and the rest requires a bigger voice, a more resolute, piercing intensity, more passion. One person's sex is another's sleep. The judge is the one who can deliver exemplary subtlety within a community of interpretation, a practice, a way of hearing that bonds people together and creates intimacy between one listener and another. It is what Ted Cohen calls the role of intimacy in art, a role extending to the judge, whose judgements, rather than true or being trued by the joint verdict, deliver a way of seeing-as which a community responds to, learns from, takes the linguistic message of, and also enjoys reading.

We choose our true judges as much as they choose us. This is why taste is truly democratic. We read this critic because his uncompromising bile appeals to us, that one because we admire her ironic turn of phrase and rant against Hollywood as a business. We like this one because he loves Hollywood and is star crazy, that one because her writing is so wry that only a few realize how mordant she is. We like this one because he is generous, that one because she is not. Critics have characters just as objects of taste do, and we've a taste in critics just as we've a taste in wine or women's ready-to-wear fashion. Do these critics deliver truth? Do any approach that idealized concept of the 'true judge'? If by truth is meant conformity to fact, then only insofar as their delicacy of taste (or indelicacy of it!) is rooted in subtle perception of the object's properties can we say this is true. Insofar as so much of criticism goes beyond any reasonable conception of what is 'in the object' to point of view and imaginative cognition of it, this is a bad metaphor, unless by truth is meant: inter-subjective acceptability or conviction. When we read a critic as often as not we half trust them, adjusting to what we know to be their prejudices and limitations. Pauline Kael, former film critic for the *New Yorker* magazine, used to hate 70 per cent of all films she reviewed, which made it a pleasure to read her. But with a slight grain of salt. It is the rare judge who brings force of revelation, in the manner of André Bazin's genuine revelation about what cinema is as a medium and how the great filmmakers like Renoir contribute to its making as a medium. Even these are not true judges if you mean persons the joint verdict of such set the standard for cinema. The true judge is, in Hume's theory, an idealized being. But my point is that since beyond a certain point there is no objective fact about which the true judge judges, and which would, if revealed, prove his (or her) claim to the title, judges are at best exemplary, and achieve no truth apart from their exemplary status in guiding communities.

We like objects of taste to be matters of debate and difference, not matters for consensus over time. Even Hume knew this, since he relished the fray of argument in his distinguished public writing (including criticism). Shifts in perspective about the arts (and about wine and food and travel and human beauty) satisfy the human desire for what Hume and everybody else in the eighteenth century calls 'novelty'. We come back to the film we saw a hundred times in the 1960s and see it with really new eyes. Did we miss what was in it the first time, are we noticing different features of it, or have our eyes simply changed, making it as new as the city of Rome after our 20 year absence? Hume's theory, and the theory of universality or consensus over time, is a mark of his empiricism, but out of sync with his own appreciation of this virtue.

So first, the standard is not something gradually trued to the facts about the object (through delicacy of taste, Sancho Panza's kinsmen and their fine art of detection). Second, it is exemplary, a standard of inter-subjective agreement in experience, and as such, is nothing more (and nothing less) than the overlapping visions of many, which do set the films of Jean Renoir above those of Adam Sandler, the music of Mozart above that of Mantovani, but very quickly avoids the vitality of disagreement, and becomes authoritarian and elitist if it tries to do much more. Within communities of taste and category of thing there is a want (up to a point) for betterment and Hume believes this commits us to a standard of taste. But does it? Perhaps all it does is commit us to betterment of taste in the sense of experience (like a Masters and Johnson course in better sex through pills and living). Perhaps our judgements do not change very much. It is not entirely easy to tell.

Given the failure of the Sancho Panza example to demonstrate that we can find out who has delicacy of sentiment by checking the data afterwards (the wine cask), Hume really leaves us with a (Socratic) circle about value and objectivity. Were we totally lacking in taste ourselves, we would have no way of being brought to see how fine he is. Early on the great critics of cinema – Panofsky, Manny Farber, Jean-Luc Godard, James Agee – were considered idiomatic weirdos, scholars slumming it for fun, commies on the warpath against high culture and the powers that be, whatever. Only over time did the eye and sensibility of the public catch up with them, catch up enough to realize that from these talented whizzes they had much to learn. A tone deaf man will benefit nothing from a master composer's lessons, nor from a master critic's judgements and descriptions of music. He or she must be well enough along, of sufficient practice and sensibility to catch on. We recognize the master by coming to trust his judgement as one we ourselves are able (now) to follow. As we shall see, this dialectic, excellent as it is, is belied by Hume's desire to root the judgements of the true judge in objective properties of the thing judged. Hume would have us believe the critic is a true judge because in some ideal sense that critic trues his judgement to the facts of the object, just as a man perceiving the moon trues his eyes to the silvery light through which its pale yellow is filtered and so 'sees it as it is'.

This, along with reference to a standard learned at the feet of history, is how we tend to put our trust in people and their 'true judgements'. We can be wrong of course, the true judge may not confirm their excellence over time through multiple articles in the *New Yorker* or *Times Literary Supplement*, but once established as a true critic, out front in the field of taste through repeated examples of excellent judgement to which we catch up, the critic becomes enshrined. Once enshrined into the hall of the rare worthies, he is treated with awe and respect, commanding the attention of the robes of court.

Now if this sounds dangerously like an entrance exam into an exclusive legal club, the metaphor is not lost on Hume, for he sees this club as that of the Inns of Court. Hume is elitist in a number of ways, one of which is his emphasis on the superiority of the very few over the very many, and the relevant casting of standard of taste in the currency of (if you will) law. In some generations, Hume tells us, the true judge may be so scarce that for decades there is none at all to be found, something I think is pure fiction, the fantasy of those who believe in the trickledown effect on culture and economy, the slow trickle down of the judgements of the very few into the bettered lives of the very many. One can easily democratize Hume's conservative liberalism by speaking of taste as established by the very many over the very many more, or in alliance with their receptive judgements. Taste is a bootstraps kind of thing: Person A is better (has better ears, better refinement for plot and character, a stronger sense of human psychology and specificity, an urgent demanding brain for the compressions of art) than B and so teaches at university, or writes for the local paper, or is even better, read across generations and not because of the lasciviousness nor merely because he was a whizz at pricing art, but because we realize how good he was. Like the unrecognized genius, there may well be unrecognized men of taste – permanently consigned to the dustbin of history. It happens (in my view) all the time.

Hume's difficulty is that he believes taste is objective because delicacy is the probing instrument for truth: for what is in the object. Rather, taste is a circular and constructivist enterprise. We are led by others because they elevate our taste to their level, and this because we already have taste. This circle constructs taste communities through training and experience. It is inter-subjectively deep, and canonical in its adulation of certain objects, but never immune from the problems of the circle: that some people can't get into it and would instead have other circles in which they fit, the Las Vegas rhinestone set, the Liberace over the top flaunt it to the hilt variety, the give me a steak and fries any day foodies, and so on. Insofar as inter-subjective disagreements cannot be resolved, we are left with little further 'proof' of who is right.

This is also the way it is with morals, as any worker in the field of human rights will tell you. We construct universal standards for human rights in the hope that they will educate and raise other publics, but when those publics refuse to play, and criticize our standards as western domination, we cannot prove them wrong apart from our own depths of inter-subjective certainty and the history of testimony and law that goes with it. We do not refuse such standards, but neither are they objective in the sense that our moral delicacy has 'grasped the facts' of violence and repression in a way no other passions and instincts have. We simply hold to our beliefs, and do so with every fibre of our beings, every reason and argument we can muster. Those are the stakes of life, the stakes of setting forth legal norms and following them. We believe better taste will deepen experience, this is the point of a standard. And that better human rights law will raise liberty and human dignity. But if someone at the end of the day chooses to live in the green Tudor mansion with the fake Tower of London soaring directly from their living room and says a pox on your tastes, we live and let live. If someone at the end of the day refuses an open civil society we fight them, or should, even if we cannot argue them into believing the value of free speech if they are completely closed to it. In neither morals nor aesthetics is there usually a leathern thong, a magic bullet to produce, that will convince an opponent otherwise, except on occasion. We rely on his or her ultimate likeness to us, meaning his or her capacity for taking instruction. And it may be the other way round. We are the ones who require this instruction without knowing it.

Hume was a conservative and believed the uniformity of human nature, while never provable (Hume was a sceptic) was demonstrable in the form of the test of time. Over time variation is corrected and judgement established on a higher footing. This conservationist stance has its worst as well as best aspects. It is about the establishment of a *canon* of literature, music, architecture, wine, food, art, about the making of the canonical, which finally precludes acknowledgement of what this century has discovered as the ineluctability of human difference. With an emphasis above all on the normative and canonical, the new is, moreover, always suspect until proven otherwise, because a single true judge may betray their prejudices or failings, or the failings (prejudices) of the age. Only when the single judgement is confirmed by many ages/generations, is it established as corrected and confirmed. This defining of taste in terms of the test of time is a prejudice of Hume's age, a high bourgeois belief in the eternity of the item, and the reach of the singular age towards truth given by civilization construed as eternity. Civilization is what is at stake here: the accretion of a list of truths over time which bespeaks 'all humanity'. Such a method for establishing and sustaining taste has been fiercely challenged by the culture wars of the American and British Academies during the second half of the twentieth century, where all the items were refused entry onto the list in virtue of their newness to history and their desire to speak, not in a universal voice to all civilized men but against this illusion, in the name of new peoples, new aspirations, new causes, particular minority groups.

The culture wars of the 1980s and 1990s have left the test of time reeling, uncertain whether its status as a justification of taste trumps all others or is simply one method for determining good taste among others. New art is not made for the ages, but to be timely for now. The belief that all historical ages correct each other out, confirming or denying over time judgements as true, is a belief about history that lacks understanding of its vast diversity, of the fact that art made in an age speaks to it, and perhaps beyond, but another age is simply another moment of aspiration and prejudice, not a way of progressively confirming or denying something judged earlier.

The canon of works which survives over the course of all time is indeed existent, but small and distinguished, and can be counted on one or two hands I think. Shakespeare, Milton, Bach and so on. What of everything else? Is it lesser, or simply more timely to the moment? Must taste be measured by universalizing standards, or is it, like other human properties, judged within diverse communities, for their own purposes, in the course of their lives?

This is an issue of diversity: diversity of pleasures, social experiences of value, preference of all sorts. It arose in the culture wars in the form of identity politics: marginalized groups claiming taste an elitist imposition which unduly elevates the systems of certain groups over those of others, and without final arbitration possible. Let a thousand flowers bloom, all good, each in its way, rather than singularizing an elite class as the unique arbiters of taste, and producers of it. The increasing interconnectedness of the world makes the issue of diversity inevitable for human practices around art, food, whatever. Ranking tastes into a standard is problematized by the contemporary understanding of human diversity. Hume's standard presupposes sufficient uniformity between judges to achieve a consensus (joint verdict). Its relation to the diversity of objects of taste, and people tasting is, I think, ambivalent and not worked out. On the one hand Hume tells us an African cannot appreciate the taste of wine because the African's experience is too different from ours. On the other that the judgement of the true judges sets the standard, the test of time. These remarks do not quite compute, unless it is taken that the African doesn't count. Which is perhaps what Hume, gentleman of his time, believed.

What does the prospect of a single standard look like once the African is given his due, and the Chinese, and the Tlingit, and everyone else? Can we imagine a single standard comparing their vastly different kinds of objects and tastes? Or is it rather that each culture has its own standard? Neither seems quite palatable. The first because we don't know how to compare, much less hierarchically rank, objects as different as opera to jazz, jazz to African drumming, African drumming to Koto music, to Tibetan chanting, and so on, in the huge department store of world culture. For the eighteenth century these vast comparisons, that is, rankings, are an article of faith which the twentieth has challenged. Recent work in Anglo-American aesthetics by Richard Shusterman, Theodor Gracyk and others has elevated popular and other arts to the status of serious objects of taste.[12] An accumulation of writing about Japanese Noh Theatre, Chinese opera, Indian wall carvings, West African folk sculptures, Ndebele house paintings in Southern Africa, Native American ceramics, Amish quilts also expands the repertoire of serious taste beyond the canonical objects of Hume's standard: Shakespeare, Milton, Renaissance painting and the like.

As for the second, it presupposes unity within distinctive cultures (which is an illusion) and incomparability between them. Both are dubious. Traditions, cultures, heritages appear unified only to the synoptic gaze of colonizer, tourist, essentializing theorist. They are not. To know a tradition is to know its arguments, its differences, its breadth of diversity, as well as its underlying similarities and forms of unity.

As for comparison between traditions, here is the problem. Some traditions – each highly developed – are not only different but oppose each other. A taste for Chinese opera may preclude or lessen a taste for the European. The more refined you get in the hearing of rhythmical clang and Chinese sing song, the less you are able to stand the big, broad, mellifluous sounds of Verdi. The more you assimilate your ears to Bel Canto tradition the less you can stand (much less appreciate) the scratchiness of the Chinese instruments, their harsh plucking sounds, the long growling fierceness and sharp, high nasal tones of the Chinese aria. How then compare tastes in this sphere? And yet others would put these in the same category: opera. What then is the meaning of this category, surely not that all things within it may be compared.

This does not imply such traditions are incommensurable, allowing for no comparison at all. Both Italian and Chinese opera have much structurally in common: a way of telling story through aria, instrumental background, an animation of libretto as music, a story, and so on. Both sing of love, revenge, forgiveness, duty and its conflicts, the moral sphere and the loyalty of family, lust, murder and death – all the stuff that plays everywhere. Diversity is a matter of quality of instrumentation, form, articulation, language and its expression in aria and orchestral voice-leading, the kind of story and moral concepts behind it. And so the conflict over categorical inclusion bespeaks a confusion about comparison: these traditions are deeply alike and profoundly unlike, which is about as rich a remark as my grandmother would have made after she'd done telling me to stop worrying about life because the sun is going to rise tomorrow. Then along comes composer Bright Sheng, musician in Tibet for seven years during the Chinese cultural revolution, later student of Leonard Bernstein, whose opera (with libretto by David Henry Hwang) *The Silver River* incorporates both traditions so masterfully that one can no longer believe they are not 'made for each other'. Sheng goes so far as to have one of the characters play a Chinese classical instrument, the pipa, rather than sing, the story is Chinese myth reset as contemporary laughter which progressively becomes more poignant and more arioso. What is commensurable with what is a matter of the human ability to imagine its connection.

This means it is too simple either to assume a single standard fits all diversity, and that it does not. We are left with lines of similarity and difference, with the question of where standards fit in, ranked or otherwise, in doubt. In our globalized world Shakespeare and Charlie Chaplin are loved by just about everybody with an education, many things are not. This gives the canonical special status, but only that. It is up to the student to pursue this thorny question further: how tastes may be related, given diversity, and what model fits diversity better than a standard of taste (or many). Such a student must also appreciate the best of what Hume points out: that without commitment to standards we lose sight of the point of taste, or a point of it anyway: that delicacy is prized and wants to be improved.

There is another problem with the account of taste which deserves mention. Taste is about *consumption*, which product you prefer and how you might prefer a better one. This consumerist stance takes the object of taste to be, in effect, a kind of product. It is an artefact of the history of individual liberty within growing systems of economy that the eighteenth century set forth such consumer centred stances. With the dawn of advertising the product status of objects of taste will become explicit, since products will be sold by their images. But consumerism is datable to the eighteenth century, where travel, wines, a good cigar, quality port, fine art and collectibles are all grouped together under the rubric of pleasures for the leisure class to enjoy. It is often thought that the commodification of the arts begins in the nineteenth century, with the birth of the gallery system and the circulation of art objects through museum (where they are eternalized) into gallery (where they are bought and sold at a good price because the price is set in terms of their 'priceless museum quality'). In fact its origins are in Hume's liberal state, where objects are grouped in terms of the pleasure they give the consumer.

This is, to repeat, a consumer-oriented theory, as opposed to a theory which gives precedence to the artist, to the expressive value of the object, to ritual or cult value, to the social benefit of art. Benefit here is for individuals, and ranked by them. And is about what you consume, how you consume it, and the delicacy of pleasure you get from it. For Hume this practice is a given, assumed and enjoyed rather than criticized. His is the enjoyment of a practice new to history, and he is ready to adulate it. The true judge is important because men of taste wish to better their enjoyment of things, to better choose and better consume. This is 'the finer things in life', about life's finery: to appear suave and refined in public, wish never to humiliate themselves in front of Lord or employer, wish to take pride in their delicacy of mind and their practised imagination. These perhaps also increase pleasure – the more refined being the more satisfying and memorable? Hume's is an approach which the nouveau riches of today will find appealing, since it elevates them to learn from the best Tuscan chefs, the best connoisseurs of fine painting, to dress themselves in the garment of a Renaissance Tuscan home with its patina of olive and orchard, to purchase a wine farm in the Cape Province of South Africa and turn the money they made as stockbrokers into good vintage.

The ultimate point is this. The setting of standards of taste is a *practice* in itself, one whose formation in the eighteenth century was a very central part of the growth of consumerism. Men endlessly sat in clubs judging cigars, wine, port, beef tenderloin, poetry, essays, the best places in Europe, and so on. This was a gesture of superiority, accompanying the course of champagne and oysters because the world was their oyster. Everything flowed into England from colony and conquest and it all got homogenized into one by the institutions of the museum, the shops in London, the judgements of men in clubs and at universities and in newspapers.

Should this practice be taken as an ultimate, unchallenged value? At what point does ranking objects (tastes) become an obsession rather than discrimination? Eighteenth-century Britain was a society in which everyone and everything had its place, in which everything was hierarchical, everyone had 'betters' and the society ran on putting people in their place. Must every object of taste be ranked (placed in a standard), and every critic similarly evaluated for his potential membership in the hall of fame, as if from Hogwarts School of Witchcraft and Wizardry? This is a boarding school where children are ranked in all things: academic performance, politeness, ability on the playing fields in preparation for a future Battle of Waterloo. Is this a practice which is the mark of a disciplinary society in Michel Foucault's sense, a society desiring the ordering of pleasures, and their distribution through forms of control? Is it a game which you play if you like or not if you don't, a matter of taste: a taste for standardization? Some people like sitting around all night ranking wines or recordings of Mozart, others find this ludicrous, disingenuous, purely subjective anyway, a game of humiliation and expulsion without further merit. Who is correct?

KANT AND THE DISINTERESTEDNESS OF JUDGEMENT

We turn to the other side of the argument: to that approach which seeks, through the concept of disinterestedness, to sharply demarcate taste as a unique and autonomous kind activity. Kant is the most powerful philosophical representative of this approach.

Immanuel Kant (1724–1804) begins with a distinction which eludes Hume: the distinction between merely liking something and finding it beautiful. According to Kant this is what is at stake in understanding taste as disinterested (following Addison). When I say I like something it means it pleases my senses. My liking it is therefore directly bound up with properties of the thing. *I like-a coffee, you like-a tea, I like-a cuppa cuppa coffee.* This American popular ditty from the 1940s says it all. What I like is my business, what you like is yours. About mere likes and dislikes there is no disputing. What satisfies me satisfies me – period. I do not speak beyond myself and my inclinations when I state my preferences. I might invite you to share my like. Yes, do try this wine, I hope you find it as silky as I do. I might be disappointed if my gesture of sharing falls flat, but I shall be entitled to no moral suasion, no sense that you have failed in any other way than to mirror me. And I shall have no way of justifying any superiority of judgement on my part.

Likes are caused by objective properties of the object of taste which interact with my psychological proclivities. This is a matter for what Kant calls philosophical anthropology. It is about organic facts of me, considered as a part of nature.

None of this pertains to the judgement of the beautiful. The judgement of the beautiful is disinterested. This means first that it is not a causal relation between objective facts about the object and objective facts about the one who judges, and second, that it expresses no 'interest' in the object. When I say I like a painting it means objective facts about the object please me. But, according to Kant when I call it beautiful my judgement is not conditioned by any causal relation between its properties and my pleasures. Nor am I pleased by what it shows me about botany or what it might get me. Because of this, Kant believes the judgement of beauty (as opposed to merely liking something) carries more than the status of an individual report (I like coffee). It carries the weight of an 'ought'. I am saying you should like it too. To be committed to a judgement of beauty is to be committed to the claim that others – all others, all humanity – according to Kant, should find it the same. This is not the claim that all others should have a similar physical constitution and social upbringing to me, one that is pleased by raspberries, high craggy mountains, red shirts with low collars, long hair (if you've got it), gold jewellery, designer glasses. I am not imposing a norm of myself onto others in the manner of the emperor who decreed all children must wear British khaki because it was a sign of their civility, and that not only must they sing of green and pleasant fields, they must *like* doing it. How you check is an interesting question, an invitation to the thought police. Mine is not a claim of omnipotence, or slavery over others: if you don't like this there is something defective about you because you are not me.

It is a claim of a different order. You too should find it beautiful because there is nothing particular to me which has caused the pleasure I have taken in this object that grounds my judgement. Rather, Kant argues the ground of my judgement is universal because it is 'disinterested'. The pleasure I have felt which grounds my judgement is based in no interest of mine, nothing peculiar to me. It is therefore a pleasure every other human ought to share who is capable of assuming a similarly disinterested stance. The claim of the beautiful is a claim grounded in a person's ability to abstract themselves, stand aside, from their interests, everything particular to them, and take this rarified, heightened pleasure which Kant calls disinterested. Disinterestedness is at the basis of the judgement of taste, when that judgement is not about likes and dislikes but about beauty. Disinterestedness is not lack of focus or absorption, it is the ability to stand aside from one's interests and take a special pleasure in an object apart from all interests in it.

This view is as paradoxical as it is powerful. How do you take pleasure in an object without grounding your judgement in any of its causal properties? How do you call a painting beautiful (as opposed to liking it) if the causal consequences of the *properties* of the painting (colour, figure, medium) do not ground your judgement? We have seen that Hume's desire to ground pleasure in objective fact partially fails, giving force to Kant's position. And yet it is strange to say the least if nothing about an object is what conditions a person's judgement that it is beautiful. For if the judgement is unconditioned by the object, why have an object at all? And why this object, the object one judges about? When I say a sunset is beautiful, yes, I may be saying something more, and deeper, than 'I like it'. But surely whatever I am saying is based in my response to the sunset, to its striated, wide angled, darkening hue, its last moment of transient brilliance, its legato descent into emptiness, its rhythm of daily ordinariness. Surely I am saying, everyone else ought to find this as I do, if it is to be believed that I am speaking in a universal voice at all?

Kant happily embraces this conundrum about the object. Whereas Hume wished to ground judgements of taste in causal properties of the object of taste, hence the example of Panza and the leathern thong, Kant argues the opposite. The judgement of the beautiful, being disinterested, is not strictly speaking a judgement about the object of taste at all! It is a purely subjective judgement, a judgement occasioned by the object but not about it. How then does an object (person, painting, rose) occasion the experience of disinterestedness, and what is this experience focused on, if not on the object itself? How does it serve as a catalyst for the play of our imaginative faculties, which is the point of the exercise, Kant thinks?

Kant answers the question through his four moments of the beautiful, in his famous *Critique of Judgment*.[13] The answer proves as deep as it is surprising.

The first moment of the beautiful articulates what is at stake that the judgement of the beautiful is disinterested. Not only is the judgement grounded in no pleasure caused by the object, but it also takes place apart from any moral interest one might have in the object. A moral interest would take the object to be something to which moral principles should be applied, and action towards the object taken accordingly. In acting morally I require knowledge of the object of my action. I must know how it will contribute to some moral end. There is no place for such an interest in judgements of the beautiful.

This is the surprising result. To be disinterested the judgement must be non-cognitive, and therefore one need not know anything about the object one finds beautiful. It can be an indefinable 'something', an 'I know not what but I love it', or a common rose. If it is a common rose, we know what it is, this is unavoidable. But our judgement that it is beautiful takes place apart from any such knowledge. The knowledge may in some vague way 'enter in', but cannot be what motivates the judgement. So even where the object is 'known', this knowledge does not generate aesthetic judgement. One might as well not know anything about it. This is serious, as aesthetics becomes an attitude towards the object which dissolves knowledge and focuses elsewhere.

These three attitudes towards a thing (concepts of it, moral interests in it, pleasure caused by its properties) are all abstracted from the judgement of the beautiful. It is therefore *dis-interested* in the object in the strongest possible sense. What then does the imagination focus upon, if none of these ways of regarding the object?

When I find myself absorbed in a flowering field of peonies, I need know nothing about them (not even that they are flowers) nor need I have any moral or other interest in them (which I might were I a financier or an environmentalist). I stand apart from whatever interest I have or determining concept I might possess and call the peonies beautiful. Not only does my knowledge of the flower slide away into a haze, becoming irrelevant to the quality and kind of absorption I have in it; the pleasure I feel on the basis of which I make my judgement is not caused by any of its properties. Were someone to ask: 'What makes it beautiful?', I would speak of its drooping, heavy blossoms, the lushness of its scent, the hypnotic allure of its soft colours. Insofar as these are properties of the flower, my answer would be inappropriate, Kant thinks. For whatever causes pleasure in me directly from the object (the peony) is relevant to why I like it, not to my judgement of its beauty. This is a strange view, to say the least, as abstracted from the object as Hume is tied to it.

The best sense one can make of it is that the qualities I refer to, in speaking about the object, are not, properly speaking, its properties, but constructs of my own imagination, my own play of faculties. Where my language becomes metaphorical, or projective, where I speak of drooping heaviness, hypnotic allure, lushness and softness of colour I am going beyond what is 'in the thing' or its positioning (it droops, yes) to what I see in it. My pleasure is subtly shifting from a pleasure directly caused by it to a pleasure I take in my own design of it, my own play of imagination in and around it. The judgement, when it passes beyond direct causality into a free play of my imagination, is what Kant calls reflective. This is because I am taking pleasure in my own faculty of construction, not in the thing.

The line between pleasure caused by the flower and pleasure generated within myself is unclear to be sure, which is finally an insuperable problem for Kant's view. Whereas Hume wanted to root the pleasure of the true judge in direct causal relation to the thing judged, and failed, Kant wants the opposite. He wants to root the pleasure taken when one finds an object beautiful in essence within oneself. This too fails, since there is finally no clear line between pleasure caused by the object and pleasure conditioned upon one's own free play of imagination in and around it. Liking something is not a different category of judgement from finding it beautiful, even if there are provisional distinctions to be had. I can find a work of art beautiful but think it too steely, severe, uncompromising, Catholic to really 'like it' very much. But insofar as I find it beautiful I am at least moved by it. Something about it causes and occasions a free play of my own faculties and interests, I don't entirely dislike it.

The eighteenth century is a century of extremes. On the one hand Hume, and his attempt to tie true judgements to properties of the object through the faculty of 'delicacy of taste', thus putting taste on the same 'objective' footing as other fields of judgement. On the other Kant, with his desire to sharply and categorically distinguish pleasure caused by the object and pleasure occasioned within the self (within one's own free play of imagination), thus rendering the judgement of the beautiful purely subjective. Between these extremes the relation of pleasure to object/work of art, of judgement to causal property and self-generated imagination, resides. It is a capacious space in which aesthetics and its partial objectivity, partial subjectivity, resides.

Kant has deep reasons for wanting the judgement of the beautiful to be categorically distinct from the judgement of liking something. These are, as we shall soon see, moral reasons, not simply reasons having to do with the disinterestedness of the judgement. It is crucial to him that the determining ground of the judgement of the beautiful resides in me, in the subject who judges, rather than in the object so that this judgement is 'reflective', a judgement about me, about the subject, rather than about the object. There is something to this (just as there is something to Hume's side of the equation as well). When I tell a joke the pleasure I take in laughing is not simply in the punch line, but in the making of it. My laughter is rounded out by my self-satisfaction in devising it. This can be mere narcissism but is often not. There is a joy in the making which comes through in all art; it is for this reason that art is, as Hegel said, essentially cheerful. What is being shared, in sharing a joke or work of art, is the pleasure in the making of it, not simply the representation it conveys, or the quality of its forms. Pleasure in art is always in part reflectively occasioned, because it is occasioned by our own sense of delight in our own faculties. Pleasure is always, in part, a way of taking pleasure in ourselves, when we make things up and they work. Conversely the depth of humiliation one can feel when one's work of art – or joke – fails comes from a displeasure at the core of oneself, at one's failed capacity at work, and in the limelight, for all the audience to see. Art renders one naked before others.

But for Kant the judgement is purely reflective, not reflective in (cheerful) part. It is a judgement entirely about me, about the person who judges. Were it partly about things specific to me: my particular interests, my preferences, wants, desires, this would more or less be the end of the story, as far as he is concerned. It is because the judgement is about me, but *not about anything specific to me* (my particulars of preference, want, desire) that I can make it 'in the universal voice', as a judgement directed to all humanity. Everyone else should similarly judge beauty here. The key is in the 'should'. I am not saying that everyone like me ought to judge as I do, which in itself would be to say a lot. I am saying all humanity ought to judge the same. Because nothing conditioning my judgement is specific to my particulars, because the source of my judgement is disinterested pleasure, pleasure taken in the exercise of a faculty all others ought to have, all others ought to similarly exercise it and feel the pleasure. What is being communicated through this judgement is a shared sensibility about the faculty itself: the faculty we all share, and which is critical to making us humans. The judgement is a call to deploy this faculty around this object. Look here, I can do it, you ought to be able to do it too, and it is a good thing for you to do this, to take pleasure as I do, because the faculty you too will be deploying is, as mine is, what makes us human. Universal judgement is a call to share universally, for all to deploy what I deploy because it is good to do this.

Why is it good to do this? Kant's answer will come slowly, although we could if we wanted stop here. Assuming love is a good thing, it would be no deficit of action to say to others, look, I am in love, see how wonderful it is. Moreover apart from my particulars (the kind of person I am drawn towards, the way I love) in its essence love is grand; humanizing for us all, and you ought to find a way to do the same. All of you, the more the merrier. This ought is not the ought of duty exactly: You have a duty to find this beautiful, to take pleasure in it, so get going and follow my commandment! That would be the Gestapo version of Kant's *Critique of Judgment*. In fact Kant, Prussian that he is, does believe we have a duty to be happy, since it makes us inclined to be more moral, which is not unessential to the *Critique*. For the *Critique* is about the moral relevance of pleasure, a pleasure which binds us together into communities of taste, making us more deeply drawn towards each other, and more motivated to right action or respect towards each other. And so this is not just a joke to him, this commandment to enjoy! However, the kind of ought at stake here is different in mood, it is an ought of togetherness, of shared enjoyment of our shared faculty, which finally, Kant thinks, makes (or might make) life more moral overall.

The third moment of the beautiful specifies that the experience of the beautiful is an experience of 'purposiveness without purpose'. This is about the way our imagination plays in and around the object. Since the pleasure is not caused by the object but within our own faculty, what form does it take? The answer is formalist. Our imagination shapes the object into a play of sensuous elements, each of which is there in order to contribute towards the achievement of an end. All the parts matter, nothing is irrelevant to the work's purpose. And yet, strictly speaking the work of art or beautiful object of whatever sort has no purpose, merely the form of a purposiveness. This is because neither concepts nor interests shape its experience. Some have called Kant's the aesthetics of 'as if'. We find in the object a sense of organization in which all the parts seem to conspire towards some end, treating it as if it had such an end. Herein resides the pleasure, the sense of perfection, the feeling that everything is there in the work for a reason.

This is Kant's answer to the question: in what are we absorbed when we find a peony or performance beautiful, if not concepts, ends or the like? The answer is, we are absorbed in the play of sensuous particulars organized in our own imaginations towards some end, without there being any actual end. We are absorbed in the way sensuous particulars form formal organization. This is what we construct: it is how the peony ends up seeming to droop like a heavy, erotic perfumed form. We have constructed that, its overall design, intensively sensualized, spontaneously framed.

Kant's idea is that everything must in a work of art or article of nature seem to be meant, seem to conspire towards development, organic fit, achievement of purpose, clarity within the frame. Music is the clearest example of his idea, since it seems to 'move' towards completion, when nothing has moved at all, simply been heard. And a fine work of music is one in which nothing seems extraneous to this overall purpose, this overall sense of purposiveness. And so the great Mozart is told 'your piece is very good, but . . . there are too many notes'. 'Which notes would you like me to leave out?' he responds, knowing the answer is, none may be left out, all are necessary to the sense of flow, build up, resolution. It is not for nothing that Walter Pater, following the formalism inaugurated by Kant, announced that all arts aspire to the condition of music. In music meaning is minimal and form overwhelming, from first to last the compositional process introduces materials so that they might be intensified, made more complex to the ear, and finally built to resolution. The fantasy of a musical movement bespeaks our projective perception of the sound which literally goes nowhere except from instrument to us, perhaps through a recording, perhaps in a concert hall, perhaps in our own ears. And yet we cannot but hear it move, travel towards some unknown place where through repetition, variation, modulation, return, cyclical generation and final dying away, it comes to its end.

The music theorist Leonard Meyer first described this process as one of music's amassing expectations which are successively unresolved and reformulated, only to be brought finally to satisfaction.[14] Tonal music seems clear: the sonata form introduces materials which lead away from the tonic and intensify, after having been stated, through the principles of variation and modulation, finally at the end returning but this time in a way that seeks final resolve rather than movement away. Cadence, that moment in tonal form where a phrase leads to the fifth degree so that return to the first (the tonic chord) feels like completion, is essential to the form. Rhythmic implication, phrase structure, contrapuntal intensification, are all about deepening, and resolution, of implications. When is music 'worked through' successfully? When we feel it so. Meyer later replaced his concept of expectation with that of 'musical implications' which are supposed to be 'in the music'.[15] But if one puts together the word 'expectation', which is about us and how we experience music, with the word 'implication', which is about the way form is descried, one gets the right picture. Whether these movements of complication, uncertainty, shock and then development and resolution are a matter of our feel for sound or that which is in its concept when composed is impossible to metaphysically determine. Music occasions a sense within our own imaginations of purposiveness leading to final 'end/resolution', even though there is none apart from our sense of it.

Form, it might plausibly be argued, is not directly a property of an object (the way colour or figure is), but a mysterious synergy between it and our imaginative minds. How much apprehension of form is objective, how much subjective, is another of the questions of aesthetics for which no satisfactory theory has been offered. Kant goes too far in thinking form entirely a property of our imaginations and not at all in the object: it is in an alchemical synergy between the two the music is made. But it is correct in highlighting the mystery of this process, the mystery of art. How can an object stimulate the sense of the beautiful on the basis of so little? How can it be that marks on paper in oil cause an entire public to swoon with the sense of power and unity? How can it be that we understand music to have a magnificent shape when all it is, is sounds? The formalist is utterly taken by this mystery and wishes to preserve it upfront in his or her philosophy of art. Art is sublime, its origin unknowable, and its force overwhelming.

To grasp the fourth moment of the beautiful another piece in the story is necessary. Kant believes the judgement of the beautiful is reflectively composed, it is a judgement flowing from our faculties of imagination and about them. That would be enough for an excellent theory. But he believes something more. Like all judgements, he thinks, this one must have a specific referent. It is not simply a call to sharing: a way of saying, my faculty has done this, yours should too, our faculties are a good thing. It is a judgement which takes pleasure in a strange thing, a thing which is not a thing, but a sublime vision of a thing. This strange referent of the judgement of taste is there in order for Kant's moral vision of the importance of the aesthetic to be given theoretical articulation.

The object of our judgement of taste is a particular aspect of ourselves: our shared, supersensible substrate, the thing that makes us human, our shared substrate of humanity. To say that the pleasure we take in ourselves is a pleasure directly referred to this substrate that is beyond sensibility would today make no sense at all. It would be considered hocus-pocus. In Kant's time everyone will have understood it as being a way of naming the soul. And everyone will have believed in this. Kant's theory is religious in a way Hume's is adamantly not. He believes the content of the judgement is the invisible, mysterious, wondrous, sublime thing that is not a thing that we all share, in virtue of being human souls. Without a Christian tradition of 'the immortal soul' to back him up, a tradition widely believed in his time, the claim would be absurd. There is no such thing that is not a thing that we all share that makes us humans. Kant believes there is, and believes, in believing it, he is simply following common faith, speaking indubitably about the deepest and most moral beliefs of his time. For Kant, the judgement of the beautiful is a judgement about our own souls, the element we share in common, specific to none, that makes us human, moral beings.

He is more specific. The pleasure we take in the beautiful is a pleasure taken in our shared capacities to be moral agents, our abilities to rise above the nature of beasts and treat one another with respect. This in Judaeo–Christian legacy is what makes us have the value we do. Since we can never experience our own souls directly, but only through our actions and those of others, since the soul is sublime, and supersensible, in being a core of self that is known only through its presentations, only through what we do, we need a way of symbolizing it, and of taking pleasure in that symbolization. The soul is symbolized and addressed through religious ritual, but through the aesthetic, we find a way of symbolically taking pleasure in it. We do this by deploying our free play of imagination in a way that symbolizes the work of this soul, the way it shows itself in the world, its action. The entirety of the four moments of the beautiful are meant to lead up to this dazzling result. The organization of aesthetic judgement, and the pleasure at its source, is designed as a way for us to take pleasure in our mysterious, sublime, moral selves, and to do so by simulating the form of moral action without engaging in any.

How does this happen, this symbolic way aesthetics has of getting in touch with our inner moral capacities and allowing us to take pleasure in them? To answer, a word on Kant's moral theory is in order. On Kant's moral theory, morality is a matter of acting out of duty, respect for the moral law, not a matter of passion or inclination (which is Hume's view). Thinking he is doing nothing more than secularizing the Judaeo–Christian tradition, Kant argues moral action is following the commandments, and that all the commandments finally reduce to one: Do unto others as you would have them do unto you. This Golden Rule becomes in Kant's philosophical theory the rule of acting out of respect for all humanity. Whatever one does, one should do it only if all others, in the same position as oneself, could be licensed to do the same. If you lie, only lie if all others could be allowed to lie in the same circumstance. If you choose not to vote, do it only if all others could do the same. There is nothing special about you, neither class, breeding, income, good looks, membership in the right club, intellect, cunning or brute strength that should allow you to get away with doing something it would not be right for all others, in the same boat, to do. We are all bound to the same principle, the principle of acting at one with all others. This is, in Kant's view, acting out of respect for other people, for their sameness with you. No one is less of a person than another, worthy of less excellent respect.

When a person acts out of respect for the moral law, which means respect for all other humans, that person is acting as an exemplar for all humanity. This Enlightenment vision of equality between all subjects, the vanguard, at that time, of democratic thought at a moment of French and American revolutions and checks on the divine rights, so-called, of the monarchy, is a vision which places the moral subject in the exemplary role. Each and every one of us, knowing we are acting in the same way as all others, acts in the name of all humanity. Our actions are in no way peculiar to ourselves, but universal.

It is easy to see that the structure of this, Kant's view, is repeated in the four moments of the beautiful. The first moment distinguishes personal likes and dislikes from disinterestedness. This distinction repeats the moral distinction between acting out of inclination (what you feel like doing, what passionately compels you) and acting out of respect. Yes, inclination may be involved in moral action (you want to save the baby, you do not just act out of principle). And yes, likes may be involved in the experience of the beautiful: you like the rose and you find it beautiful. But the ground of judgement is in both cases not a matter of inclination or likes. Whether you liked it or not, were inclined to do it or not, you are acting/judging out of the motive of respect for law, or disinterested appreciation. And so the first moment of the beautiful repeats the structure, Kant believes, of morals.

The second moment does the same. Just as when you act morally, out of respect, you are acting in the name of all humanity (doing what you are doing because everyone else should do the same in the same circumstance), so in the experience of the beautiful you are judging in the name of all humanity (everyone should similarly find this beautiful, in the way I do).

The third moment of the beautiful symbolizes the structure of moral action by simulating purpose through purposiveness. Just as moral action organizes what is done in a way that should lead to the right end or conclusion, so in the experience of the beautiful all the parts are symbolically organized so as to seem to lead to a conclusive end.

It is because all of these moments simulate the structure of moral action that the fourth moment can conclude: beauty is the symbol of the morally good. The experience of the beautiful is our way, our only way, of taking pleasure (disinterested pleasure) in our shared moral capacities. We do so by actively and through the free play of our imaginations symbolically engaging in moral action, that is, *simulating its form and judgement*. The call for others to find something beautiful is really the call for them to engage in a reflective judgement about their piece of the shared substrate of humanity, the soul. This is why we have a duty to take pleasure in the beautiful! Because it is a training ground for moral action and judgement, a way of taking pleasure in that side of ourselves, a way of acknowledging our shared capacity for moral judgement when we can never 'see or know' that capacity directly, but only in the form of indirect symbols devised by ourselves, and finally, a way for a community of like-minded judgers of the beautiful to form, which draws humans more deeply together and on the highest possible ground. The model is religion, something ubiquitous to Kant's day. A community in prayer is a community in awe of God and in encounter with its moral self through this ritual and song. That community exists on a similarly high ground, and binds itself together in a way that cultivates moral spirit through fellow feeling. Kant adopts the religious standpoint in his secular vision of aesthetics.

THE MORALLY GOOD AND THE SUBLIME

We have seen that Kant invests the disinterested experience of form with a massive perspective. This perspective sets a template for future aesthetics. Kant's writing and vision lead directly to Friedrich Schiller (1759–1805), the great playwright of high ideas and human freedoms of the early nineteenth century. His plays, and aesthetic theory (in the *Letters on the Aesthetic Education of Man*)[16] are about moral uplift through experience of form, but also through their high-minded content and sublime (so he hopes) moments of glory and tragic recognition. Schiller wishes his art to provide humanizing sensitivity towards others, and a trumpet call for all humanity. Schiller believes that through the content of his plays as well as their formal unity (purposiveness) humans are brought together to take pleasure in their deepest capacities for morality, and so uplifted. Again and again his plays are about injustice, the difficulty of moral action, the high-minded willingness to die for a cause. It is not simply through formalism that beauty becomes a moral symbol: Schiller believes Kant is wrong in this, but through a combination of theme and formal means. Schiller is surely right, insofar as the mere play of imagination, without a guiding idea, leads to no moral uplift, simply the pleasure in imaginative freedom. Whether that can move people to resist oppression or act more morally, who knows? Formalists like Kant tend to put too much trust in the power of abstract form to deepen their self-recognition and improve their souls.

It is a combination, Schiller tells us, of high-minded ideas or ideals, and excellence of form that compels the human imagination and spirit. This is a way of saying that the aesthetic category of the beautiful and the aesthetic category of the sublime are more closely linked than Kant thought. The *Third Critique* is about both. Since the object of the judgement of the beautiful is something sublime: the supersensible substrate of humanity, one cannot finally understand the beautiful without the sublime.

The sublime has a long history, dating to ancient times and the writings of Longinus. The sublime differs fundamentally from the beautiful. It is an experience not of harmony and pleasure (purposiveness shaped to conclusion without purpose), but of something taken to be so overwhelming that it dwarfs the subject into a state of awe and trembling. The sublime is the experience of an object whose size (magnitude) or power is so great as to dwarf the mind, even the cognizing imagination. Faced with the grandeur of the tallest mountain, the power of the greatest symphony, the astonishing, overwhelming sky, airbrushed with a thousand galaxies in the cold, laser light of the southern hemisphere, the number line stretched to an infinity we cannot imagine, we bow down in awe. We cannot properly conceive of, cognize, the thing presented to us. Hence the mixture of pleasure and pain built into the experience. Our emotions are flooded with the sense of exaltation, we are levitated. And we are reduced to near nothingness by our inadequacy before this enormity. 'Before thee God I am nothing' says the high priest on the holiest day of the Jewish year, Yom Kippur, the only day he is allowed to enter the room of he who must not be named, the holy of holies, in the temple. Overcome with humility he hits the floor in shame for his sins, the sins of all, beseeching God for another year in which to atone through action. This is the sublime.

The experience of the sublime is one of bowed head before the overwhelming character of a thing, is a state of awe before that thing. If aesthetics is in the first instance about the judgement of the beautiful, religion, its double and mirror image, is about the sublime in the first instance. In the state of awe the enormity of an idea arises in the mind: the idea of an overwhelming power, a nature too vast to be cognized, the power of number itself (stretched to infinity), the enormity of the mountaintop. The sublime, Kant says, is an experience in which great ideas, ideas so marvellous that they have no clear presentation or instance in the world, may be cognized, or better, received, since we finally fail to cognize them at all but are simply overcome by their visionary power. The sublime is our way of coming before the power of a universe whose spirit rushes beyond us: it is the experience of the utopian, the moment when nations, worlds, the future, the mysterious fact of life and its elevating power, is revealed. It is our reaction to the supersensible substrate of ourselves when we contemplate it straight on. Above us, yet also within, our attitude towards this thing that is not a thing because we cannot know it directly like other things, is one of worthlessness and exalted identification with its power. The sublime is a force of empowerment. Such ideas are for Kant: the perfect moral world, the divine itself, the supersensible substrate of our own humanity. They are important human motivations, utopian motivations, and so, the sublime is our way of becoming overwhelmed by their force, a force which can compel us to act in its spirit.

The sublime is about power, and for Kant, this means the motivating power of ideas: ideas worthy of worship.

It is crucial to the power of art that it intertwines the beautiful and the sublime. This is what Schiller immediately understood from Kant, and from his own work as a playwright. It is what the world of Europe heard in Beethoven, believed true of the young Napoleon, found in the impassioned writings of Rousseau. This is Kant's world, the moral urgency of the late eighteenth century. When the theme and variations in the final movement of the Beethoven *Third Symphony* come to a hush and the theme is heard as a yearning, the moment is poignant, but also sublime, as if the heavens have opened and justice has been heard. This is the music of all humanity, its rush of visionary motion towards an unimaginably wondrous future. 'How could he have done that? How is such music possible?' is the question we ask, overcome by the sublime. Beethoven originally titled that work 'The Napoleonic', until Napoleon declared himself emperor and Beethoven withdrew the title in disgust.

History has shown since Kant's day that the sublime plays a generative role in mass historical movements: for good or bad. When the sublime is connected to social ideas which become adulated as scripture, it is central to the formation of modern cults, cults of aestheticism, nationalism, temples of art. It is a cult of pleasure, and of transcendental awe before the glorious. One finds it for example in the articulation of the sublime glory and utter beauty of the French Revolution in the historical writings (works of art really) of Jules Michelet. Abel Gance (democratic nationalist) relies on the aura, the charisma of Napoleon to charge the then newly wrought project of the League of Nations (formed since 1919) with his over-arching spirit. Throughout his film (*Napoleon*, 1925), the figure of Napoleon is shown apart, as if under a halo. He interacts with others, but through gestures of superior resolve carrying the certainty of commandment. He is small but filmed always from below, to appear grandiose, or in a profile filling the screen, dwarfing all else. By dominating space Napoleon commands time. Finally the film exfoliates him, splitting the screen into triplicates, each filled with his colourized form or with the armies that are his alter ego. It is thrilling; the already larger than life domain of cinema has proved too small for his tumultuous presence, his monumental talent, his dreams for the future of humanity. The sky is, literally, the limit, as the film cuts between it and he, perched on horseback and surveying the future, the Italian campaign (or is it the twentieth century?), from the mountaintop. The film is about Napoleon's second life, about his future, a Europe prophesied in his name, by giving him this second life on screen. His multiplication on screen signifies his universalization. He is everybody, everywhere, for all: like film, his double (equally exfoliated, equally large). That the colours of the three split screens comprise the 'tricolour' – the French flag – means Michelet's version of the endless sublimity of the French revolution is being called to completion. Napoleon and the nation are one, he is the flag. 'From now on', he announces after having been given command of the Italian campaign, 'I am the revolution'. Scary, yes, this great man thesis which the film cultifies, although for democratic ends, is nevertheless idolatry. The film ends with the Italian campaign under way, but as yet incomplete. We are to complete it in our own time, the film is telling us, through the unification of Europe and the (then) new League of Nations. So will our own time redeem Napoleon the fighter by gathering power under the banner of his aura. Our completing it is his completing it. And so the aura of Napoleon pervades the entire map of our utopian historical future: our future is his, we are him. This subliming of the idea of a perfectly just world into the face of an individual is a way of concretizing awe through his aura, of transcendentalizing *him*.

The twentieth-century critic Walter Benjamin will argue that such tactics recruit the sublime for the purposes of deifying the historical idol, and energizing mass emotion and action around his signification. Through identification with him, and all he stands for, we have the illusion that awe is ours for the reaching, that the impossible distance between ourselves and the sublime idea is being mediated by this priesthood. It is Catholic, a direct telephone line between we tiny morals and the great one. Both fascism and totalitarianism rely on this kitsch. Nothing can be more historically dangerous, in that ideas are no longer debatable, persons no longer capable of being judged. They are idols, and this idolatry (the breaking of the first commandment of the ten: thou shalt have no other gods before me) may lead men into the siege of Stalingrad (two million dead, starved to death, trying to keep alive by eating rats), the killing of Tutsi, the ethnic cleansing of Bosnia. Voltaire, empiricist to the core, and deeply sceptical of human fantasy, once said something like: if you can get a person to believe an absurdity you can get them to commit an atrocity. He knew: he'd seen what Catholicism had wrought. Happily he missed the twentieth century on account of being dead.

The sublime is that which resists incarnation in an individual, a nation, a group. Because it is an experience of an idea which has no presentation, no instance in the real world. It is meant to cause humility. When concretized as the aura of nation, of group, of individual, it causes the opposite, mass identification. Much of twentieth-century aesthetics described the importance of the beautiful in this. Beethoven is both, yes, both beautiful and sublime. When politics become beautified through representational kitsch and the recruiting of Beethoven, Bach, even Wagner (already an idol himself) for Nazi culture, the sublime idea is concretized in beautifying things, giving the illusion that its achievement is similarly beautiful. These symbols of the fascist nation, cast in the glow or aura of religious perfection, seduce and energize, generating the aura of cult and its hysteria. And so the Italian fascist turns the sublime idea of the classical world into a series of wedding cake architectural forms which are meant to tell the populace that they are really Roman warriors in disguise, the Nazi takes dumb German peasants and elevates them into holy gods, the Stalinist (on the other side of the pendulum) casts a dirty worker as a marathon man ready to push the state forwards with the strength of Arnold Schwarzenegger and the perfection of Mr Nexus Six Model himself, Rutger Hauer.

This is what the Frankfurt School famously called the aestheticization of politics.[17] It is a modern twist on the formation of these categories in the eighteenth century, telling us that these categories are not simply abstractions, they respond to deep movements in modern culture and life. In Chapter 5 I shall speak about what is at stake in understanding a new medium of art. There I shall focus on aesthetic features of film. Since I shall not speak of it in that chapter, let it be noted here that from the first the political power of film was at stake for aestheticians of the Frankfurt School, and liberal democracy. Writers like Benjamin, and Siegfried Kracauer were concerned to understand the revolutionary potential of this mass medium, a medium capable of sublimity and seduction as well as powerful social revelation. If their utopian hopes – and fears – about the medium were not substantiated by later history, it is nevertheless true that to grasp a new medium, central to the public imagination, is to make claims about its politics, and these are connected to the aesthetic features one discerns in it. Hence the power of the sublime to move Frenchmen, and Frenchwomen, and Europeans, to reclaim Napoleon for the early twentieth century. Aesthetics is never totally dissociated from politics, given the powerful social roles of the arts, and the way aesthetic categories are needed to understand these roles.

There is nothing more human in the making of art, or religion, or aesthetic philosophy than the desire to invest abstract judgements about form with deep cultural, symbolic meaning and value. For this is the desire to make art and nature the vehicles for communion around the largest possible ideas, thus turning art and nature into temples of religion, homes of human intimacy and vehicles of power. The later formalism that flows from Kant will largely give up Kant's big picture of art and morality, scriptured onto the experience of form, and simply say: the value of art consists in the unique power of absorption in form it provides. When we engage in the experience of purposiveness without purpose no further meaning attaches to it. This experience is not about the symbolization of the morally good, its value consists in the fact that it is an end in itself, a way of deepening absorption within one's own imagination that is not about anything at all, but is instead a mystery. This desire to free aesthetic focus and pleasure from the burden of meaning and symbolization is as deeply human, and central to aesthetic theory and artistic practice, as the counter-tendency to invest the experience with sublime values. It is because focus on form is abstract, it is because so little meaning is present when one follows through musical phrasing, or the abstract designs of a Mondrian painting, that form can become a mere cipher for all manner of further symbolization and signification. Where there is no meaning to begin with, or little as yet, the possibilities of supplying a script are vast. Now no experience of form is simply that: we always bring meaning to the occasion. But less is more, meaning the more reduced the form is of meaning, the more someone can attempt to supply it from the outside. The philosopher who ascribes meaning onto the object then becomes the artist of the occasion, or wants to be, by being the one who creates the meaning that is supposed to be there. Kant does this with his picture, applied to the experience of form, that takes this experience to be symbolic of the morally good and explains why. Or partly does with his picture, since there is a cultural context out of which he is writing which also sees the aesthetic in this religious way, a civilization Schiller is referring to which is brought up on this vision.

Kant's project of responding to this already existent cultural framework and also for helping it along by providing a theory of how the aesthetic serves the appropriate symbolic purpose, is a template for the history of art and aesthetics which follows. We shall see it happen in the avant-gardes (Chapter 5) where theory and manifesto aim to invest abstraction with political force. And to do so by turning abstraction into a cipher for the sublime, by supplying the 'great idea' which the work is supposed to mean. This desire to conceptually control an abstract experience comes close to the corruption of the sublime that happens when all manner of politics are pasted onto art. Where great ideas flow from abstract experiences and where a culture tries to artificially paste them on in the manner of kitsch is hard to determine, since great ideas (Kant's moral ones) flow from works of art and experiences of nature in cultural contexts, for cultures prepared to feel them and know them. Anyone might feel the breath and emptiness of the universe when gazing into a starry sky in the southern hemisphere. Kant will say he sees (looking into that sky in Prussia, or writing as if he has done) the moral law within. This seeing-as, this way of perceiving more than is in the thing itself, is generated by our cultural positions, not simply our shared humanity. Even in Kant's time Hume will have understood another way that persons regarded works of art and beautiful things: as mere commodities to be enjoyed, as civilizing instruments, things to be discussed in men's clubs. Whose heaven is starry-eyed and about the moral law within, and whose an occasion for a good port and cigar?

The avant-gardes will attempt (with uncertain success) to invest their works with deep political significations. What meaning attaches to the empty cipher of an abstract experience is a matter of what a culture is prepared to accept, or not, or debate about, or remain uncertain over. Modern culture wants to have aesthetic experience both ways: as a singular, magical thing in itself with no further meaning attached, freed from the burdens of interest and purpose, and as a massively symbolized ritual which serves the largest imaginable purposes. There is finally no true judge of such matters, which is why aesthetics has been since Kant allied with social criticism.

CHAPTER 4

ART AND EXPERIENCE

FOUR KEY STROKES OF DIFFERENCE FROM THE EIGHTEENTH CENTURY

The nineteenth century separates itself from the eighteenth in four decisive strokes. First it separates the study of art from that of nature. No longer will a single aesthetics suffice for both. Second, in focusing almost exclusively on art, it invokes the concept of art as human expression. Third, it demonstrates why, and how deeply, art has a history, and how much understanding that history matters for the understanding, experience and appreciation of art. Fourth, it makes clear that the arts must be studied in terms of individual media of art rather than simply as a singular, categorical whole. To know what art is one must know what makes one medium (painting) different from another (music), and why, in virtue of its particular features, this or that medium predominates at a given historical moment. Writing in the wake of Romanticism, which blends the arts together by turning painting into myth and poetry, poetry into music, music into painting, and all the arts into forms of uncanny memory, the nineteenth century begins the great, and ongoing act of sorting the arts out, sorting them for the differential possibilities and differential limitations, sorting them for their possibilities of pre-dominance, and also combination. All of these ideas find their most detailed explanation in the masterwork of G. W. F. Hegel (1770–1831), from whom much of the aesthetics of the nineteenth and twentieth centuries follow.

One would do well to view the history of aesthetics as a triple legacy of Hume, Kant and Hegel. From Hume questions of taste and of quality of judgement (the true judge) remain in place today.

And from Hume aesthetics retains a bent for naturalistic explanation: the attempt to root aesthetic experience in facts about human nature, particularly facts about human perception and psychology (Hume's 'strong sense and delicacy of passion'). This attempt to find psychological bases for the making and experience of art may be found in the work of John Dewey and Richard Wollheim, both of whom will make their appearances in this chapter, both of whom are naturalists.

From Kant we have inherited the legacy of formalism and of the symbolization of morality through art. One finds formalism in the work of Eduard Hanslick on the musically beautiful (in a book with that title),[1] in Clive Bell and Roger Fry on visual art, and in the writings of many others. Post-Kantian formalism wishes to restrict art to a small, and closely defined set of properties: properties of the medium. The goal of formalism is to argue that art is typically misperceived. While we believe representation, or expression to be central features of music, or painting, or architecture, they are not. The point of art is significant form in Bell's sense, and only that, an experience of fluency, purposiveness, finality which enraptures. Art's real value is a mystic thing, overwhelming, sublime, unfathomable and untranslatable.

The problem with formalism is always the difficulty of adequately distinguishing formal from non-formal features of a medium. Chamber music, abstract art: these are the most persuasive examples. But even in the symphonic repertory masterpiece after masterpiece has been made which challenges the distinction between formal and non-formal features, persuading that it is the synergy of these (however they have been defined) which counts for the art. On any formalist theory of music, words become marginal to that medium. Musical form is a matter of phrasing, harmony, rhythm, pitch, voice-leading, timbre, cadence, repetition, variation, and so on. And yet: in the Beethoven *Ninth Symphony*, final movement, the famous drinking song of joy ('Freude, Schoene Gottenfunkeln . . .') first appears in the cello section, which sings it alone. There is no doubt they are singing a song, one cannot hear it otherwise. We simply do not know what song, whether there will be words, until the music is repeated by the singers who sing the Schiller drinking song with the words. Retrospectively we realize that the cello section has been longing to sing words, as if the instinct for the word has been in the music all along. This is critical to the integration of orchestral and choral elements in this movement, hence to its form. For the celli are invested with the glory of words, and sound and word seem to become one. As soon as a feature is branded 'non-formal' and consigned to a marginal status within a medium of art, one can usually find a major example in which that non-formal feature blends into the construction of form in a most central way.

Moreover it is perverse to want to eliminate non-formal elements (however they are defined) such as concepts, interests, passions, emotions, ends and social role from aesthetic experience as a general rule! For example: formalism has little to say about the communal power of Greek Tragedy, which is about acknowledgement, recognition, process of purgation. Formalism is a powerful vision of purity and untranslatability that inevitably fails as a theory. It is best understood as a point of view on art, one which seeks to highlight perception of organization over perception of theme, expression or story.

From Kant aesthetics also retains the moral legacy: his idea that the beautiful object, being a judgement finally about the self and its inner sense, is the symbol of the morally good. One stands before the beautiful object as an exemplar, and the work, being a subjective experience symbolic of our moral capacities, stands as exemplary. For Hegel it stands for something more: the aspiration of an age; and something less: less universal, rather that which speaks at a moment of history.

This brings us to Hegel.

HEGEL'S AESTHETICS OF SOCIAL EXPRESSION

Hegel's masterwork is titled (straightforwardly enough) *Aesthetics* and is subtitled 'Lectures on Fine Art'. This is enough to tell us how the focus of his work has shifted from Hume's and Kant's. The book is no longer about something called taste, or the experience of the beautiful. It is about art. Hegel introduces the distinction between a book about nature and one about art by relying on the commonly held idea (in his own time, as in ours) that art is a product of human activity and appreciated as such. Art is made by humans as a way of accommodating themselves to their world and art (correctly) is understood on those terms:

> [M]an brings himself before himself by *practical* activity, since he has the impulse, in whatever is directly given to him, in what is present to him externally, to produce himself and therein equally

to recognize himself. This aim he achieves by altering external things whereupon he impresses the seal of his inner being and in which he now finds again his own characteristics. Man does this in order, as a free subject, to strip the external world of its inflexible foreignness and to enjoy in the shape of things only an external realization of himself. Even a child's first impulse involves this practical alteration of external things; a boy throws stones into the river and now marvels at the circles drawn in the water as an effect in which he gains an intuition of something that is his own doing. This need runs through the most diversiform phenomena up to that mode of self-production in external things which is present in the work of art.[2]

Art responds to a universal human need to 'lift the inner and outer world into [our] . . . spiritual consciousness as an object in which [we] . . . recognize again [our] . . . own [selves],[3] and '. . . in this duplication of [ourselves] . . . bringing what is in [us] . . . into sight and knowledge'[4] for others.

Hegel believes human activity is organized along a broad goal. The goal of human activity (that is, human history) is to conquer our environment, to create a world for ourselves in which we are free to be free. This means removing (overcoming) the alienation of our social as well as natural environment, making these conform to our deepest aspirations. The goal is to build a social world in which we find our deepest aspirations capable of expression. And this means simultaneously coming to know what our deepest human aspirations are. The goal of history is to build a world in which human empowerment is possible, and we can only do this by simultaneously coming to understand what makes us tick, what we truly want and how we together, as a social world, may facilitate this. Hegel's theory of history is simple, and a result of the Enlightenment announcement of universal human freedom. The goal is to make the world ours, thus enabling our own empowerment and becoming.

Writing at a moment when he believed the entire history of the world, with its blood, suffering, apparent waste, has in fact exhibited progress, Hegel's view is that the formation of the modern individual can only take place through human action. Only by trying to make the world one reflective of our interests can we realize we have failed, and get a better idea of how to do it through what went wrong. Human action is the piston of human knowledge. By making a world, we come to know better who we are and what we want, by realizing what the limitations of this world are. Progress is historical.

This is the shape of the Hegelian dialectic, crucial for aesthetics as well as religion, philosophy and politics. From stage to stage, by casting the world in a particular form, a form of monarchy, religious domination, philosophical culture, and particular institutions of law, humans have attempted to articulate their own freedom, to know, through this creative act of making their world, who they are and what institutions, forms of culture, concepts, arrangements of power will express them. The goal of history is knowledge: the knowledge that will allow for, and be shaped by, the world we simultaneously make. Homo faber: man the maker. This motto extends from the making of laws and courts to the making of art. Only through making a leap of faith into a new historical form, a new consciousness of utopia, a new set-up for human life to play itself out in a particular kind of game (Greek, Roman, Mediaeval, Renaissance, Enlightenment) could the limits of each be known, and something better be imagined out of the details and ruins of the old. Only at the end of history may we properly understand what the human action which led up to it was really about. At the time we stake a risk, unsure about the consequences of our conception of law, equality, human community, culture, philosophy. Happily for Hegel the final victory of history, the grasping of its golden snitch and end of the game of this wizardry, occurred – so he felt certain – right in his lap. This happened with the French revolution and with the enlightened ideas of Immanuel Kant. However Kant's thought, about life, justice, knowledge, art, remained too abstract, lacking in a sense, Hegel believed, of how morality, beauty, culture, constitutional law simply hang abstractly in the air, without grounds for real interpretation in life, apart from the sociological institutions (courts of law, churches, universities, museum, concert hall, chapel, forms of knowledge and science) which give abstract ideas and ideals the meat and potato of human belief and action. A true judge of culture is one who is not simply possessed of faculties by nature and training, but a person grounded in, and limited by, their society and its aspirations. Art is not a consumable thing made for taste, it is an integral part of the history through which humans have tried – and for Hegel, succeeded – in making a world that reflects their aspirations. It is a form of world-making and of knowledge, a way for people to come to know who they are and what they want.

Hegel's term for this is that art is a form of absolute spirit. Through sensuous symbols, art provides images not of abstract morality itself (Kant's idea of the beautiful), but an idealized image of a new social order, one of harmony, unity, purposive form in which the alienated fragments and contradictory aspects of the actual historical world at a given time are symbolically unified. In art, place and time find themselves embodied in a way that tries to bring together contradictions and resolve problems. Art is utopian in that it expresses what the world might look like at that time, were it better, and how humans might enjoy it. As such it is a way of bringing to light contradictions, problems, and the aspiration to resolve these.

An example is needed. Hegel's two volumes are filled with these, they constitute to him the past history of the arts. But a more contemporary example might do better. Since I lived in South Africa during the 1990s, at the tumult of transition from Apartheid to democracy, let me turn to the art made at that moment of whirlwind. We go back to 1992, one year after the formal end of the Apartheid state. Nelson Mandela has just been released from jail. There is an 'interim government' in power to work out terms of transition, with the National Party, under F. W. De Klerk in the process of hammering out an arrangement with Nelson Mandela, representing the African National Congress. This is a moment when the delicate negotiations about the new democratic state might at any moment collapse. It is a moment of ongoing violence. The moment will lead, as it happens, to the Interim Constitution of 1994, mandating the first democratic elections of that year (with Mandela elected State President) and the Truth and Reconciliation Committees which began their work in 1996. The final constitution will be completed in 1996. But no one yet knows this, the air is heady with change and rife with uncertainty.

In this heady moment the art scene seemed to express the yearnings of a people to come into contact with the styles and lives of each other, to hear in each other's art the possibility of connection each *with* the other, to hear in that art the chord of liberation from the strictures of separation imposed by social life, racial and cultural ideology and political fact. As the new South Africa gradually lumbered into being, artists seemed to have discovered the fact that they shared – if from highly skewed perspectives – a common landscape and a common history. Such was a moment for the expansion of styles in a host of original ways. An African painter would appropriate Abstract Expressionism, recasting it with the patterns of

Ndebele villages, Zulu pots or the landscape of the bush; a young sculptor whose parents are from England but who grew up in this world of snakes, red earth and the sublime violence of nature would find West African forms natural.

In this liminal, mixed place called South Africa, formerly one among the ultimate experiments in Western modernist/racist state domination, the postmodern dreams of pluralist toleration (lack of exclusivity) and the pan-availability of diverse cultural styles finally came into play – at least in art. I think of that moment in the South African art scene as utopian: utopian in the way that its optimism, its heady indeterminacy and its exemplification of the capacity of artists to restitute connection between styles and persons, all exist as ideal models for the future of the nation itself. The sense of emergence from a white-hot past liberated a tenebrous desire for the future, and the South African art world was for a brief time fuelled by vast quantities of that desire: desire for a better society, desire for a new nation, desire for better terms of agreement between persons, desire for the fun and the natural.

It is only at certain times in the history of nation states, and usually at the moment of their formations or re-formations, that art can experiment, while also expressing new terms of citizenship. Artistic experimentation in South Africa has been profound because it has been a way of experimenting – in the sphere of art – with new and idealized relations between persons who will jointly inhabit a nation. And it is experimentation without a single narrative of national unity, but instead with the genuine dynamics of compatibility and interrelation. As persons would find themselves sharing styles, they would become more alike, and paradoxically more able to voice, communicate, their differences. Which means that art is a practice which sets the utopian terms of national communication by making diverse populations more alike, and difference more communicable and negotiable. Such practices of friendship, of bonding, of alliance, of becoming like the other, and other to the past self that one was, such practices of becoming a richer, less repressed self, are in the field of subjectivity a kind of experimental work. Such work is far more difficult to carry out in the social and political fields, and as in the progressive movement in India, art therefore becomes a beacon for what is more difficult to achieve elsewhere. Its energy is fuelled, its utopian role made possible, by that. The politics of establishing (re-establishing) the nation require that an actual agreement be forged between vastly different racial, ethnic, linguistic and geographic groups (the ANC, the National party, the Inkatha Freedom party, the Zulu, the Afrikaaner, etc.), each with vastly different interests and, indeed, little internal uniformity. Out of these groups must emerge an agreement to set the foundation of the nation – if the nation is to endure. Even where the desire for agreement is there, who can agree what the minimal announcement of rights will be, when some reject the very idea of the right to private property, while others wish to keep the means of production largely as it is?

This leaves the sphere of art in the position of an idealized exemplar for what happens slowly or not at all in other arenas of South African life. And this is the Hegelian point: the art is producing, in idealized form, a gesture which reveals the national aspiration by fulfilling it in a way hardly (so easily) possible in other parts of social life. Art stands as an exemplar by bringing together contradictions and overcoming problems. And this happens, at this moment, for South Africans, through the cross-pollination of styles.

Nowhere was this state of affairs better exemplified than by the Everard Read Contemporary Gallery in its inaugural show in September 1992. The gallery's inaugural show contained painting, sculpture, pottery and mixed assemblages. It ranged from resistance art (a fine mixed-media painting, 'Riot' by Kendell Geers, with a hole in the shape of a bomb blast cut out of its pictorial surface), to furniture (made by Stephen Cohen and covered with wild images of dancing and riots). To my mind the most exciting work in the Everard Read Contemporary's inaugural show was the sculpture. In a country where the twisting of trees, the availability of hardwoods of all kinds, the anthropomorphizations suggested by animals, and the *ambience* of traditional African carving are ubiquitous, sculpture suggests itself as a dramatic possibility of response. Joachim Schonfeldt's 'Pioneers', a carved cow with various heads, set on a pillar, is a statement about the old roots of 'Boer' farm life, and correspondingly, the framing of black Africans by colonialism. The sculpture is carved from brown wood and partially painted white. On its sides are small paintings of black Africans in suits and ties, done in a style and frame that one would find at an out of the way country auction. The work is both unabashedly nostalgic, and critical. In short, it is open to the total fact of its past. In a similar vein, Guy Du Toit's sculptural suite, 'Shipwreck' consists of 36 concrete pediments of about 1.5 metres in height arranged in rows. On these are placed small, commonplace bronze objects from the Boer/ African past: anvils, bells, drums, saddles, a goose, etc. The piece can be seen as an occasion to place on exhibition the objects of that past, objects signifying a harsh, simple, but also beautiful life. But the pediments also look like miniature versions of the huge, cruel and unornamented concrete slabs that compose fascist and totalitarian architecture of the Apartheid state.

This was work relinquishing the past in a decisive gesture, while also sanguine about the way that past remains as a trace in the landscape, and also in the actions and attitudes of South African populations (then as now). Then there is Johannes Maswanganye's sculpture 'The Rich Man'. A carving in leadwood of an oversized, leaden man who is dressed in a suit, a tie (which he also holds) and a yellow shirt. The man's face is a distended parody of a white man's face, and the whole work rings with parody. Yet Maswanganye has given that white man's face the features of a black African. One sculpts the other – finally – in the image of oneself, and it is oneself, including one's differences from others, that one must, finally, learn to take pleasure in. Yet the image of oneself projected onto the other – it is also the point of such wooden sculptures and newly composed paintings to show – is never, as it were, cast in stone. Identities were at that moment ready for change, for a perilous intermingling with those long excluded from one's own self-image and sense of power.

This show illustrates Hegel's third decisive break with the eighteenth century. Because art is an expression of the aspirations of place and time, art has a history and that history is essential for its understanding and appreciation. South Africans will instinctively get this art, either enthralled with its vision or angry enough to exit the gallery (in the hope of cocooning themselves against the winds of social change). But others, in other parts of the world, and later, at other places and times? Explanation of context will be required to animate the gestures, express their inner messages, and explain what the intermingling of style is all about. This is the project of art history. And so if we ask the question, 'Why should art have a *history*?' and 'Why should this history matter at all for our appreciation of its beauty and power?' this is Hegel's answer. Art is not mere entertainment, a consumer item for the pleasures of taste (Hume). Nor is it a universalized moral exemplar in virtue of abstracted form, as Kant would have it. Art is a concrete action in concrete media, which is expressive of the aspirations of the age: this is for

Hegel why history is essential to its understanding: because it speaks to history (to place and time).

THE KEY CONCEPT OF A MEDIUM OF ART

The importance of locating expression, and all other values of art, in *particular media* is the fourth innovation of nineteenth-century aesthetics. It was Hegel who gave this idea its most powerful articulation, when he said the history of art was a history in which certain media are favoured at certain moments in history. This is because they are paradigmatically able to formalize the cultural aspirations which at the relevant moment in time want expression. Sculpture, Hegel claims, is the central art for the classical world because it harmonizes the ideal world of the pagan gods and the physical world of man. Architecture is the art for the ancient Jews because of their injunction against graven images and their worship in the sublime house of the Lord. For the Romantics it is poetry, and so on until the end of art, which ends in Hegel's own time, so he says, because art is, given the complexity of modern life, unable to express deepest aspiration anymore. As we shall see in the next chapter, the avant-gardes would have a bone to pick with this view.

Hegel asks the reader to accept a hierarchical analysis of the arts. Each age shares a single aspiration, which a particular kind or kinds of art uniquely are able to express – hence their predominance at that time. Whether one accepts this hierarchical analysis of the arts, each age with its single and shared aspiration, each age with its single main art to match it and all the others in a subordinate role, has been a matter of intense debate within the culture wars of the past 20 years. There the claim has been that hierarchy is the mask of power: a means of crushing human difference by setting forth certain cultural prototypes as dominant, others as insignificant. This marginalizes other voices, inhibits the recognition of diversity. Identity politics in the United States, Britain and other places has resisted the claim.

Nevertheless there is something to the idea that at certain times certain media do dominate. Today the media (film, television) are probably the central art forms. In the German and Austrian worlds of the nineteenth-century concert, music and literature were perhaps central. But why? Because these media have uniquely the pulse of their times, the shared desires a culture holds dear? Or rather for reasons of economic system and sociological organization: because money is poured into them for all manner of reasons and they are favoured as sites of circulation. With the media (and internet) this is obvious: their technologies have an expansive range unequalled by any other. It was also true of print circulation in Germany, and the performance of music in the home, church, school, concert hall. Better to conceive of the relationship between favoured media and social aspiration as dialectical. These media are to a degree favoured because they express what a society wishes for; but they also play a critical role in shaping the way that society conceives of its aspirations, which is why they are favoured! It is not simply that the media express our aspirations better than other forms of art today (this may be true). It is also that our aspirations are themselves formed by their mechanisms of their representation. The favoured media *form* the way we think about our future. Television produces our horizons of social expectation as talk show, serial, and in two-minute sound bites – for better or worse. Aspiration and medium form a dialectical system.

There are in fact many reasons why Hegel's concept of a medium is indispensable for modern thinking about art. One is this: knowing about an art through its history, and its contemporary projects, is knowing what is difficult to achieve in it, or impossible, and conversely what comes naturally, compared to others. Ease and difficulty are relative terms, how they are thought depends on comparison with other media. And where one stakes the comparison has a great deal to do with how one answers the question. Any photographer with a digital camera that works, and glasses on to correct for total myopia, can take a picture of a crowded subway it would take the most accomplished painter to paint – a Chuck Close, a Superrealist, a Dutch master of the stuffed bird, the rounded apple, the table overwhelmed with goods. A violin can do things a guitar cannot, for example slide though tones, generate an entire palette of sound. A guitar can make melody which it will take years of scratching on a violin to do, even for a fine student. Television can exfoliate stories in the manner of the Dickensian novel of the nineteenth century in a way film cannot for the simple reason that it is episodic. Ted Cohen's work on virtuosity takes off from these remarks: it is about the ability to make something look easy which within its medium (of art, sport, whatever) it is in fact very difficult, and about the implications for appreciation. To appreciate a Chuck Close is to appreciate how much virtuosity there is to it. To appreciate my photo of my house is to realize there is nothing much to it. Understanding and appreciation in art require acknowledgement of the medium in which the work is made. This the eighteenth century hardly noticed.

As we shall see aesthetics has persisted in thinking that the question, 'What is art?' can be raised independently of the differential traits of media: Arthur Danto does this in the twentieth century. But it is a question largely destined to failure. Differences between media preclude any easy answer to this question directly. Moreover, the ability to define precisely any medium of art is also a problem perhaps insoluble. Media form a complex system. Were each not in many ways different from the others, there would be no coherent fact of the arts whatsoever. We know many ways in which each differs. But that does not mean these differences form a crisp definition. Rather the system of the arts is a complex system, defined through overlapping strands of similarity and difference from the others in Wittgenstein's sense, or through *'différence'* in Derrida's.

It was this modern system of the arts, each embroiled in the others, wishing to appear in the guise of the others (painting as novella, novel as music, music as theatre, theatre as, etc., etc.), each stressing the desire to surpass its limits, each wishing to take on the qualities of the others, but also each anxious about its identity, wishing to clarify it, that gave rise to the central concept of a medium for aesthetics. Hegel turned towards the concept of a medium of art on account of his historicism. In turning towards particular media of art and challenging them as to what they can and cannot do, Hegel is following events already present in the aesthetics of his day. Schiller, Lessing and others were busy questioning drama, sculpture et al. for their capacities and limitations. This interrogation of a medium of art for its capacities of beauty, expression, signification had not happened before in the history of the subject.

Earlier work on what we may now consider media or genres did think about its subject in this way. There was no anxiety about what an art is vis-à-vis the others, no differential concept of 'the media of art' at stake. Rather a direct encounter with the terms of this or that art: period. Aristotle's work on tragic drama, Plato's on poetry/performance, these took for granted what a particular art was and were not interested in comparing it to a field of other arts. Aristotle and Plato were each concerned to understand if the art had social value or not. Aristotle argued tragic drama did have value for his society because of its powers of communal purgation which were conditional upon the knowledge or recognition of tragic fate which the drama gave its audience. Plato argued poetry should be banned because the social 'knowledge' it gave was fraudulent. Neither fore-grounded the concept of a medium in the more modern sense, even though the work Aristotle did in dissecting tragic drama hierarchi-cally (plot and character are the most important elements, others less so) proved a template for the later, modern study of a medium.

As we shall see in the next chapter, a central stand of modernism and the avant-gardes make a racket out of pushing art beyond extant norms and limits, probing how far an art can go by pushing it further, and doing so by even more centrally foregrounding the concept of a medium. But artistic experimentation is for the avant-gardes about *purity*: reducing a work of art to its basic building blocks, essential ingredients, while simultaneously pushing it beyond all recognizable shape. It is as if the other side of experimentalism is chemical proof, with the artist a philosophical chemist, securing essence of an art form once and for all, so as to make his or her experimentation less anxious, less embroiled in unknown and unknowable terrain. As the arts expand, so their desires to retrieve 'identity' also expand, and they aim for reduction to essentials. Formalism satisfies this need, both within artistic experimentation, and in aesthetic theory, even if it is destined to fail on account of always leaving out too much from the story. Its desire (in artistic practice and aesthetic theory) is to retrieve that which pertains to this and only this medium: its essentials, and in doing so, in highlighting these, and making all others supplementary rather than essential, to return to 'what really matters in the medium'. As it happens this is also to return to some-thing mysterious: the ability of such simple building blocks, the stones of architecture and its space, the time, tone, pulse of music, the paint of canvas and frame of painting, to make music and convey absorption. Something more is always at stake than these mere chem-ical combinations of elements, as if art were at basis chemistry. And by leaving it out from the story, the art looks all the more alchemical, strange, magical. Art is magical enough without formalism to wish to leave all else out. The point is, formalism is as an aesthetic theory a legacy of Kant's which also pertains to the modern system of the arts and the way media become highlighted as a system: vis-à-vis each other, with each wanting to become the others and wanting to remain utterly and uniquely itself. Autonomy is as hard to maintain, and as exciting to maintain, in a medium of art as it is in a person's life! We are creatures in modern times of conformity, but also of obsessive difference. The story of why is a story no less complicated than modern life itself!

One significant aspect of this has to do with the consistent rise of new media in the nineteenth and twentieth centuries. From photography to film, film to television, television to internet, arts have been gifted birth through new technologies. The avant-gardes have been motivated to consistently work between media, and to force the birth of new media. In each of these cases how a medium is understood depends on the kinds of comparisons we draw between young and old, between the new medium on the rise and those already extant and normative. Film was for years misrepresented as a kind of theatre, and always to its detriment, since it always fails when its actors are compared to the members of the Royal Shakespeare Company, its screenplays to George Bernard Shaw, its plots to Greek tragedy. Film is a great art which is understood as such only when, historically, its difference from theatre becomes comprehensible. It took some time for film criticism to come to realize silent film's debt to opera, with the powers and limitations of that medium, its ability to animate the simplest themes in the world (love, death, vengeance, madness, jealousy) and to do so through the physiognomic aria of the silent film actress's eyes, her elongation of motion, her stylized contour of gestures. To see this as aria rather than theatre acting became crucial to the grasping of depth: depth is grasped in short through the realignment of the system of differences according to which identity is grasped, or what Jacques Derrida calls in French '*différence*'. The foregrounding of the concept of medium is a modern idea, crucial to modern aesthetics, because the arts exist in this web of difference.

Indeed how aesthetic theory approaches any art depends on its point of comparison and contrast. If the question 'What is literature?' is raised through comparison between literary language and philosophical language, as has been the wont of literary theory and deconstruction in particular, the space between literature and philosophy becomes opaque. Philosophy turns out to be more literary than one thought; literature more philosophical. This point of comparison however, is quite different in perspective from the one associated with Aristotle: the one which thinks of literature, theatre and even poetry as matters of plot and character. When one starts with the thought: what makes literature literature is a gripping story with vivid characters; the comparison with philosophy looks different from when one starts from the question: what kind of language is 'literary' and how does this language relate to what philosophy calls 'philosophical language'. When one begins from plot and character the more close comparison will be to history, where the storming of the Bastille and the heroes of the revolution are worthy of any novel, and have been the subject of a million films. There the question of similarities and differences between these 'media' will take on a sharp cast, focusing on the question of fact vs fiction, interpretation vs. making it all up. Were one to call into question this line of demarcation one would have to argue the writing of history is in effect also fiction, which is close to what Hayden White has said.[5]

I will not explore questions of fiction, history and philosophical language here, merely point out that much of the aesthetics of literary criticism, historical studies and the like depend on the way comparison and contrast are framed. This again points to the way the modern arts form a *complex system*: from various perspectives differences and similarities take on different forms and different aspects of media are highlighted. It is only when literature is located in relation to philosophy but also history, painting but also film, social criticism but also poetry, poetry but also theatre, that its identity within the system becomes properly thought. That and our *intuitive experiences* of literature, the way it takes us over into its story, brings us characters, passes time in rapt reading, which should not be forgotten as central to what we know to be true of it. It is in the totality of these overlappings that the identity of a particular art is understood, which is why no art can be sharply defined.

LEGACIES OF EXPRESSION AND IDEAS OF PROCESS

Now for Hegel a medium is understood uniquely in terms of its expressive possibilities. The link between medium and expression has proved critical for subsequent aesthetics, although it has not always been properly appreciated. Moreover, expression has not always been thought of as a social property: the expression of an *age*. As the nineteenth century rode on, art took an expressionist turn; as individual liberty and desire became thematic in societies, the concept of expression became more personal and individual. One finds this in the work of R. G. Collingwood, writing in the Oxbridge of the 1920s, and going so far as to claim that expression is art wherever it may be found, whether in painting, language or therapy.[6] Collingwood arrives at the remarkable idea that art is language, because for him the work of art is the vehicle for the communication of inner expression, and this is in effect language. This is an idea not worth unpacking here except in one respect. With the thought that a work of art is a vehicle for expression comes the idea that it is a particular kind of action, in which the artist/maker works through his or her inner emotional states. This thought, congruent with the birth of psychoanalysis and its emphasis on human interiority and human expression, remains of interest; for the arts of the twentieth century have at times emphasized exactly that: the bringing to paint, sculpture, music, even architecture of human feeling in need of acknowledgement, in need of sharing with others. The artist is sometimes seen as a person alone, whose alienation and despair require confirmation through intimacy, whose Dostoyevskian soul needs plumbing, and whose inner states demand outward expression.

The fascinating correlate of Collingwood's idea is that art is process, not product. The viewer recapitulates the artist's act of expression within his or her own imagination, in experiencing the work. Indeed the true work is this free play of imagination through which the viewer expresses the same emotion as the artist. Collingwood is Kant turned psychoanalyst. Neither trusts the physical art object as the centre of aesthetic experience, but rather the free play of imagination that takes place around it. For Kant the physical object is simply an occasion; for Collingwood a kind of road map, directing the viewer to the same (or similar) experience as the artist had while making it. For both the real aesthetic experience is an act taking place within the twinned souls of artist and audience, rather than on the page of the book, or in the frame of the painting.

This idea, that knowing a work of art is recapitulating it in the same way as the artist did while composing it favours *process* over product. It favours the process of embroilment with an object, the fight with it to the finish line, the use of it for the imagination, which is set to work. The view turns art into an active gesture, emphasizing 'work' above all else. Art is a kind of labour, a labour of the imagination with materials and forms, a gesture of investing them with traces of one's own spirit, and forcing them into patterns of conclusion. And for the modern audience to grasp the work is for that audience to submit to a similar labour, call it a labour of work or of love, depending.

To express an emotion in a work of art is for Collingwood to work it through. Sadness, joy, despair, love, jealousy, fear are transposed from human breast to active imagination, then communicated by the artist through the road map of the physical object. If Aristotle thought tragic drama an act of purgation, Collingwood thinks all art a purgation through which fire is transmuted to gold and in the wake of which we can live without insuperable burden. A work of art lives in history through each person's history of its remaking. And so re-enactment allows for knowledge of self and other, the sharing of feelings in every case worked through. Collingwood's vision of history is similarly that of re-enactment. To know the mediaeval age is to know its mind, and that is to re-enact its course of actions, from motivation to intention to effect. To know another soul is to make art of their art, thus sharing their spirit. The audience is transformed into active artists working through their own similar emotion.

Naturally this view suffers the oversimplification of any radical account. To know an emotion in art (or life) is not necessarily to feel it. When I find Brahms' music sad, yes, it calls forth some sadness, I am tinged with melancholy as often as not. But I also feel empathy for what I find within it. I feel Brahms' sadness through my sympathy, not through becoming similarly sad – sometimes anyway. When I am moved by Strindberg's tortured theatrical writings, his vile self-loathing, hardly containable cruelty, his fierce longing for peace, does this mean I am calling on similar things within myself and 'expressing them' in the course of sitting in the theatre shocked? Is he revealing to me a hidden note in my own soul, one the mirror has long concealed? Perhaps, but also perhaps he is calling forth something in my capacity for empathy, some faculty of imagination on my part, some sense of human concern I ought to be in touch with within myself. Rather than thinking art causes an act of self-expression on my part, it is plausible that it excites my imagination. How much this involves self-expression may be hard to say. Anyway, one needs a psychological theory of human emotion to even begin to decide this.

Collingwood's vision of history, and of human acknowledgement, is strait-jacketed in a vision of re-enactment, when our mode of knowing – and feeling – is far more variegated. Nor is it always true (essential) that an artist uses a work as a vehicle for self-expression, even if this is a central concern of at least one region of modernism, that of Proust, abstract expressionism, modern theatre, certain strands of poetry. Peter Kivy has argued in an excellent book that the birth of Italian opera took place under a speech theory of music, according to which the goal of composition was to invent the craft of transposing human speech made under the influence of emotion into the musical aria and accompaniment.[7] The goal, similar to the literary invention of characters, was not self-expression but control over material. It was about learning how to make music *seem* expressive, how to make the aria seem as if the singer were overcome with emotion. This goal, control over craft and the representation of human depth, is as central to art as that of self-expression. It has the goal of adding something deep to the world, be it a trace of self or an angle on life. Brahms is surely about both: about his own deep need to find peace and relief of loneliness through the sharing of passion in sound, and about the desire to make music sound so moving that he himself will be moved by it as I am.

And this is the real point: expression in art is also about the Kantian pleasure we take in our own capacities for free play of imagination and free creation. This cheerfulness suffuses whatever else is being presented in novel or drama, poem or painting, even if in the form of resoluteness, obsession, manipulation. Expression is a reflective act, not simply a direct working through of suffering or sadness. It is an act that takes shape through the making, and celebrates its own talent and absorption in the medium. This is one of many reasons why Collingwood's theory cannot leave out the central place of the art object. We shall shortly see Richard Wollheim correct this. Whatever an artist is or is not expressing drives creation but is also (dialectically) shaped by it. Through the process of working on a thing (canvas, film, novel) fascination, joy, relief, love, grandiosity and many other emotions take over, along with the careful shaping of spirit to materials. The net effect is the result of deep impulses, yes, but also of the way many other emotions enter the process of making, and are crafted by what it is possible to represent and express in this act. Collingwood's theory ironically deletes what Hegel had already foregrounded: that everything happening in art happens because it happens in a particular medium.

Collingwood's theories of art and of history depend on the absolute symmetry between the expressive forces an artist feels as he or she makes a work, and the expressive forces we recreate within ourselves when we hear or see it. The focus on product as *that which must be unpacked as process*, is a central theme in aesthetics. It can also be found in the work of Collingwood's American contemporary John Dewey, philosopher, educator, aesthetician. This emphasis on process is a modern idea, one coming from a romanticization of the stream of life in which we live, and in which art is set. It is a perspective which sees life as an effervescence of spirit, a soul continually spilling out beyond itself in the throes of reality, a view which celebrates the transient, shifting and wilfully chaotic contours of life, rejecting fixed meanings and values as stalemate. Dewey wrote his book, *Art as Experience* under the influence of Albert Barnes' important and then new collection of modern art.[8] He wrote in the context of Proust's vast novel of return, recovery, self-knowledge through a journey that could be called one of self-expression, concentration on self anyway. He'd seen the wildly coloured and intensely figured distortions of post-impressionist paintings by Gauguin and Van Gogh. And floating in the air of the times were the words of Baudelaire, whose poetry speaks of a world of correspondences within the temple of nature, where human emotions and feelings find themselves projected into natural shapes through a fit of form and feeling, the willow tree drooping now in sadness (although it feels nothing), the long lake speaking of solitude (of which it knows nothing, not being a thing that can know at all), the mountaintop of glory (when it is simply a piece of rock and dirt), the falling leaf of the dance of love (although it is simply past its due date), the elongated, hunched figures of Sienese painting of a mourning intensity and lyrical longing that can be otherwise called devotion and humility. That works of art exploit the basic human feature of projection, through which nature and artefact take on the properties of conveying, stimulating, suggesting, representing human moods, appearing as if they themselves carried the gesture in question, was to all indisputable.

Dewey's work is of interest to aesthetics because it locates expression within experience and thinks of the aesthetic as a moment of embodiment shaped into a complete experience. Art is experience, a completed piece of life provisionally abstracted from life as a stream, but in every way continuous with that jet stream. What does this mean? Although Kant had also emphasized experience as the domain of the aesthetic, he had reserved an autonomous place for aesthetic experience: in the domain of the disinterested. For Dewey, nothing could be further from the truth. Art has value only because everything happening within it has already happened outside it, in every other significant sphere of life. Indeed the aesthetic is a feature of experience per se, wherever that feature may be found. Aesthetics are a matter of experiences lived to the hilt and brought to completion. It is in the depth and closure of the event that the aesthetic resides. Art is simply one way to make this happen. Dewey calls this the satisfaction offered by real experiences. The kind of which we say: 'That . . . that was really something'. Dewey is a naturalist: value is explained by reference to the human organism and his or her biology, psychology, faculties.

If the explanation is naturalistic, the theme is in its own way not entirely un-Kantian. For an experience that matters is one which is formulated purposively, designed, shaped, happening towards conclusion:

> [W]e have *an* experience when the material experienced runs its course to fulfillment. Then and only then is it integrated within and demarcated in the general stream of experience from other experiences. A piece of work is finished in a way that is satisfactory; a problem receives its solution; a game is played through; a situation, whether that of eating a meal, playing a game of chess, carrying on a conversation, writing a book, or taking part in a political campaign, is so rounded out that its close is a consummation and not a cessation. Such an experience is a whole and carries with it its own individualizing quality and self-sufficiency. It is *an* experience.[9]

And,

> There is that meal in a Paris restaurant of which one says 'that *was* an experience.' It stands out as an enduring memorial of what food may be. Then there is that storm one went through in crossing the Atlantic – the storm that seemed in its fury, as it was experienced, to sum up in itself all that a storm can be, complete in itself, standing out because marked out from what went before and what came after.[10]

The aesthetic is marked by intensity, fulfilment, and its memorable character. The enemies of the aesthetic are neither the practical nor the intellectual (contra Kant). They are 'the humdrum; slackness of loose ends; submission to convention in practice and intellectual procedure'.[11] It is tax accountants we fear, anaesthetists, the drudgery of repetition, the boredom of predictability (unless perhaps marked with the power of ritual).

Of course certain heightened experiences, brought to conclusion, prove less pleasurable than traumatic! The film *Titanic* is one thing (perhaps a disaster in its own right but whatever else, an entertaining movie), the ship's actual severing by an iceberg in real life is quite another thing to experience. Both experiences might prove 'memorable'. Both have the shape of an experience brought to conclusion! And yet the real thing is hardly an aesthetic experience, unless you are a masochist. Dewey obviously has in mind those experiences which, although mixed with pain, do finally achieve something leading to satisfaction. Which means it is not the shape of experience alone that counts but the pleasure or at least positive intensity involved. This at least Dewey learns from the eighteenth century. No one would *pay* to be part of a sinking ship; many paid to watch the movie.

So the experience needs to be both formally organized towards completion, and also an experience of satisfaction. This distinguishes it from trauma, but is not yet enough to explain what is unique about art. Having opened up a deep vein of continuity between experience in art and the aesthetics of experience generally, Dewey must now explain what is unique about experience in art. Otherwise art simply disappears into the general category. What is special about the arts on his view? Why do we care about them as we do?

Dewey's answer is that art is controlled experience, that of making, the creation of worlds. Similarly the beholder, facing the work of art, goes through a labour of remaking the thing into the intentional object it is, the finished product it is, the activity it has relied on to become what it is:

> [T]o perceive, a beholder must *create* his own experience. And his creation must include relations comparable to those which the original producer underwent. They are not the same in any literal sense. But with the perceiver, as with the artist, there must be an ordering of the elements of the whole that is in form, although not in details, the same as the process of organization the creator of the work consciously experienced. Without an act of recreation the object is not perceived as a work of art. The artist selected, simplified, clarified, abridged and condensed, according to his interest. The beholder must go through these operations according to his point of view and interest . . . In both, there is a comprehension in its literal significant – that is, a gathering together of details and particulars physically scattered into an experienced whole.[12]

Faced with a finished product, a work of art, the viewer uncovers the process through which it was made, which is what the work invites the viewer to do. In doing this, the viewer animates it, experiences, knows it, can value it. All aesthetic experience is action, Dewey tells us, an act of becoming which the viewer unfolds. In this way all art aspires to the condition of music. Music is something we hear through as an active process of unfolding, the building, transformation, conclusion of implications, expectations, phrasing, however one wishes to say this. And so it equally is with all other arts.

As in Collingwood the core idea is symmetry of process between artist and audience. Process is not simply expression in Collingwood's sense though, it is the process of shaping something to 'experience'. Paradoxically art is reflective because it occasions an experiential process which shapes the object so that it will occasion an experiential process, brought to conclusion. To enter into the texture of the work is to re-enact this process brought to conclusion or product. A work of art is like a video game where you are given a completed element and have to rework its process of making to the point of its closure (to the point of its completeness as the thing you have been offered). This dialectical spirit is what marks art as unique, and active. A work is like a master giving the student instruction in how it can become itself, and through this, how he or she may grow.

There is something to this idea that product is a mere route to the process of its making. Picasso's *Les Demoiselles d'Avignon* was for a generation understood on formalist lines. Its recruitment of African sculptural forms and Romanesque architecture were explained to be vehicles allowing the painter to reconstitute pictorial space cubistically: composing figures across multiple, intersecting spatial planes and integrating figure and ground into a single geometrical fabric in which everything is from one perspective foregrounded, from another recessive.

The great art critic Leo Steinberg asked a simple, Dewey-like question, to this generation of formalist critics of Picasso. Why are the women in the picture situated in a *brothel*? Why do the women stare back with these intense, cruel, implacable, resolute eyes? Why do their gazes almost feel like a threat? What has this to do with form?[13]

No one had asked these questions, which arise directly from the picture itself. They argue against a purely formalist reading of mask and sculpture, since mask seems to conceal a primitive power circulating at the core of this picture, which comes from the women. The intense sexuality of the subject suggests that more is at stake in this resolute, uncompromising, obdurate geometry of solid forms than mere establishment of perspective.

Picasso, Pablo (1881–1973) © ARS, NY
Les Demoiselles d'Avignon. Paris, June-July 1907. Oil on canvas, 8′ x 7′ 8′′. Acquired through the Lille P. Bliss Bequest. (333.1939)
Location : The Museum of Modern Art, New York, NY, U.S.A.
Photo Credit : Digital Image (c) The Museum of Modern Art/Licensed by SCALA / Art Resource, NY
Image Reference : ART162072

Steinberg returns to Picasso's youth, to his life in Catalonia where gazes given and received between men and women already carried the act and culpability of sex. To *look* at a woman was to penetrate her; one could be punished for it. Looks were in Picasso's brutal universe, primitive forms of an already primitivist act, the act of copulation understood in its intensity rather than sensual refinement. This is not, contra the Italian rococo, the leisure of lounging with a lover in some villa of Palladio's making. It is an act so terrible, so potent, that the eye cries out to turn to stone, or to be met with a brutality that pays back the violation. Women take on the power of castration in this work, and the power of partnership in a destiny of sex so primal that one is in danger of death. Everything hardens as eye meets eye, repulses it in rebound, receives it in gasp and shock, returns the look of the oedipal victor who already expects retaliation for conquest. The philosophical brothel is the arena of painting where man meets woman and achieves form in the manner of combustion. Masks are, Steinberg tells us, almost ineptly superimposed upon faces, as if concealing their even deeper, and more terrifying primitivism.

So far the reading is brilliant, but not yet about process in Dewey's sense. It is rather about what one sees and feels in the picture. But here is the point. Steinberg returns to the many sketches for this painting Picasso produced in the course of his artistic process. For a time Picasso's drawings contained a medical student holding a skull in the picture. This figure was finally removed and does not appear in the finished product, the *Demoiselles d'Avignon*. Now the medical student and the skull suggest mortality, and Steinberg's reading of Picasso's process concludes that what Picasso has done is encountered, then banished, death from his picture, a picture so intense as to virtually identify sex with death and retribution. By returning to process, product is animated as an expressive act, an act of inclusion, exclusion, fear and trembling.

A brilliant analysis, which, even if you disagree (I do not), makes the point: art may look finished, but its intensities, even of form, are unlocked only through return to process. And process is not external to the picture, it is implied by pictorial details found in the finished product. Only by seeing the finished product as an act in which something is left out can its true meaning be known.

The problem with a theory of art that turns product into the materials for the story of its process is that such a theory fails to appreciate the dialectical relationship between this point of view and the finished product itself. The point is captured in the very term 'work of art', which refers to an act of making and a thing made. Process is only relevant if it deepens the understanding of product, which is what Steinberg shows about Picasso. This is quite different from asserting that product is the mere vehicle for the story of its making: its making to conclusion. Moreover the right story of process cannot be told without acknowledging the obvious and ineluctable point that process is designed to produce/achieve product. An artist paints with his eyes, Richard Wollheim tells us, constantly checking to see how the work looks as a whole, and continuing or revising accordingly. The process of making is focused on the product made. There is no process independent from it. This is where art parts company with therapy, where the process is the goal (change gradually achieved through encounter between patient and therapist, perhaps with the help of prescription drugs). Or the story of a life, which may be understood as goal oriented, but also a process forever under-way. Expression and craft both depend on the goal of finishing something in coherent and quasi-independent form, which will be sent out there into the world as an orphan for an undisclosed audience. An artist makes with this idea of completion, and separation in mind. When we love art we do not love it because we love repeating the struggle leading up to it. This is the Hollywood version of Michelangelo, with Charleton Heston cursing in tough theatrical Americanese from the scaffolding of the Sistine Chapel. It is the apotheosis of biography over all else. Biography, including the biography of making (version after version of the *Demoiselles*) is critical to deepening the story of what the completed product is. But only takes on relevance in relation to the thing made, the completed thing, whose integrity and formal magic must not then dissolve into the story of process.

PAINTING AS AN ART

A theory of art should therefore be a theory of this or that art, of a particular medium and how it shapes process in the light of completed product. A theory of art should not in the first instance be categorical: about art as a general kind of thing. No art does quite the same thing as another. The best psychological account of a *particular art* in the twentieth century is I think Richard Wollheim's account of painting. It reserves a central place for process, and for expression, while standing critically towards Collingwood and Dewey.

In Wollheim's work two of Hegel's ideas are conjoined: that the study of art is the study of a medium, and that the study of art is the study of expression. For Wollheim expression is always liberal and singular, that of a single person's frame of reference in the world, his deep psychology. And process is that which is crafted through an emerging concept of product, which overrides process, even if process deepens the sense of the end result. Finally, Wollheim's work aims to provide a theory of meaning for an individual art (painting) which grasps meaning through psychological categories. What is distinctive about the arts is the way, Wollheim believes, meaning is generated through psychological capacities and acts, desires and intentions, rather than language, which is about socially given semantics. In language we conform to the speech of others, in art that matters, what is revealed are the microcosms of difference, the distinctiveness of individual voice, which the true critic may commune with – given time and effort. Art is about these individual idioms of voice, wherein resides its uniqueness.

Wollheim's masterwork, *Painting as an Art* aims to produce a theory of pictorial meaning that is, in being psychologically grounded, naturalistic. He roots the forms of pictorial meaning in specific psychological faculties, and by reference to the artist's intentions. The place to find an artist's intentions is, however, in the picture itself, in what he or she did, not in what he or she wanted to do – although this too can be relevant, along with background information about the artist's marriage, psychology, place, time, class and workplace.

We shall turn to these psychological capacities shortly. Note that his work is unique in its blend of connoisseurship and psychoanalysis. The point of a work of art is to provide deep and enduring experience, and this, he believes comes from deep in the soul. It comes, I have said, from the individual soul: this man's experience, not another's. His debt is to Collingwood and Dewey, and their notions of process/expression. But also to connoisseurship and its emphasis on the fine-grained details of a work of art the artist strives to produce and which are his or her particular signature elements. In the preface to *Painting as an Art*, Wollheim reveals his method:

> Going back to works I already knew, or in a few cases . . . seeing a work for the first time, I evolved a way of looking at paintings which was massively time consuming and deeply rewarding. For I came to recognize that it often took the first hour or so in front of a painting for stray associations or motivated misperceptions to settle down, and it was only then, with the same amount of time or more to spend looking at it, that the picture could be relied upon to disclose itself as it was. I spent long hours . . . coaxing a picture into life . . . To the experience, to the hard-won experience, of painting, I then recruited the findings of psychology, and in particular the hypotheses of psychoanalysis, in order to grasp the intention of the artist as the picture revealed it.[14]

This recruitment of psychoanalysis was meant to derive from the idiom of the picture 'as it was'. And to pin-point the depths of art. This view, held by the likes of Walter Pater (formalist) and Adrian Stokes (psychoanalytic critic) finds its legacy in Wollheim's aestheticism:

> [I]f I am right in thinking that art presupposes a common human nature [as Hume believed], and that pictorial meaning works through it, then it must be absurd to bring to the understanding of art a conception of human nature less rich than what is required elsewhere.[15]

What Wollheim accomplishes in this book is nothing less than to restore to psychology its obvious and irresistible place in the explanation of art. The attempt to secure the right level of depth is admirable. This depth is achieved through basic psychological capacities the artist shares with the viewer, and through deep psychology, the deep revelation of vision, motive point of view, persona. Therefore a concept of psychology rich enough to speak to basic, shared capacities and the subtlest revelation of motives must be relied on in explaining pictorial meaning/value.

Wollheim focuses on three categories of pictorial meaning: pictorial representation, expression and what he calls pictorial metaphor. Each derives from some aspect of human psychology and is secured with respect to the artists' intentions as the critic reads them.

The ground of representation, he tells us, resides in the psychological capacity of 'seeing-in'. This is among his main contributions to aesthetics. Viewers simultaneously see the surface of a picture and the things within it. All painting is surface in that it is paint on something (canvas, wall, or ceiling). To understand the heavy melancholy of Van Gogh, and its wild ecstasies of vision, is to simultaneously feel through the thickly applied paint on the surface, like dull platitudes of heavy, Dutch earth. And to see the shoes within, endlessly toiled, laces undone, tongues open, as if awaiting the human who shall wear these yet another day in a state of exhaustion, solitude, loneliness. Wollheim's innovation is to have rewritten the Wittgenstein concept of seeing-as, according to which we see an object flickering between one thing and another (duck and rabbit), and to have also rewritten Ernst Gombrich's concept of pictorial perception as a constant switching between seeing the surface and seeing into its depths. We simultaneously do both. This is the distinctive feature of painting. Sculpture has no depth to see into (normally), simply surface and mass. Film has no surface, only depth since it is light projected onto a screen. Painting is the only art established through the interplay of both. Wollheim calls this 'doubleness'. Leonardo told painters to make a study of walls. For there, this already seems to obtain, as the cracked surface of stone or stucco seems to afford exactly this kind of pictorial doubleness.

Expression is grounded in what Wollheim calls the psychological capacity for projection, something Baudelaire already knew when he wrote of the mystery of correspondences, ways we have of amalgamating what we see in the world with our own expressive states, our own imaginative capacities for seeing the world as expressive. And so the weeping willow, the patriarchal face etched into the mountain, the furry, cheerful cloud, the ecstatic, starry night which makes Van Gogh reel in the south of France. For Wollheim projection is always also expression of feelings deep inside us, often unconscious. This is an artefact of the psychoanalytic theory he believes. One may take it or leave it.

One of the richest thoughts in Richard Wollheim's book concerns the capacity of certain pictures to corporealize their surfaces, that is to invest their picture surfaces (or parts of them) with the anthropomorphized traces of the human body. When pictures are rendered flesh or skin, when they are touched with the resonance of life, the viewer will, in accord with Wollheim's idea of perceptual 'two-foldness', at once see *into* them and discern on their surfaces the living traces of life. The interaction between representational and expressive meanings with corporeal effects will synergize pictorial experience and pictorial interpretation. Wollheim illustrates this in a brilliant reading of Titian, who is shown to invest his paintings with the feel of the eroticized and abundant body. Working out from the figure in broad, swirling contrapuntal rhythms, Titian seems to make his canvases glow with life. The effect is that nature and body, world and person, subject and object, enter into mysterious, eroticized *correspondence* or oneness. The viewer's feeling that the canvas is itself alive with the traces of the figure's movement cannot help but be read back into what these pictures are about. They are about a being resonant with desire, with eroticism, fear, excitement, a being capable of anthropomorphizing the world and finding its traces in that world. For Wollheim, the corporealization of the pictorial surface allows paintings to exhibit nothing less than the terms of human embodiment, to show (that is, to remind) the viewer what it is like to be physically and psychologically embodied in a world of people and objects whose terms of intimacy, eroticism and merger are established and sustained through the perceiving body, through the eye, through desire and through the sense of touch. And to sustain, as in dreams, the wish for tactile and emotional plenitude.

Such intimacies between viewer and picture excite the viewer's own body and kinaesthesia, making the viewer aware of his or her own body as a feeling, desiring thing positioned before, and within, the pictorial gesture, and also a source of meaning and interpretation (of the world that is kinaesthetically experienced). Life is like this.

It is a great aesthetician who can limn a unique power of a medium in a way that demonstrates how perception in that medium leads to one of the medium's great themes. Painting is about embodiment because of the way viewers find themselves positioned in front of paintings kinaesthetically. Sergei Eisenstein will find and exploit a related kinaesthetic power of film. Hegel did it with Greek sculpture, Kierkegaard with opera,[16] the art he calls paradigmatically erotic because of the operatic seductiveness of voice, melody, orchestra. Hence Don Giovanni, for Kierkegaard the paradigmatic opera, the opera that reveals what opera is.[17]

Painting matters as an art because it evokes such particularities of experience, shaped through what it and it uniquely, especially, without peer, can do. Why else, Wollheim asks, should it matter?

Yes, why else? Hegel tells us painting and other media matter as arts because they speak the principles of the age, idealize them, bring them to recognition. What Hegel is saying is that an artist's intentions do not rest with their psychology but have to do with their historical formation, and the genius, the one who matters for the age, is the one who has grasped the historical possibilities of the medium in ways that allow it to address that age's problems and prospects. Art as experience is at its best the shaping of deep, *public* desires for liberty, equality, new social relations, new ways of envisioning self and other. This was my reading of the South African moment, a moment in which art history is critical, along with social and political analysis, because human intention has a direction and the art is at the forefront.

Now one could take the perspective of an aesthete and simply stare at these pictures for hours, training a brilliant, devastating, seeker of an eye on their forms. But will that activity reveal their inner intentions, their needs, their shaping of forms, their messages? One will fail to understand their shifts in form, their strange, abrupt borrowings (each from the tradition of the other), their coded speech. If one thinks all that is irrelevant to painting as an art then one's view of art is finally, socially and historically datable, and dated. It is datable to a vision of art called aestheticism, the position of Pater and Stokes, which addresses known, and past traditions requiring little new historical knowledge, knowledge that is taken for granted, and then relates to those works with the aura of the nine-teenth-century grand tour. And so you go to Venice and stare, and absorb, and make your mind into a receptacle for the subtleties of form, thus clearing a path from the past to a museological gaze upon painting and cathedral which licenses endless looking. This is also very much of the tradition of the eighteenth century, it is the aes-thetics of removal: removing art from its stream of life by either placing it in museums where the imaginative gaze of the viewer is licensed over the object, because the object can no longer speak back from its place in the stream of life, or casting it in the aura of the grand tour, as a venerable site, a strange, shimmering ruin, an eternal portal into things of forgotten lore.

Wollheim's abstracted approach is perfect if the perspective one wants to bring to art is *psychoanalysis*, for that is an activity which involves long hours of absorption, so that gradually, conclusions (interpretations) may be made. It is an approach which above all favours individual expression and revelation. I would like to say that in its own way psychoanalysis can contribute to art, sometimes greatly – but only when knowledge is settled, and in no way to the detriment of art history. To understand South African art from the outside, one must bring more to the story: a reading of social context and artistic contribution to it. This is not a psychological reading, although it is reasonable to impute those intentions, or something like them, to the artists, who are ciphers for the whirlwind of change.

Wollheim's psychological theory is finally a way of casting art in the role of museum object contributing to absorption and medita-tion, based in human psychology. It is not simply a theory of picto-rial meaning but of how to approach art, to the exclusion of other approaches. What matters are individual signature elements and these are grasped through the abstracted, focused gaze of the viewer/ psychoanalyst. All this takes place in the rarefied space of the museum, apart from the social stream of life in which the painting was in fact made, and to which, more often than not, it speaks. There is thus another, competing way one might grasp signature and meaning: as a complex social transaction between artist and patron, work and world, painting, church, Catholicism, devotion, economy. Wollheim explicitly rejects this approach in his preface, but on no grounds beyond the personal. This allows his abstracted, museological stance to take absolute precedence, which it must not.

The social purposes a work of art serves are critical to unfolding the qualities of experience it once offered, to illuminating its aesthetics. What is possible in film depends on the Hollywood selection process. What films do with viewers is a matter of large scale pressures of ideology, voyeurism, power. Art articulates knowledge and is limited by the shape of knowledge in relationship to power. Its possibilities of critique are to be understood in the light of the principles of social constraint in place at a given time, along with pressures of economy, patronage, commodification. These things are by now well known within the discipline of art history, from Michael Baxandall's work on the devotional meanings of Renaissance art, and the linguistic concepts by which such objects were valued,[18] to T. J. Clark's lifetime of study of the moderns, set within the commercialization of art and the rise and fall of political utopianism which form part of the mass history they were so totally of.[19] When Clark shows us that the impressionists routinely cancelled out the blight of factory and smoke which was also part and parcel of their Sundays outside of Paris by river and in park, painting landscapes of pristine redolence, and idealizing a world which was already beginning to recede, even at its moment of glory, into the status of past impression, he is telling us something about how their aesthetic experiences were formulated by deleting social conditions and projecting fantasy into a picture. An impression abstracts from what is there, just as memory does (one does not remember the grimy factory one passed briefly on the train, but instead the spume of water and picnic by the river).

There is no clearer example of the importance of social role in shaping artistic intention than the work of Eduard Manet. Wollheim reads Manet's work psychoanalytically, as an invitation into a space where the fleeting and the dreamlike generate reverie, but also a kind of emptiness. It is about fantasy. There is something to this. When the woman at the Bar at the Folies-Bergère (1882) in the painting of that name stares into space, caught between an impossible collision of mirrors and perspectives, she is inside our world but also out of it, her otherness confirmed. Manet is addressing the viewer, allowing him or her access to this space within the bar that is also a space of the mind outside it, within subjectivity, showing us that subjectivity is otherness, the thing painting cannot, in spite of its fantasies of omnipotent understanding, capture. He is leaving her alone, by placing her apart from us. Showing us that in a society such as nineteenth-century Paris, where the museum, the gallery, the systems of knowledge assure the bourgeois patron that the world is his oyster, that his gaze over prostitute and painting is licensed, that his understanding unproblematical, that there is no problem of otherness, no unknown quantity where everything is to be bought and sold (including women), valued through the eyes and the desiring fantasy of possession, figures are trapped, left to dream, float apart from us, in an empty world. And by manipulating space like a cook, he allows us entrance into his pictures and then refuses to secure perspective and position for us, so we dream, float, become disoriented. This is his way of probing the otherness of things, our lack of understanding of them, his way of sticking it to the art world he despises, and is utterly of, and saying: the world in my pictures is not assured, you shall not use them to buttress your complacency. His work is part of that system, but thus in its form and content, critical, an act of refusal. This act of dreaming, reverie and also refusal, is paradigmatically modern. It is a psychological invitation but also a social lesson, highly didactic at that.

This social lesson, which Wollheim does not play up, can only be understood if one is placed in the burgeoning experiences of Parisian modernity. This is highly travelled terrain for aesthetics, not only by Wollheim but by those great critics and historians of Parisian modernity, T. J. Clark and Walter Benjamin.[20] Their Paris looks something like this: the Parisian art world was a world, and a world unknown until the nineteenth century. The earlier was one of church and noble, an art world of commissions by popes, of glorification of palazzo and cathedral. The cultures of modernism arose in the context of urbanity. Critics, journalists, novelists, and private citizens conversed over endless coffees and bottles of Pernod, spreading news and fomenting public opinion as they talked and scribbled for their newspapers. The bourgeois grazed, sampled and consumed. The institutions of production (studio, atelier) produced. The institutions of exhibition (museum, gallery) exhibited. All were part of a larger pattern of spectacle, speed commodification, urbanization, nationalism, and industrial capitalization that constituted Parisian, and global modernity. For better and worse, Paris was traversed by a system of gazes: museumgoers gazing with a sense of ownership at objects taken from the colonies, the bourgeoisie watching itself and sampling the goods for sale in the newly created department stores on the newly created boulevards, men turning an appraising eye on the city's many prostitutes. These placed art at the cusp of pleasure, ownership and commodification.

Modernism in art and architecture arises and dwells at the centre of this urban world. The critical paintings of Edouard Manet could have arisen only because of the web of museums, exhibitions, critics, bourgeois interests, buying, and selling was in place in Paris, 'capital of the nineteenth century', to use Benjamin's term.

Against this background we can understand Manet's desire for escape into fantasy, a place beyond commodification but also licensed by the institution of the museum, where a person like Wollheim may become wrapped up in contemplation in ways more momentary than the worker at the bar. She has less time, less education but wants a similar thing. She wants out, she is bored with all this male carousing, these endless middle-aged men hitting on her, these people casting her in intoxicated dreams because they're drunk. It is work to her, and loneliness, and an endless stream of days. And we can understand his desire to interrupt the complacency of the bourgeois, secure in his intoxications, happy with his prostitutes, fully in belief that the world is his. This is an act of interruption of experience, an address to economy (the transactions of art which will place his, and everybody else's in the gallery), it is a response to the critics that mock him, forcing him and his impressionist pals into the salons of the refused. His *Christ Mocked* (1845) is about that, with he in the leading role and the critics of Paris carrying him through the stations of the cross; it is about the system of prostitution that turns an *Olympia* into a bed for the hour, and also projects onto her the belief that she loves it, for as prostitute she has been taught to play the game of gasping with pleasure 12 times a day so the men can play at the idea that they are wanted. Look into Olympia's eyes, see the rigidity of her positioning, its strident floral arrangement (flowers where the sex is), her coldness, and you are repulsed, repulsed by her. The more you stare at her the less you can make out what she is really feeling, whether anything at all beyond boredom and hostility (towards you). Whatever the case, she is repulsing your fantasy (you the French bourgeois viewer) of entering this picture and finding confirmation of your lust there by a willing flower of a woman waiting for you, the viewer, to arrive and look her over. It is this fantasy which the museum has cultivated. Tired, bored, feeling a little down, girlfriend left you? Fine, just saunter over to the museum and stare at the Titian painting (after Giorgione) and you will feel loved again. For Venus will be there, all cuddled and nice, gorgeous, perfectly rendered, waiting. She's always there for you, that's the beauty of art.[21]

And so at stake is a critique of the way beauty is rendered, and institutionalized, as a form of aesthetic experience. Manet is a philosopher, a philosopher in paint of the aesthetics of the world he is of, and its limitations for he himself (his own work, its fate in society) and everyone else's. He is about the way belief systems, social security, and a world creates and sustains forms of experience of art, and the contributions of art to these. He is a social critic addressing the society in which he and his work circulate. Aesthetics is in general about forms of experience cultivated as social practices, through art worlds, and the role of art objects within them, for them, cast through their lenses. Wollheim's perspective arises through one such practice, Manet's through another. And Benjamin's, and T. J. Clark's. Hume's is yet another. For Hume, the question of Olympia would be a matter of taste. I like it, I don't, and why. That too is a practice.

Which practice is right? Is there a coherent way of answering this, or is it rather a matter of moving deftly between perspectives, historicizing each so as to get some sense of where it is coming from and what it wants to leave out. Perhaps it is movement between multiple aesthetic practices which delivers the most meaning, and deepens experience and the recognition of how others have experienced the work of art one is contemplating. This would be a point in the spirit of Friedrich Nietzsche, whose perspectivism stresses shifts in perspective rather than ultimate consensus between them. Perhaps the reason why one wants to study the history of aesthetics is to become aware of such multiple interpretive practices, so as to deepen the repertoire of possible ways we have of approaching art: also to understand, through debates, something of the limitations of each. It would place the kinds of attempts at definition made by Wollheim, Kant, Hume in their places, show us where they come from and what their limits are. Whether art can be defined, and how, has been an ongoing issue within modernity, within modern aesthetics. It is to this we turn in the next chapter.

But before turning there, it is worth noting that the question of aesthetic experience, related to that of aesthetic practice, is very much with us today. I think there is a gap between the experiences of young people and my own which is inadequately discussed by philosophical aestheticians, or even by critics of art. One of the reasons students today find museums so odd, spend so little time in them, is that the contours of twenty-first-century experience have so speeded up, are so much a matter of clicking from website to website, product to product, everything has become so rapid, that art is seldom made today which solicits the kind of intensities of experience, the long sit in the museum for hours, that a Jackson Pollock, a Michelangelo, a Louise Bourgeois, wanted, demanded, an Agnes Martin whose minimalist changes in a uniform surface across a canvas require the longest time to animate, with a strangely tiny meditative state that is in its own way, enormous, about the enormous, poetic, lyrical. No one has time for this, either to make an object that will do it, or to spend the time engaged in it. There is a generation gap today regarding the nature of experience which the old fail to understand about the young. I am a child of television, but I still grew up in a time before computers, before endless circuitry of airplanes and cell phones, Bluetooth, Blackberry and the fruits and vegetables of modern technology, when people wrote (more slowly) letters to each other, when we typed books with carbon paper for the second copy, when we walked more than we drove. Maybe Damien Hirst is a kind of art object I am too old to appreciate: an object fiercely addressing experience in the manner of an immediate consumable. Maybe it is for this reason that young people go to museums increasingly because of the DVD collections and multi-media fireworks. They walk through the Renaissance section as if it were a mini-mall. It is easy to call this a loss of depth. Perhaps it is a change in the quality of experience of more subtle register. Chamber and orchestra concerts are kept in business by grey haired physicians. The average age makes me feel a youngster. Who is speaking then, to whom, through what art? Aesthetics as a history matters because amidst the vast sea changes in the nature of human experience, as time compresses and images bombard, it is important to recover something of the world of the past, when experience carried the elongation of devotion, instead of the sense of quickly grasping some consumable. Perhaps art today needs a new aesthetics of experience, and perhaps you, the reader, will be the one to write it.

CHAPTER 5

MODERN DEFINITIONS OF ART AND THE PROBLEM OF NEW MEDIA

THE DOUBLE USE OF THE MEDIUM IN THE AVANT-GARDES

The problem of defining art, present in aesthetics since the eighteenth century, becomes a challenge in the light of the new art of the twentieth century. In the early part of the twentieth century, Dewey's book is not so much a definition as an approach, but Collingwood absolutely seeks definition: art is expression, and being expression, is language. His definition moreover is wilfully independent of particular media, which finally don't matter to him, except in the way one hotel on the highway differs from another because it has a bigger sign or different coloured rug in the lobby. But Collingwood's formalist colleagues Clive Bell and Roger Fry were attentive to differences. Their definitions, formalist ones, specified art as 'significant form' and nothing but that, meaning that each of the arts was defined as the kind of form which made it significant (and nothing but). Now there are at least three ways in which the concept of a medium has currency, and here I am relying on ideas of Ted Cohen.[1] First, a medium is thought of as the physical stuff that any art is made of, as in, my medium is oil paint, or fresco, or wood or ceramic glass. Here literature is left out, since the physical stuff of which it is made are, one might say, marks on paper, but really its medium is language, words, sentences, paragraphs. Second, there is the notion of a medium in a more abstract or metaphysical sense, the kind of sense that would encompass literature. It has been said that the medium of architecture is space; of music, time and tone; of film, projected light onto two dimensions (in a more physical sense celluloid); of digital arts, computational systems. Third, a medium is something like the viscous substance through which flows a message, a medium is a particular field of representation and expression, social action and individual meditation. Hegel thinks of media this way: as routes to communication.

These notions are not entirely separate: physical and metaphysical elements conjoin to make meaning and limit its possibilities, to formulate terms of design and expression, and similarly limit these. Formalism wishes to exclude the third sense entirely. A medium is not in essence true to itself if it is busy conveying messages. Rather its point is in the formalization of physical and abstract constituents. This reductivist sense of art was one side, I suggested in the last chapter, of the modernist adventure, since it aimed in theory and in practice to legitimate each and every medium in terms of features specific only to it, thus proving it unassailable as a kind of thing in the world, unique in its whirl of magic. Fry was a cubist painter and the formalist reading of cubism (see last chapter) told a story about the cubist re-establishment of pictorial space through a geometry of multiple, intersecting planes. Content was mere supplement, whether a cigar or a woman on the beach, who cared really? The point was to foreground significant pictorial form (the cubist representation of reality). In these formal energies the picture lived as art, not because it showed you a nice, sentimental hat. This hard-edged vision of art was Fry's own, a philosophical vision radically opposed to Leo Steinberg's reading of Picasso, and of painting in general let's say. Formalism began – and ended – with the importance of the specific medium.

Clement Greenberg, writing for the *New Yorker* in the 1930s, 40s and 50s, argued in 'Avant-Garde and Kitsch'[2] that the turn towards abstraction in painting and sculpture was a self-protective mechanism for an art now required, on what he called Kantian grounds, to 'justify' its existence in a culture of materialism, commodity fetish and economic rule. This justification also had to do with the way the kinds of experiences works of the new art wanted to engender were increasingly out of sync with public demand. Greenberg's view of the abstractionist turn was a preservationist one. By removing the world (or making it peripheral) and focusing on specifics of the medium, the arts highlighted the things that made them autonomous from the getting and spending of capitalism, the brutality of war, the cannibalizing commodity function which was subsuming the arts. But his view was also an essentializing, philosophical vision of the arts, which had them acting as self-discoverers of their own chemistry,

Cartesian explorers who would arrive at their own first principles and build a philosophical art from them. The key word for Greenberg was 'reductionism'. In essays like 'The New Sculpture'[3] he praised the abstractionist turn as one which reduced sculpture to its unique elements: materials, three-dimensional embodiment, form. The 'what' of representation (a Bernini pope cast in bronze, a Canova reclining nude, a Rodin Balzac heroically achieving revolutionary humanity) was happily removed so that sculpture could exist purely as itself, in short, in a state of purity.

This inward turn, celebrated as formalism, was always, I have said, more that that, since the gesture inevitably also carried representational, poetic, rhetorical meanings, which deepened it. It is almost a definition of the avant-gardes that they push–pulled in both of two ways, towards simplification and reductionism, and towards the weight of political rhetoric that would assert itself in and change the world. Abstraction was a contraction from meaning and a deepening of it, and if this seems paradoxical it is no more so than the way human beings often live in the world at times of rupture, wanting to get away from it all while also inflating their identities with greater and greater images of (illusions of) power.

The works of the Constructivists, the movement around Mondrian (De Stijl), the Futurists, the Bauhaus wanted to remake the entirety of human geography, from buildings to music, to clothing, to point of view. Since their experimental gestures were perforce ahead of the times, ahead, that is, of public knowledge, experience, opinion, they required a turn to theory and criticism in order to explain, invoke and provoke, in order to communicate, indeed define, their own works.[4] At the same time they aimed for reductionism to line, primary colour, transparency of steel and glass, the simplest uses of their media imaginable. These simplifications spoke to identity, but also became as it were empty ciphers which artists thought could be filled with the generating power of theory. A depictive painting of Christ on the Cross can't be read in a thousand different ways but a mere black spot on a white canvas, a diamond of intersecting lines can be told a thousand stories about, so that it seems, in each case, to mean what the words behind it say. Abstract satisfied the mysterious formalism goal of magic and simplicity, transcendental gesture untranslatable and sublime, while also a mere lens for whatever the words behind it seemed to want it to mean. In this doubleness the aura of transcendence fed into the weight of the words, making the gesture seem nothing short of religious. The avant-gardes were a kind of secular religion, a series of cults.

It was not for nothing the movements revolved around those who wrote: poets, critics, theorists. A new genre, taken over from Marx's *Communist Manifesto*, came into the arts: the manifesto, which announced creed, defined intentions, spoke of what the new art was going to be, explained, excoriated, cleared the way for the new. Images of art as a laboratory, allied with the sciences in some mysterious way, part of the new engineering, came into being. Images of erasure: erasing the past, clearing the deck for new architecture and new people, images of historical construction and constitution, came to dominate. Just at the moment Hegel believed art was already completed, no longer speaking of the highest aspirations of mankind because not philosophical enough, the avant-gardes took up the cudgel by combining experimentalism in style and materials with experimentalism in theory. The theorist was now an artist, a kind of philosopher, scientist, sociologist, literary critic, journalist, and rhetorician all in one. He explained, described, defined, aestheticized. And so the new aesthetics were those, on the one hand, of silence: a refusal of voice at all, an abstract turn to the transcendental and sublime, while on the other of an endless barrage of words, a *bavardage* as the French would say, a torrent meant to unleash the political power of art through the message.

I have written about the fragile alliance between these voices, often within the same artist: Mondrian and the artists of the Dutch art movement De Stijl around him, is in one voice an abstractionist par excellence. His paintings reduce content to an abstract pictorial square and diamond grid, his colours are nothing but primary colours, the edge of his canvas disappears into this abstract logic in a way that eliminates the figure/ground relationship, and all figuration. These pictures have a musical energy and elusive dynamic register that is about nothing at all but simply invokes music for the eye. It is not for nothing his late painting, *Broadway Boogie Woogie*, is a homage to jazz and to the jazzy character of the New York skyline and dazzling street at night, when all that can be seen from above is a rhythmic tangle of lights. And yet, this very turn to abstraction allowed Mondrian to also treat, or believe he was treating his canvases as mere empty ciphers for meaning. Mondrian the avant-garde theorist believed his works were philosophical demonstrations of everything from social harmony to the victory of technology over nature, and were icons ready to bring about a new and perfected world in the light of this pictorial/theoretical message. For the avant-gardes, a picture is silent, but also worth a thousand words in virtue of the way its abstraction serves to 'speak the language of theory'. I have written a book on this subject: the avant-garde game was to make abstract art which would therefore seem to be a mere cipher for theory, while simultaneously making abstract work, and work in new technologies, that would preserve the autonomy of the artwork and allow it a transcendent force (the sublime). Since the sublime is precisely that aesthetic attribute which brings forth great, unfathomable ideas, these two sides of the game reinforced each other. For theory was, through the sublime nature of the abstract object, presented in the work as a kind of halo, a great, unfathomable image of the sublime future (of which it spoke). The silent aura of the avant-garde work allowed its theories to appear in the form of something utopian and grand.[5]

What does this have to do with aesthetics in the twenty-first century? Two things at least: first that aesthetic theory happens within art, within its practice, in the form of its theoretical turn. This is a requirement of interpretation, since visual objects need explanation if they are to have the slightest hope of 'speaking' to the future. The visual medium is not normally one of speech, and so writing is required to empower it with a message. Second, that the new art required new philosophy to make sense of its flouting of past art, of its bringing art to the brink of absurdity and revelling in that. When Duchamp offered a urinal in a museum exhibition, either he was mad, or a charlatan, or doing something which required philosophical unpacking, as to how this thing could fit into canons of art, or even speak to them. The new art already had philosophy in it (in the form of theory of art) and called for more, to explain what it was doing.

Where an avant-garde opens up a gap between its gestures and the audience who are meant to understand them, and be moved by them, theory becomes required, aesthetics demanded, criticism wanted, to bridge the gap and bring the audience to the portals of experience. The twentieth century vastly empowered the role of the critic, and Clement Greenberg ended up having the power to begin or end the careers of artists in a single review. This was because the avant-gardes already relied on words to spell meaning into their reductionist gestures, their experiments with new materials, technologies, forms. The true task of aesthetics became to understand this double game the avant-gardes were playing, between reductionism and manifesto, and to find a path to criticize the bravado of their conclusions, the hubris of their politics through art. To criticize it but also to historicize it, understand the context of its announcement. To see the quality in the silence and explain the gesture.

The avant-gardes arose between the two world wars, in the aftermath of the seismic shock which that first world war (the war to end all wars!) produced. How could modern life have led to such devastation when everything the world of Paris, 'capital of the nineteenth century' had taught was that life was an ongoing intoxication with speed, colour and the spume of champagne glasses overflowing with luxury and effervescence. And now that speed had led to bombs, mustard gas, and death on an overwhelming scale. Germany lay devastated, France in ruins and Winston Churchill had lost an entire generation of comrades. How had modern life done this, managed to blow itself up so completely, and with all the techniques of positive thought and engineering to do it? Of course they hadn't seen nothin' yet, all they had to do was wait another 20 years for the genocides, the camps, the tanks on the Russian Front, the bombed cities and human rubble, and they would virtually collapse. The avant-gardes had their heyday between the two wars, one calling for radical change in society, a better use of new technologies, the other closing the book on utopia more or less altogether.

Greenberg argued that the turn towards abstract was a way of safe-guarding the dignity of experience, the power of absorption, which art had inherited from Courbet, Manet, the nineteenth century, by seizing on the autonomy of the arts granted to them in the eighteenth century, and using this as a protective mechanism. The purity of abstraction was a defence against the onslaughts, Greenberg argued, of social kitsch. Kitsch was in the 30s and 40s, deeply associated with politics, with the turning of the sublime into a concretized image of Roman empire (Fascist Italy), German rural hamlet and art deco Wagnerism (Germany), smelting plant with Russian worker (Stalin), the stuff discussed earlier in this book when the sublime came up. It was the charade of representations proclaiming all manner of absurd ideologies and decorating them with ordinary forms, so that they appeared part of daily life. It was also a way of riding the crest of radical politics, both on the right and on the left. The avant-gardes had two faces: on the one side the face of abstraction, autonomy, silence, the sublime, of purity, simplicity, and the dignity of refusal. On the other side the face of the avant-gardes was a political one, the face of the manifesto, the social demonstration (dada), the rhetorical challenge to the institutions of art (the museum, the gallery, the commodity function) and the face of a revolutionary resolute and optimistic about his or her challenge to authority and ability to ride the crest of the future. On the one hand the avant-gardes chose retreat and silence, refusal of meaning and message, on the other nothing but polemics, theories, in your face gestures of political empowerment. These two sides of the avant-gardes were variously emphasized by significant critics of the time, and ongoing to the end of the twentieth century. Greenberg emphasized the aesthetics of the one side, those of absorption and sublimity through reduction of art to its simplest formal means; critics like Peter Burger and John Berger the political.

This is why as many positions opened up in aesthetics as did in the arts themselves: formalism, expressionism, anti-art theorists, and so on. The modern landscape of the arts called for this. But when philosophy entered the game, it tended to use the tools set forth by eighteenth-century aesthetics, and traditional Platonic definition: seeking an essence of art in the form of a definition of its basic ingredients. This was not the way theory happened within the arts, which was more of the nature of rhetoric, buzzword and experimentation. And yet philosophy's traditional methods came up with equally (and appropriately) radical results. To say all art is language, because the artwork is a mere vehicle for expression, as Collingwood did, was to say something about as radical (if not nutty) as you could get on this subject, given that most people who enjoyed most art went to museums and studied it, contemplated it, got wrapped up in it in the way connoisseurs do, or fans, or people wanting to get off the street and have a nice time. To say art is simply a form of experience, part of the stream of life (Dewey) was to say something nearly as shocking. The shock of the new, to use Robert Hughes' turn of phrase, happened in philosophical aesthetics just as it happened in art, and because it happened in the new art.

DANTO'S AVANT-GARDE DEFINITION OF AVANT-GARDE ART

The most celebrated and finest theorist of the avant-gardes, the best of those wishing to define art in their wake, is Arthur Danto. His attunement to the new art has been unparalleled, his voice as radical

as any avant-gardist's. Arthur Danto's philosophy of art is so important to the latter half of the twentieth century that I for one cannot
imagine philosophizing about plastic art apart from it.[6] For my generation it has been his writing about the avant-gardes more than
anyone else's that has caused us to think about the putatively philosophical character of that art, about its historical explanation and
about its relevance for the philosophical definition of art. His views
have been so surprising to us, so original, that we have felt them to
be of a piece with the originality and scandal of the avant-gardes
themselves: Danto is an avant-garde philosopher of the avant-gardes.
His art criticism – written largely for the *Nation* magazine and collected in a number of volumes – is about local context; his philosophy seeks universality of scope. He seeks a philosophical definition
of art: about the general conditions according to which objects can
be rightly called 'art'. For him this is a matter of the body of theory
behind the object, not, as it were, the object itself. It is the theory
which allows a 'real thing' to become a work of art. This theory is historically evolving in ways which alter the kinds of things that can
become art, and (related) the kinds of statements artworks can make.

This theory, while utterly rooted in the new plastic art of the twentieth century and having little or nothing to say about music, architecture, theatre or film, and congruent with the avant-garde goals of
those media when they function as parts of the avant-garde, is unin-
terested in the details of any particular medium in its fundamentals.
It takes the line of reasoning that art is a property established at a
more abstract level of human thinking than human interest in the
particulars of media. This is important to understand. Here is a
philosopher working between two levels of thought. On the one
hand he writes out of concern for a particular art in a particular
century, on the other he takes it that what makes that and all other
art art is something more abstract than the specifics of these media
and this history. The two levels are tied together in his thinking
because twentieth-century visual art is supposed to be the art which
finally became philosophical and in its own way hit on the philosophical truth about what makes all art art. Whereas I have said the
role of avant-garde theory is to politically empower art, Danto
believes that it, along with the reductionism and purification of
modernisms, has served the purpose of reaching the highest level of
abstraction that art can reach in its own philosophical self-discovery
and definition. Danto, like Hegel, provides a big reading of history.

Danto's is that art in his century achieves philosophical self-definition, and does so at a higher level of abstraction than any particular medium. Wollheim is about painting as an art (the particular kind of art it is), Danto is about art per se and universally. Danto is therefore the heir of the eighteenth century, the period which made aesthetics a project of general definition.

Except that his modernist style of definition precludes all aesthetic quality! This too is a legacy of the avant-gardes, of his reading of Duchamp and Picasso as chemists and alchemists of significant form and thought. Just as constructivism claimed (in one voice) to have little time for the beautiful and despised taste, so Danto thinks that what the likes of constructivism have shown is that art is definable apart from any and all aesthetic dimension. Whereas the eighteenth century had little interest in art; now Danto has little interest in aesthetics, until recently that is, when he and others have returned (weakly I think) to the topic of beauty. Particular works of art might be tasteful or beautiful, but this does not make them art. What makes them art is the theory behind them, the way they are constructed by that interpretive community behind them called the art world. A work of art is 'propositional', it makes a statement. This statement becomes art through a theory of (its) meaning, a theory investing its syllables, forms, materials, assemblages, with interpretation. At one time in history it would not have been possible to turn hammers and wrenches into works of art; the community of belief would never have interpreted them as such. History had to cause the interpretation of art to change, meaning the theory held by the relevant community to develop concepts that would allow for the inclusion.

Art is defined by one thing only: a historically evolving community of belief, or theory, which sets its terms. At one stroke aesthetics becomes irrelevant unless the community, at a given time in history (say, the eighteenth century) lends these features a central role in the art-making interpretation (in the manner of Hume and Kant, and their theories of taste). Art is a theory-laden entity and always has been, since it is theory which makes an ordinary thing (ceramic pot, tract house, piece of driftwood) into a work of art.

Struck by the gap between Da Vinci and Duchamp, between a *Mona Lisa* and a 'ready-made' (Duchamp's snow shovel, *In Advance of a Broken Arm*), he thinks no single kind of meaning or aesthetics could ever account for the paradigm shifts in interpretation which have resulted in such different items being conceptualized as art.

Another kind of theorist might throw up his hands and say: there is nothing in common between these items: art has simply changed too radically for any universal definition of it to be found. Danto's response is: what holds all these differences together is the shared property of shared belief or theory! At one moment theory decreed X, at another Y, how these changes occurred is the work of art history. That they occurred is what the definition of art encompasses.

Now nothing is more modernist than Danto's view, because it is exactly what the avant-gardes taught him: a work is generated by the idea behind it, and that is argued into existence by a community of voices, a movement. Danto's is the avant-garde concept writ large, and combined with recent debates in the philosophy of science which stress the theory-driven nature of language and knowledge. Danto's most recent formulation of this view can be found in the book that came out of his Mellon Lectures at the National Gallery of Art in the 1990s. There he formulates the claim in a way that is somewhat critical of his earlier view:

> My concern in [my early article, 'The Artworld'] . . . was with works of art that so resemble ordinary objects that perception cannot seriously discriminate between them. The thesis was enunciated thus: 'To see something as art requires something the eye cannot descry – an atmosphere of artistic theory, a knowledge of the history of art: an art world.' . . . I now think what I wanted to say was this: a knowledge of what other works the given work fits with, a knowledge of what other works makes a given work possible. My interest was in the somewhat attenuated objects of contemporary art – the *Brillo Box*, or Robert Morris' very uninflected sculpture . . . These objects had few interesting affinities with anything in the history of art . . . my thought in 'The Artworld' was that no one unfamiliar with history or with artistic theory could see these as art, and hence it was the history and the theory of the object, more than anything palpably visible, that had to be appealed to in order to see them as art.[7]

The earlier thesis, based on a remarkably inventive use of the philosophical conundrum about the identity of indiscernibles, proposed that what makes Warhol's *Brillo Box* art as opposed to its supermarket cousin is nothing the eye can discern, since both Warhol's *Brillo Box* and the Brillo box in the store are (to all intents

Andy Warhol, Brillo Box, 1964
Andy Warhol Foundation/CORBIS

and purposes) visually the same, indiscernible: and yet one is art, the other not. Hence the art-making property, the thing that makes *Brillo Box* art while leaving the box in the store out of this category, must be non-perceptual. That property is it seemed reasonable to say, a theory. Reasonable because the histories of art had become clearly theoretical in the twentieth century, playing games with theory and highlighting its crucial role in jacking up their meanings, values and politics.[8]

Andy Warhol's work seemed to Danto tailor-made to be a demonstration of the point. The difference between the two objects, *Brillo Box* and a Brillo box, given the immensity of their similarities, was that the one made a statement about its relationship to the other, while the other remained essentially mute about everything. The one was propositional, the other not. This was what placed the Warhol in the ballpark of art, rather than its supermarket prototype. Scribbles do not acquire meanings through mere perception but rather in virtue of a conceptual background; Warhol's object gets its meaning from the background of theory held by the art world. It was all this that Warhol's work implicitly *demonstrated*. Warhol laid the groundwork for Danto's own words, as if Warhol already sort of 'knew it' behind the dark glasses. There is a clarity about Warhol's work which Danto alone saw in 1964. For what makes Warhol's work fine art is not only its one-of-a-kind status, but more than that, its complex *questioning*, its invocation of thought as well as its refusal of thought, its ambivalent game playing, its conceptual magic, its parodic hilarity. None of which applies to the supermarket prototype, and all of which one locates in a distinctively modernist regime of art-making and reception, one rooted in the history of dada, surrealism, Duchamp, Rauchenberg, Clement Greenberg and so forth: what Danto calls 'The Artworld'.

Were one to ascribe a similar conceptual background to the mass-produced box in the supermarket, one would be willing to call it also fine art.

That Danto could presume Warhol to have been implicitly in the same business as himself, that he could believe Warhol's work succeeded in demonstrating the essence of art for all times and places, was about as audacious as Warhol's own antics. I think of Danto as very much of a piece with Warhol: they share a similar modernist sensibility, playfulness, capacity for imaginative scandal. I mean the Warhol who presumed to produce works of art so close to the landscape of signage that it was only the dazzling hand of the artist himself that would spell out whatever differences, small or large, could be found between his own work, commodities and signs. Warhol's seemed a stroke of genius for a world so permeated by the icons of film that Jackie O. could be embalmed by his silk screens in the way Egyptians once were in sarcophagi. His was a response to a commodified world in which signs and adverts were also themselves kinds of art: including the Brillo box (the one in the store) which had been designed by an abstract expressionist painter, thus already half collapsing the distinction between industrial and fine art, between art and advert, between painting and selling. Warhol, commercial turned fine artist, well understood the slippage between these categories, the overlap between them.

Danto's philosophy is a philosophy of modernist art history. It takes modernism to have had a project, a project that is philosophical, not political or transcendental, which is my reading of that same material.

The goal of modernist art history has been to arrive at a self-definition of art. There is a legacy of the New York School of art criticism in Danto's view, of the Clement Greenberg who in writing about modernist sculpture claimed its abstraction of form was about arriving at a revelation of its basic constituents, in the manner of a philosopher. That this project of self-definition through abstraction and reduction culminated, according to Danto, with Andy Warhol is another of those modernist surprises history has gifted us. Not only is Warhol in the same business, Warhol completes modernist art history by finally arriving at a discovery of the essence of art. Combining Hegel's view that the point of history is self-knowledge, and the actualization of self-knowledge in the institutions of society, with Clement Greenberg's formalist criticism that abstract art has been about philosophically establishing the underlying possibilities and nature of the medium per se, Danto thus reads avant-garde art history as the search for a philosophical self-definition of what makes art, art. A correlate is that art history achieved its purpose with Warhol, arrived at its final conclusion. This project must now be given over to philosophy, whose terms of argument and elucidation can take the definition further than visual demonstrations could ever go. Art no longer has grand project, a grand narrative. It is therefore freed to be whatever, for whomever, in the way it likes. Let a thousand flowers bloom, none any more definitive. This is Danto's rosy picture of postmodernism in the arts.

This is a big, fascinating, audacious metaphysical story about history, a philosophical reading of it that speaks to its purpose (self-definition) and its achievement of that purpose (with Warhol). In its brashness and audacity, it is a story worthy of any avant-garde manifesto, just as Hume's work is worthy of the best connoisseurship of its day, the best criticism. Aesthetics is always of its time, in spite of its universalizing claims. One can read the times through it just as if it were the morning newspaper. One can only wonder if modernism has had a single, overriding purpose, which it has brought to completion, or if modernism instead is a thing of many parts, many projects, many points of view, some over, some ongoing. Such a competing picture of modern art would be Jean-Francois Lyotard's, with its emphasis on the refusal of a single grand narrative to be found in history, and its corresponding belief that there is no simple way either to say that modern art history is over or that it is not. It all depends on your point of view. I am sympathetic to Lyotard's way of thinking about this problem.[9]

Now this big thesis of Danto's comes down to a reading of Warhol, a reading which takes him to have proven what makes his artwork art (and all art, art) by setting up the problem of the identity of indiscernibles: what makes his work different from the ordinary Brillo box on the supermarket shelf? Danto noted something important in noting that Warhol's work differs from the supermarket Brillo box in virtue of its voice (a work of art makes a statement, on his view). That voice was possible because of the *art world* behind it, and to which it spoke.

But commercial art also has its forms of rhetoric, and fine art is also in its way commercial. I think that rather than marking an essential difference between a Brillo box and his own oversized sample, Warhol is coming dangerous close, dazzlingly close, to showing the *opposite*: these are so similar that it is impossible to establish an essential difference between them. They are cut from the same cloth, in spite of the fact that his speaks about the other, in a way that the other does not speak about his. This *is* a difference in kind, but then think of all the similarities. Both objects are about buying and selling. Both are circulated in shops specializing in the selling of goods (supermarket and gallery). Both are designed by persons who are, or have been, commercial artists. Both are playful, they make you want to touch and buy. Both are seductive. Warhol's work is about its cousin, yes and playfully so, through the gesture of oversize, parody, self-parody. But the attitude it offers is comradeship, as if to say we two boxes are cut from the same materials, and made to order, each in its way. Mine is in love with yours. We are cousins, mirror images, two of a kind. There is a kind of incest, not entirely proper, intimated between Warhol's work and its double, a hidden male/male eroticism, a love of the same if you will, a love of passing oneself as another, of going in drag, performing oneself through another, thus revealing how one is, in effect, to all intents and purposes, the other. There is liberation in this parade and charade, a kind of coming out from the closet of museum security and fine art practice.

Nothing is more American in its brashness than this, nothing more hidden from America (at that time) than the identity politics of consumerism, and of gay culture. Late capitalism was fun then, a kind of romp through the department store of culture before culture became the rather more cruel commodity fetish that it is today, and art became the commodity traded on eBay, and featured on *Antiques Roadshow* around Britain and the United States. In the modern art world art is always also a commodity, which is what Monet already understood. Warhol is fascinated by this identification of art and commodity.

It will be retorted that finally, there is an indisputable difference between the Warhol and the supermarket variety. Warhol's work is free to entangle itself with the supermarket box, the supermarket box remains mute. It is engaged in no spirited discourse with Warhol's work, and that is the difference. Works of art are propositional (they say and imply things), mere commodities don't. Were one to exhibit the supermarket box in a gallery, in the manner of some conceptual artist, that might be sufficient to give it 'voice', but as it happens, the thing is meant to be used, not displayed, appreciated, treated in some romping, duchamping manner as the voice of art, the take-off on the gallery, the whatever on whatever.

True, but again not quite, for to repeat: the Brillo box was made by an abstract expressionist painter and who is to say that it does, nor does not commune with abstract expressionist art? Although its purpose is consumption, its texture is not, one could argue, free of voice. Warhol's designs have become canonical for a whole design industry these days which 'refer' to Warhol, whether in the design studio or on the supermarket shelf.

It is a feature of the way Danto sets up the problem of the identity of indiscernibles that 'for all intents and purposes' Warhol's box is visually identical to its supermarket cousin. This is meant to prove that nothing perceptual spells out the reason why one is art while the other is not. But it is worth noting that Warhol's playful, zany, comic, provocative voice depends on the oversized and partly painted character of his *Brillo Boxes*. These are perceptual qualities. The gesture would have been provocative enough were the objects he chose to exhibit (in the manner of some conceptual artist) actually the same as those in the supermarket, say, in the manner of Duchamp's 'ready-mades'. But even those shift the meaning from snow shovel to Duchamp object, and in doing so do not simply do so through the flat (although at the time outrageous) gesture of placing such things on exhibition. Rather in Duchamp's metaphysic their choice is highly calculated, like a move in a game of chess. His 'ready-mades' suggest coded messages, even a poetry of eroticism, breaking and entering, the body, male and female, etc. They depend on their titles as much as how they look, and the interplay between title and object is what counts. A hat rack is called Medusa, and of course it looks like her hair turned into metal tongs. The object assaults, jokes and does nothing (says nothing) at the same time. This is a game which is pure performance. Even Duchamp's 'ready-mades' rise above the occasion of their mere thingness through the games they play with art.

It is in virtue of these games, interpreted by theory of course, but also up close and in your face, right in the museum, that the works become art. With Duchamp theory becomes an essential ingredient of meaning in that without an outside reading, the objects reduce to non-art. This is their point. That theory plays this kind of role in his modernist game does not, however, mean it plays a similarly essential game in say, the paintings of Joshua Reynolds of young, upper-class English women standing before the hunt. No universal point can be made about the role of theory from the modernist case. It is a particular, extreme case. Danto is failing to appreciate what is unique in history (i.e. not generalized across history) in this avant-garde example. He fails to appreciate its historicity. It is a particular art practice, taking place against an art world (museum, gallery, commodification, criticism) at a certain historical moment that allows Duchamp's work to be called art.

The practice set in the institution is what counts. Hence George Dickie's institutional theory of art, which picks up on the importance of institutions (the art world) and practices (Duchamp's) in together making something art. The problem with this, as yet another in the endless stream of definitions of art, is that it fails to allow for the centrality of aesthetic experience in also discerning whether something shall be called art or not. A practice has to hit us in the right way, and there are no pre-given criteria for how it does or should hit us. We must find experience of it and reflection on it convincing, hence the importance of the critic, theorist, middleman in helping us to the portals of experience when we are unsure. What makes something and sustains the interpretation of it as art is a way a culture treats it. This is not a definition, it is a way of pointing to what Wittgenstein called the 'form of life' in which we dwell, and through which we come to understand new things as art over time, or keep them in a state of permanent uncertainty.

The problems, then, with defining art as a historically evolving theory held by a community, are at least three:

First, art is a practice, not simply a theory or set of beliefs, or belief/attitude conjunction about object, representation, value and so on. It is practices of selection, inclusion, experience, aestheticism, avant-garde gesture, whatever, which at different times spell out the characteristics of what can become (new) art, of what the (new) horizons are for the subject. It is not that Danto's view is wrong exactly, it is incomplete. The entire story of art is required for an understanding of what becomes art, and when. This story is about what Ernst Gombrich in *Art and Illusion* calls the artist's 'stereotypes', which are belief structures, visual representations encoded in the mind, narrative styles, and ideologies, that conjoin to produce a sense of what can be represented or expressed or whatever, and how. But it is also about the institutions of art and their ways of codifying tradition, refusing or accepting new product for all manner of purpose, including commercial; it is about what a public wants, whether it has a theory about it or not; it is about public beliefs of course, but also wants and desires. What becomes art is a matter of how experience and market conjoin, not simply how theory rules. This is dialectical, an interaction of variously supported theories by artist, critic, public, of other sorts of beliefs and desires (about representation, devotion, social good, pleasure, taste, whatever) with the history of practices, like those of Hume's bourgeois compatriots, not to mention himself, which license a way of treating objects (as the material for taste). To define art as a property of theory exclusively (hence to produce a universal, philosophical definition), is to lose sight of the complex circumstance in which theory adheres.

This is an avant-garde position. Danto is an avant-gardist at heart. For just as the avant-gardes claimed (in one voice at least) that the meanings of their abstract paintings and glass sculptural designs were given by their theories, so Danto claims the same about art generally. His is an extrapolation from not only the specific circumstance of the avant-gardes; it is a generalization of their ideology. Ironically even the avant-gardes were far more complex: which is why a Jean-Francois Lyotard can pick up on this side of the avant-garde practice and generalize it. Danto's reading of the avant-gardes, of Warhol in particular, eliminates the aesthetic side which was inevitably central to what they did. This was even true for Warhol and Duchamp. These two sides or games, the theoretical and the aesthetic, did not always sit comfortably, or even coherently, with each other. But together they defined the multiple aims of the practice.

This leads to the second problem with defining art in terms of theory. It eliminates, and means to do, the aesthetic as an essential ingredient of art practices. This is not even true of the world where Danto lives when he writes as a philosopher. For the avant-gardes are as concerned with making beautiful, overwhelming, expressive, powerful, shocking, sublime things as everybody else is, although not in the same way as those before them. The aesthetic is as central to the fate of how things become art as theory or any other ingredient is. When a philosopher produces a definition it is as much to leave something out as to include or highlight something, and the aesthetic is not correctly eliminated, however striking this makes the definition.

Third, to define art in terms of theory means one has a clear enough idea of what theory is, and also can show that such theory has been that which drives art history. The one part is philosophical, to make perspicuous what one means by a theory, since this is a notoriously sliding signifier. The other is art-historical, to make a convincing case that this property, so clarified, actually does define art at various historical moments. I have written about this elsewhere,[10] and urge the reader to think hard on the matter. Danto began his philosophical career, when he turned from printmaking to philosophy, in the philosophy of science. And his ideas of theory derive from the work of W. V. O. Quine there. The theory is a kind of holistic form, which as it evolves comes to include new features, first representation, next expression (expressionism), finally abstraction. It is more or less a reading of art history from the Renaissance (depiction) to the post-impressionists (the wild beast Fauves with their contorted expressive figuration and wildly evocative colours), to abstraction (Pollack et al.). Suffice it to say that the more Danto tries to clarify the theory in its various formulations, the more its insufficiency as an explanation of what counts as art at a given time becomes evident. The Baroque counted the musical gestures of a church built of contrapuntal forces which soar to the ceiling in the manner of Christian triumph and domination. Is this a matter of theory, say of the counter-Reformation Christian faith in relation to an art of its empire, or is it an understanding of the pleasure and sublimity that comes from the overwhelming experience of such spaces and how they might therefore express and invoke a community of the devout? At any point in the history of art it will be, to return to the first and second points, the practice and the aesthetics which matter as much as theory. More than that, theory will be defined in terms of the practice (which is how one will come to understand the beliefs involved), and vice versa. This is an organic relation, what Wittgenstein calls a 'form of life', it is not a matter of three conceptually independent elements which combine, like the parts of a mechanism (automobile), to make the mechanism (automobile) run.

Danto's more recent work has reformed the idea of theory into a looser concept called a style matrix. This he states in his recent Mellon Lectures, a position quite different from that stated in his earlier 1964 essay, 'The Artworld', written in blown away response to the Eleanor Stable show, which captivated the young Danto as 'world historical' if you will. In the Mellon Lectures he states that while the visually distinctive character of the Warhol work does matter, the brunt of what turns Warhol's work into art, what he calls a style matrix – a lineage of art work and art theory – is more important. The style matrix into which the art world places an object is more important than the object's palpably visual properties. More significant than, bigger than, a *y* as opposed to an *ie*. No longer are visual properties excluded from having a defining role for art: they are simply less important. Now once the formulation is as vague as Property A being greater than Property B, the philosophical position seems diluted as impossible to verify. Theory and history (the style matrices) count more than what one palpably sees. Perhaps for the Warhol, but in general . . . a lot more, a little more, almost the same, very much more? Depending on circumstance? Visual properties, now re-enfranchised as essential to art, might for a given case run at 49 per cent importance to theory's 51 per cent. Sometimes an Electoral College might have to be called in to pronounce final judgement about which wins, or there might have to be a Florida recount. Furthermore, once one has gone this far, why should one not go the whole way and say that for certain kinds of works, perceptual properties count *more than* theory, while for others, less. And soon enough one will have to ask how theory and the palpably perceptible are to be distinguished each from the other. For by the lights of many, percept and concept are beyond a certain point not clearly distinguishable.

There are differences in kind between works of art and Brillo boxes. But it is rather the pattern of similarities and differences which together count. Viewed from certain perspectives the kinds are the same: both are commercial, part of a commercial world, designed graphically, etc. Seen from another perspective they differ in terms of the way a practice takes them to speak, and the intention imputed to an artist (Warhol) to have them do this, to turn art into play, a kind of coming-out party played over shopping. The point is

Wittgensteinian: instead of definitions of essential differences we have patterns of similarity and differences between overlapping language games (practices) which count in spelling the one object as art, the other not, or less so, or more peripherally so (how one puts this can be a matter of debate).

FILM: A CASE STUDY OF THE AESTHETICS OF NEW MEDIA

Danto's story is not about the philosophical relevance of new media, but these are in fact what has produced his, and just about everyone else's theory today. It is because of Duchamp, who gave rise to Warhol, that Danto could think as he did. Duchamp invented a new medium, a kind of theatrical game played in and around painting or sculpture, between word and image, that is about both by being neither but almost both! Take that as you will, the point is that ours is, as Rosalind Krauss and others have argued, the age of new media, media which arise, split, multiply, hybridize, mediate one another, exist betwixt and between. The work of William Kentridge, neither film nor animation nor drawing nor silent cinema but all these, the work of every installation, performance, multi-media artist is of this hybrid creative category of thing. Identity is less clear than it is for any individual medium, which although it exists in a complex system of difference between other arts, nevertheless does have at physical and abstract levels, properties unique to it. Painting after all is paint on canvas, in two dimensions, framed or located on a wall, sculpture three dimensional but not architecture; film is, whatever else one wants to say, celluloid which has preserved photographically sequences of framing and converts these into light projected onto two dimensions. Nothing else does this. But to say that, like saying music is time, tone, pulse, is not to speak to its significations of form, its mode of rhetoric, its complexities of vision, its peculiar magic and powers of absorption.

The problem of new media remains central for aesthetics, and may be illustrated by the story of film, no longer new, but new enough to serve the purpose. This story is of importance not only because it reveals how film became realized as a practice, and also understood by aesthetics, through evolving systems of comparison and contrast with other arts (theatre, opera, painting, even photography). But also because the story illustrates the wide concept of aesthetics I am embracing in this book. Thinking about what film is, and can be, happened within film, art history, journalism, theory, and finally philosophy. It is salient to study how philosophical problems arise for aesthetics through this wider ambit of aesthetic thought about a new art.

Film was invented by Thomas Edison (1891), whose Edison box transposed images caught on celluloid into a stream of projected light, which, when it hit a white surface, appeared as a moving image. Within a few years the two-reeler came into existence, and from the first films he began to understand that the stationary box positioned in front of a scene liked to capture things that move. Perhaps the first film ever made was *The Great Train Robbery*, which excelled in loads of motion: a train pulling into a station in the west, its being held up by outlaws riding on horseback and waving guns all over. The close-up of a woman terrified, another being robbed, the positioning of the camera on the top of the train so that when it pulled away you were there with it. Motion was understood to involve bodily action, violent, comic, athletic, dramatic shifts in perspective which would transport the viewer from this angle to that, this place to that. The close-up was quickly discovered and exploited as the way human emotion and gesture would be built into story, and by the time of D. W. Griffith shots were edited into a seamless story form rather than simply compiled. The manipulation of time, the shift in tense from past to present to future and back, the dreamlike nature of a face, these things recruited opera, whose simplicity of plot and depth of gesture were tailor-made for the lyrical and dramatic raising of the eye, opening of the mouth, registering of desire through the tensile body, prolonged in the manner of an aria. Quickly, in short, human physiognomy became the locus of the lyric, the dramatic, the inner script of human feeling which made a story sing out to its mass public, in the manner of the grand opera of Verona, adored by cab driver and princess alike. In film it was even more democratic, because being in the dark, there was no difference in quality of seats. Everyone became part of the experience of darkness illuminated by the panoply of light on screen. This act of illumination proved auratic: people were blown away by the ghostlike presence of spectral beings on screen, whose existence became endlessly repeatable on the silver screen, and whose presence proved eternal, because already evanescent.

From the first, this spectral presence of those photographed in the past on screen became the material for another of film's unique themes: the ghost story, the one possessed, the woman driven mad by gaslight because already haunted by something that was, and that is so much part of her that it remains invisible. This revelation of invisibility was itself an act of illumination, shown in lighting, gesture, plot, the haunting of the image by the weight of something old or forgotten, recurrent only in dreams. Just as opera gravitated from medium to theme, just as painting found one of its great themes in the embodiment of the human flesh in the tumult of life (Wollheim), so film found its subjects in motion, emotion, simplicity of story, innocence therefore, and sheer culpability, the dreamlike, the haunted, the past. No villain was more villainous than the banker, come to steal away the family farm, the politician, ready to manipulate Gary Cooper aka Mr Deeds so that he might prod the public into his degraded subversion of their interests, the actor with his greasy black moustache, there to steal away the girl to the precipitous dangers of the city, where he would have his way with her and leave her an outcast, no hero more good than the same Gary Cooper, this time in *For Whom the Bell Tolls*, holding off the fascists long enough, his leg broken, his life shattered, so the others could get away, or Paul Muni, emaciated, underfed, writing late into the night, his pen mightier than the mightiest sword, raging against the French medical establishment which refuses to believe that smallpox is caused by microbes, or Ronald 'It is a far, far better thing that I do, than I have ever done', Coleman, dashing as he faces the guillotine so that others may be saved and true love may endure, even if he is the one to be nothing but envious, since he is rejected. Film's intensity of gesture, simplicity of plot, sheer juxtaposition of light and darkness within the compositional frame, allowed a century so complex that it would otherwise host the avant-gardes to rediscover that life is simple, good is good and evil worse, that tragedy is unredeemable and comedy side-splitting, that happy endings will always remain happy because you can see the film a hundred thousand times if you live long enough.

These discoveries of the medium were quickly noted by the likes of Erwin Panofsky, the great art historian, who was there in the back rooms of Berlin warehouses in 1905 watching two-reelers.[11] He writes from experience, having been there 'from the beginning'. Cinema was from the beginning, Panofsky tells us, an ebullient game of discovering what worked. It quickly gravitated to things that move (train robberies, comic incidents with gags), close-ups (the expressivity of the face), cutting across locations (transporting the viewer aesthetically from one location to the next in the way theatre could never do), moving between past and present (the flashback), and exploiting human and natural physiognomy for expressive values in a way that called forth human temporality (desire – the future, remembrance and being marked – the past). Panofsky, writing an essay in 1934 called 'Style and Medium in the Moving Pictures', argued that film discovered three essential features of its medium: dynamization of space, spatialization of time, and what he calls the principle of co-expressibility. Most important of all, he ended the essay with a claim about the medium of film which is both surprising and wondrously obscure. By dynamization of space he means the ability to transport viewers into motion, and to establish scenes through motion. While in the theatre the viewer is stationary, in film he is sent from New York to Rio and then to the South Pole in seconds. Or placed on the top of a moving train as it is about to enter a tunnel. Space is established dynamically in film, through a camera's motion into it, a mid-range shot, followed by a close-up perhaps, a shot from under a lamp or focus on a detail (a pen on the writing table, a ball dribbling through the room) and then perhaps, if the place is Monument Valley, an enormous pan, worthy of its monumental subject. And film adores things that move. When a film contains itself in a small space, like *My Dinner with André*, where Wally Shawn sits and mostly listens to his pal the theatre director André, as they consume wine and food, animation is given by André's irrepressible personality. He is in motion even when sitting, his rhythm of language is as dynamic as any rodeo or jet plane ride.

Spatialization of time has to do with the way film conveys a sudden shift of perspective that articulates time, but time from the point of view of human emotion or desire. The flashback is the most evident and dramatic example. In *The Quiet Man*, John Wayne is alone in a village in Ireland. As it happens this is the village from whence his family had come to America. His return signals flight, there is a gravity he carries around with him we do not as yet understand. We do not know why he has left to come back to this place. We can tell he is running away, and that whatever it is that has plagued him he will not share. He wants to start over, in the past. All we know is that in spite of his fantasy that he will find refuge here, it is far more foreign than he expected. He is in love, and does not know how, nor is he willing, to conform to traditional courtship and marriage practices. This is sinking him. At a certain point in the film the local clergyman invites Wayne into his home and shows he's a boxing fan, by showing Wayne a picture of himself in his former life as a boxer. Cut now to the flashback, Wayne is fighting a man, fighting to an ugly conclusion. His aggression is profound. It is a tough, gritty, terrible scene in which he is caught up. The man is killed. Wayne is overwhelmed with guilt. We see him now, in this house, with this man, and his face registers something we had not known before: bitterness. And that he seeks in this place of his origins, refuge, the erasure of time, of all that has happened. This is the spatialization of time, through film's movement in and around time, human emotion is conveyed in its literary depths.

My own favourite example comes from Francois Truffaut's *The Four Hundred Blows*. Antoine Doinel (this is the first of five films about his life) is here a teenager, say 15, maybe younger. His mother is cold and punishing, his father ineffectual. Always trying to get away from this little, petit bourgeois enclosure that is his life, he knows not where to turn. And so the stealing, the hanging out on the streets, the cigarettes, no one to understand. He is sent to reform school, and there, in the final scene of the film, he runs away from a soccer match he is playing, in his school uniform. He runs and runs without knowing where he is running to. The camera tracks him in one of the longest tracking shots in cinema, and so we follow at his shoulders, in front of him, sharing the perspective of his blind escape. Eventually, exhausted, running more slowly, he reaches the sea. The camera pulls back slightly to mid-shot as he runs across a long vein of sand until he can run no further, he has reached the sea. The film ends framing him looking out towards the sea, still in the adrenaline of motion, a motion unable to be continued. The sea is a limit, and becomes the horizon of his future, the shape of his desire, as real and inchoate as water itself, as impossible to cross as his own enclosure, as wanted as vision itself. This is the bringing up of time, and through time, the Heideggerian temporality of being in time, according to which humans are creatures thrown into the world, not of their own making, and condemned to the project of ceaseless self-understanding through a life in the present which flows from future to past (meaning a present in which being in-formation and always lacking in understanding), means to be pointed in the direction of a future unknown. It is where time, desire, emotion converge in the moving frame. Only cinema can do this.

Panofsky was a creature of silent film, where there is no screenplay, only story framed by snippets of plot and dialogue which appear from time to time on screen. In silent film, story is a frame which is realized essentially through gesture, close-up, editing, camera. The actor's exaggeration of mouth, her slow movement towards the centre of a room, her turning of the eyes spoke volumes on screen – spoke all that cinema could speak. The star drew out her gestures, prolonged them to make them 'sing'. Everything happened visually, making silent film almost a different medium from sound films. Panofsky, in wishing to define film through contrast with the theatre, found an ally in silent film, where the screenplay is non-existent.

Panofsky clearly believes screenplay secondary to what happens on screen visually. In spite of Panofsky's failure to properly value the screenplay,[12] his principle that in film the actor's *physiognomy* is central in creating the character remains a good one. A screenplay adds the critical dimension of talk, and this talk must be integrated into the visual flow of the film. Talk demands its own physiognomic realization – it has rhythm, inflection, idiosyncrasy which must synergize with visual physiognomy into narrative. A good screenplay is written or adapted with this in mind, and a director is in the business of syncing visual physiognomy with the rhythm of sound. This is what prepares the distinctive feature of sound film comedy for example: screwball films where Cary Grant yaps at Rosalind Russell who yaps back in a way that sets pulse to their super-animated faces. How an actor talks is part of how they look, the overall feel of their presence. A better concept for the syncing of sound and visuality is that of a complex system, in which each mirrors, and contributes to, the other. Panofsky's point still holds: when sound dominates and little is happening visually, the film almost always dies. Documentary filmmakers know this instinctively. When they have people talk for long periods of time, they counterpoint that with things to look at: either the close-up of the person is so taut and mesmerizing that it holds its own, or they dovetail speech with images from the past, newspaper clippings, fade-ins and fade-outs, that sort of thing.

Panofsky's work, and that of other significant intellectuals of the time, Rudolph Arnheim, Walter Benjamin, Siegfried Kracauer, André Bazin, is already philosophical in that it seeks metaphysical implications of the screen and its dimensions. None is as yet work which sustains contact with the history of philosophy however, at least not *directly*. Film criticism becomes philosophical when a problem is hit that requires the making of new philosophy to even begin to think about it, much less pretend to 'solve it' once and for all.

An example of such a problem is found in the conclusion to Panofsky's essay, with this remark about the medium:

> The medium of the movies is physical reality as such: the physical reality of eighteenth-century Versailles – no matter whether it be the original or a Hollywood faxsimile indistinguishable therefrom for all aesthetic intents and purposes – or a suburban home in Westchester; the physical reality of the Rue de Lappe in Paris or the Gobi Desert ... the physical reality of engines and animals, of Edward G. Robinson and Jimmy Cagney. All these objects and persons must be organized into a work of art. They can be arranged in all sorts of ways ('arrangement' comprising, of course, such things as make-up, lighting and camera work) . . . The problem is to manipulate and shoot unstylized reality in such a way that the result has style. This is a proposition no less legitimate and no less difficult than any proposition in the older arts.[13]

The medium of film is physical reality as such, meaning the desert stones of Monument Valley, the harsh sun and the facial grimaces of the smouldering John Wayne (Ethan Edwards), the materials of the past which compose it. The issue is, as I have said, about the way an aesthetic problem, a problem of style, becomes a philosophical conundrum. That is to say, it is about how the aesthetics of an art historian, trying to understand the nature of a new medium, turn philosophical, becoming a topic for philosophical aesthetics.

Recall now Ted Cohen's remark that there are at least three distinct notions of a medium at use in the literature.[14] First, a medium is physical stuff, as in, my medium is oil paint, or fresco, or wood or ceramic glass. Second, there is the notion of a medium in a more metaphysical sense. As in, the medium of architecture is space, music time and tone, film, projected light. Third, a medium is something like the viscous substance through which flows a message, a medium is a particular field of representation and expression, social action and individual meditation. In one sense the film medium is light projected on a two dimensional surface from film stock (or analog tape or digital formats), nothing more. But Panofsky does not mean this by his use of the word 'medium'. His use is imported from the study of the visual arts to refer to the stuff from which the thing is made, and which shines through in its realization. He means that the medium of film is reality in the way the medium of sculpture is wood, that of building, steel and glass. When it is said that the medium of Michelangelo's *David* is marble, this means that marble is the stuff from which Michelangelo composes, the stuff whose 'form' he liberates from within the stone. Marble is there in the finished product in every possible way. The kind of sculpture that is made is conditioned by it, its expression inflected by the materiality which shines through. The gleaming surfaces of Bernini, the smooth, lyrical fleshiness of Canova sculpted from pietra dura, hard stone, are tours de force in marble, given what that material is. Try conceiving of a reclining Canova female figure made instead out of steel, or wood, or bubble gum, or Styrofoam and you have three entirely different finished products, all by Claes Oldenburg. Change the material and everything changes with it. The materiality of the finished form is something that cannot be abstracted from visual experience, or from meaning and effect. That Bernini can render the hard clarity of marble soft, making hair bounce, is a work of magic. Were he a modernist working in string and wood it would not be so hard, nor make us catch our breaths. These things give truth to Hegel's adage that 'not all things are possible in all media of art', and related, that it is the discovery of the potentialities of any given medium, their exploitation and indeed, creation, that defines the history of an art form as much as anything else.

When Panofsky asserts that the medium of the moving pictures is physical reality as such, he is speaking to the central role of physiognomy. It is Garbo's eyes, Jimmy Stewart's twitch, Gary Cooper's tight lips, John Wayne's swagger that are the substance of their cinematic expressivity. Catherine Deneuve's frozen face is pure marble. Even the voice becomes what Cavell, following Panofsky, calls part of the 'individuality' of each of these stars. We listen for the peculiar twang of Stewart, more high pitched, breaking slightly in the upper registers when he is anxious; for the low-throated ripeness of Joan Greenwood's high-Ealing-studio Englishness. Cavell calls these 'individualities'.[15]

Sound contributes to their sense of presence, which returns us to that most striking of Panofsky's remarks: the medium of film is reality as such, which makes it seem that an actor's presence on screen, for this art historian turned film critic, is that of marble in sculpture: right there to be touched, which cannot be right.

For one thing, marble is inert, while the actor actively participates in the making of his or her character. We have famous stories of Hitchcock treating actors like things, positioning them as if blocks of wood or statues. His film *Vertigo* is about a man fixated on such manipulation of women, which takes the form of necrophilia. The protagonist aims to recreate the dead through the living from shoe to hairstyle, then to possess her. The film is a metaphor for film generally. Actors in fact have a strange status between becoming thing-like and remaining persons on screen. They act, are *active*. And yet they exist in a film as appearances, bugs under glass, objects of porcelain. The star is fixed and free at the same time, figure and figurine.

But the real conundrum is that marble is physically present to the viewer in a way the actor definitely is not: you can reach out and touch the marble, just as you could jump on stage and touch the theatre actor. But you cannot reach into a movie and make contact with Grant or Russell. They are not in this immediate sense, present to you. Then what kind of material presence is this which causes Panofsky to use the metaphor of an actor shining through the screen like Michelangelo's marble through the sculptural form?

In short these early remarks about the medium very quickly led to philosophical problems which remain present in aesthetics today. Panofsky was not a philosopher, and so the kind of aesthetic work he was doing had to do with limning the features of a medium as it was growing to fruition. Philosophical aesthetics then took up such questions as the 'reality' of the medium, just as films have continued to explore this strange spectral intensity, exploiting it in their work. I take up these two points in turn, first the philosophical conundrum about the medium, second, and later on in this chapter, ways in which films, especially those of Terrence Malick, continue to address, through exploiting, these strange features of the medium, thus keeping it auratic, uncanny, fresh, mesmerizing.

It is worth reciting a remark of Stanley Cavell's (from *The World Viewed*) about films and photographs both:

> The reality in a photograph is present to me while I am not present to it; and a world I know and see, but to which I am nevertheless not present (through no fault of my subjectivity), is a world past.[16]

One might take Cavell's remark (a riff on Panofsky) to mean something like this: central to film is that although not literally present, the actor (or mountain, or field and stream) *seems* present to us. It is only that we are absent from him (it). Cary Grant, is, unfortunately dead, even as I watch *The Philadelphia Story* (I am certainly not present to him, not able to address him). And yet there is a strange way in which he *seems* present, strange in a way not true of his oil portrait, nor any sketch of him. 'Look', I exclaim with delight, examining a photo from an old album dug up from the attic, 'It's Uncle Harry, how young he was then, the ruddy cheeks, swift glance of his darting eyes, hair parted in the middle, the dashing figure. It is as if he were with us today.' But now is many years later; I am revisiting a tattered home movie, or perhaps a black and white photo in a brass frame. Harry is long departed, yet I've the sense that time has collapsed and he is with me, or I with him, it is unclear where we are, the photo is a window into the past, or a way of bringing the past to the present. Roland Barthes says photography is a memorial to the dead, a way of making the dead present again among us while also confirming their absence, since the photo reminds us it was *then* that we knew them (and no more). This ontological disturbance, this sense that the barriers of time are being occluded, associates photos and films to dreams, séances, to the intensity of memories unfolded in mesmeric absorption, as if memory were a film replayed within the self. As a child I had an overwhelming belief that I could replay my life at will, and would sit in bed reviewing and rewinding the course of my life in memory's chamber, each time speeding things up, or slowing them down depending, and all with the most intense visuals. Time gained was also time lost, since the automatic replay of my own past confirmed its pastness. I was passive before my own memories, unable to enter them, able only to allow them to consume me.

Cavell calls the world in a photo or film a displaced form of presence: Garbo is present to me, but I cannot be present to her, I cannot speak to her in the film, nor reach out and touch her. Then is Garbo, who was once physically present to the camera (at the moment she was filmed) really there before us, as if directly out of the past? What kind of *there* is this?

Certain philosophers, most notably Kendall Walton, have argued that physical reality is *literally* there to be seen in a photo or film. According to Walton film is neither a copy of the world (in the sense that a drawing of the Vatican is a copy), nor is it a representation of the world in the sense of a painting. Photos are transparent windows to that which is no longer there. In his words: 'We see the world through them.'[17] To see Garbo in a film or photo is to see through the photo to her as she was then. Photos are mirrors reflecting back into the past – strange mirrors, because what we see in them is no longer there. That the thing which caused its 'reflection' in the photo is of the past makes our seeing of it, in Walton's phrase, 'indirect'. '[T]o look at a photograph is actually to see, indirectly but genuinely, whatever it is a photograph of.'[18] This is because photos are counterfactually dependent on the things photographed (something not true, Walton says, of paintings). Photographers stylize, yes, they frame their subjects by positioning the camera, choose film stock, set the time of exposure, the light meter and so on. These choices generate perspective, mood: art. But once they've been decided there is no more human intervention. The camera goes snap and that is that. This is not true of oil painting, where the entire act of painting is a human choice, a human intervention. Paintings may represent people who are not there; photos capture only what is. (Let us avoid the dilemma of photoshop, which convulses the very medium of photography by turning a photo into a baseball field of cut and pasted images from the computer file and the worldwide web).

Walton's aim is to identify a class of perceptual experiences which share the property of counterfactual dependence. These include mirrors, telescopes, microscopes, and (he thinks) photos. All of these devices, he believes, share the property of transparency. We see through them to reality. Walton seeks to demonstrate that photography is a case of transparent perception by assembling examples of seeing through space meant to prepare the claim that photos allow us to actually see through time to the past. The simplest example of visual perception is two people each looking directly at the other (in a café, across a crowded room). One can then move on such examples as observing a suspect through a one-way mirror, a ship through a periscope, the human heart through an ultrasound machine, a cellular micro-component through an electron microscope, a distant star through the Hubble telescope. In each of these cases the gap widens between perceiver and perceived, becoming less and less reciprocal, more and more 'distant'.

Walton's leap is to move from these cases to seeing across time, which is best imagined, Walton tells us, through the experiment of looking through a 'multiply mirroring device'. The device (on this scenario) reflects the world through so many mirrors – each mirroring the next – that we lose all orientation as to where the object perceived is with respect to ourselves. We can't trace the figure seen through this hall of mirrors back to any particular location. The world seen through this multiply mirroring device is presented to perception while also screened from it. The example is meant to warm us up to the idea that seeing across time is but one stage further than seeing across space (through the device). Seeing across space can also eclipse perspective, derange orientation as to source.

It is important to note that behind the multiply mirroring device is still the sense that the thing seen in it really does exist somewhere out there, right now, in its material robustness: it's just that we can't pinpoint the object's whereabouts through the device. There is a route one could take to the object perceived; it is only that the device fails to yield it and in fact obscures it. This is quite different from saying we can see through the photo or film back into *time*, where there is no possible road map back to the thing which we could take to arrive at the past. In looking through a photo towards the past, our estrangement from that past is metaphysically permanent.

In his 1984 paper 'Transparent Pictures' Walton finds no particular problem with this: 'I don't mind allowing that we see photographed objects only *indirectly*, though one could maintain that perception is equally indirect in many other cases as well [such as mirrors, images produced by lens, etc.].'[19] For him photographic transparency is no more problematical than the transparency of a mirror. This is unpersuasive. Seeing into the past is a concept a hundred times more bizarre than seeing through a mirror, which is not bizarre at all, or even seeing a fetus through an ultrasound machine.

The best case for seeing into the past is Walton's example of seeing a degenerate star. One looks through the Hubble telescope to a star but by the time the light from that star reaches the telescope the star has in fact disappeared. It is in the past. We are seeing, in this sense, that which is past. But note, here we are seeing it directly, through its original light source. It is just that this light has taken a long time – too long a time – to reach us. The case is different from looking into a photo. The star appears to us in its original light: the light which travelled from it to the device, just as a person appears reflected in a mirror through the original light which emanates from the person.

This is what makes the person 'present' in the mirror. Seeing something or someone in a photo is not seeing them in the original light which travelled from them to the photographic device. That happened long ago and led to an imprinting of the image (like a sound recording) onto the photographic emulsion.[20] At a later time the film emulsion has been developed and at a still later time that film has been projected. We see the original imprint through new light. That is what we see; the imprint and nothing else. A photo is, Cavell says, a mould taken of reality, which means, not a mirror of it. One does not see through the photo to something beyond (Where? How would you get there?); one sees into the photo as if into a Heideggerian house of being.

If one wants to call this indirect seeing, well and good, but one has then changed the language, for this is emphatically not the kind of 'indirect seeing' one has looking into a mirror. We see into the photo, and then, knowing that it is a mould of the past, have access to the past without quite seeing it. One feels the presence of the past in a photo because it hovers elusive and unseen in the manner of trace or aura (that which signifies that which is not). In this felt conviction resides the strangeness of a photo, in its aura.

That we look *into* photos and films rather than through them is a general feature of our experience of films. We are absorbed in the living presence of those on screen, as if into a mirror of ourselves. We do not look through them towards the past, we do not typically *seek* to do this. Only if someone asks: can't you see the way New York looked then, in the 40s, in that film shot? It is of the apartment building I grew up in! I sometimes see films about old LA that way: as signs of the LA I loved in the early 1980s, where old Hollywood was already a living ruin, a neighbourhood of fading blondes reeking of cigarettes and booze, walking ancient, tiny dogs along the moonlit streets, as if last living legacies of films noir. Perhaps it was all in my head. The point is, sometimes we do seem to see transparently back to the past through the photo, and/or film. Other times not. The evidence from experience is totally indecisive.

We look into films, as if the world there were more real than real, and also look beyond them, as if they were a haze or penumbra of shadows, pointing towards a past which is similarly eclipsed. This doubleness of perception is critical to the absorption of the medium.

I should like to call film an intermediate case, about which it is too simple either to say we see the past in it or that we don't. In saying this I am recruiting a thought of Wittgenstein's, the relevant passage being from his *Philosophical Investigations*:

> A main source of our failure to understand is that we do not *command a clear view* of the use of our words. – Our grammar is lacking in this sort of perspicuity. A perspicuous representation produces just that understanding which consists in 'seeing connections'. Hence the importance of finding and inventing intermediate cases.[21]

It was an important part of Wittgenstein's teaching at Cambridge University in the 1930s and 1940s to try to 'find and invent' examples of objects about which it was too simple either to say it was a 'p' or a 'not p'. He was interested to explore items about which it was, or seemed, too simple to say it is or is not a number, is or is not a person, is or is not alive, is or is not a game, is or is not language. Film perception is exactly this. It is too simple either to say we see Grant on screen or we don't. His presence is absolutely peculiar.

Wittgenstein distinguishes two uses of the word 'peculiar', one transitive and the other intransitive. Richard Wollheim long ago grasped the importance of Wittgenstein's intransitive use of the word 'peculiar' for the experience of art.[22] When one speaks of something being peculiar and means it transitively, there is something to say about the respects in which the person or thing is peculiar. 'How is he peculiar?' 'He talks to himself all the time and he's not on a cell phone, he wears no socks in winter and always carries a purse, he only eats borscht and goes around pretending he's Jerry Seinfeld.' The transitive use solicits an answer to the question 'In what respect?' The intransitive use does not. Wittgenstein illustrates it in this way:

> Describe the aroma of coffee. – Why can't it be done? Do we lack the words? And for what are words lacking? – But how do we get the idea that such a description must after all be possible? Have you ever felt the lack of such a description? Have you tried to describe the aroma and not succeeded?[23]

He is setting the reader an assignment ('Describe the aroma of coffee'), then asking what is at stake in the failure to complete the assignment. One can of course begin to complete it. One can speak of coffee's burnished sweetness, and behind that of the bitterness of the beans, one can compare coffee to liquorice, chocolate, tea, talk of its shot-in-the-arm quality. However, at a certain point language stops before the portal of experience. Either you know the aroma or you don't.

A medium of art sustains absorption, makes magic through its peculiarities. The film medium is peculiar in its mode of making the world present to the viewer. While sculpture sets materials directly before you, film does not. And yet physiognomy is 'there'. While painting is not counterfactually dependent on sources in reality, film is directly tied to its sources, and yet we cannot see them (but we almost seem to). Film convulses the imagination, which is unable to sort out its relationship to things screened, to their mode of being-there before us, real and spectral. In this resides its aura or halo of power.

This has been a story of how reflection about film by film criticism, which in its own way can be called aesthetics of film because it is about the medium, generates particular philosophical puzzles which philosophical aesthetics then addresses. Aesthetics was happening all along, within early films, and in the writings of Panofsky about the medium. Now it becomes a philosophical problem.

The power of film magic is not automatic, it must be sustained by new inventions in cinema. It is the total film form and film sense which carries forward, and reinvents, the magic. In our age of an endless spate of film products, increasingly indistinguishable from advertisements and shopping malls, filmmakers must work harder and harder to reclaim the ancient magical power of the screen.

It is Terrence Malick who most recently has remade this early magic of presence and absence everybody felt and so few feel today, in our age of an endless line of cinema products. His work has always explored the haunted, spectral character of the film image, and its implications for a temporality in which past and present exist in uncanny merger. Malick is master of turning present into past, a master who sketches states of presence which are already those of evanescence. With Malick landscape rings of eternity, it is just that humans stumble about in it, occasionally blessed by its magic before losing their grip. Malick's film *The New World* (2006) begins with a map of the new world, then water, shot from below, with light reflected onto Pocahontas, swimming underwater. Three ships arrive, bearing English settlers to establish the first Virginia colony, then the eternity of a river, flowing through the pristine forests of primaeval Virginia. It is a page taken from Wagner and his opening measures of *The Ring*. Music is not add-on in Malick but a central constituent in achieving ecstasy, and temporal texture. As the camera lingers on that river which will lead John Smith from Jamestown colony to the native tribe where he will meet and fall in love with the young Pocahontas, the music rings out as a source of everything. Smith enters, a voyager in time searching for a route to the 'other sea', into a timeless domain where he has not been asked to arrive and of which he knows nothing. The sense of human intrusion is powerful, also of the strangeness of that initial moment of contact between European people and the landscape of the Americas. Its dense forests consume him, its grasslands half occlude him. He could not be more out of place in his heavy armour. As things deteriorate for the colony in the first few months, a convoy is sent up river, in search of the great city and king. Smith goes and is taken prisoner by the tribe, then spared when Pocahontas throws herself on top of him before her father, the father who will with Shakespearean pain, expel her a year later, after she's saved the colony by bringing grain and corn against his wishes. As Smith, living in this strange place, begins his dance of attraction with Pocahontas we hear his own voice-over in the present tense. 'Shall we refuse love when it makes a gift of its presence?' He has already been established as diarizer of things happening around him; in an earlier shot we see him sitting in the grasslands, writing, and before that hear his voice-over, again in the present tense, but knowing that the present he describes is ongoing ('We are planting wheat', 'How shall we proceed with the naturals?').

The pair explore each other, touch, react. The film cuts between his perspective and hers. 'Mother, where are you?', she asks in silent dialogue with her own soul, seeking solace and explanation for the feelings growing inside her. Against voice-over and haunting motifs of piano they circle around each other, touching with the delicacy, the tentativeness, of two blind people exploring the world through their fingers. Love is blind, especially between persons as different as these, without a common language.

Malick has the ability to provide point of view without using the classic shot-reverse shot that usually establishes it. There is no 'point of view shot' in this sequence, no Hitchcock cutting between Bodega Bay as we see it and Bodega Bay from Melanie Daniels' point of view (*The Birds*). Instead Smith follows Pocahontas through river and forest with the camera placed just aside his shoulder in steady cam and with some use of hand-held shots. This yields the sense of the world seen from Smith's point of view, and in intimacy, almost merger, with it, as if our consciousness were his twin, his ecstasy ours. The refusal to clearly delineate shot from reverse shot delivers a world that slides between actuality and perception, reality and consciousness. This merger of world and world perceived renders world into a fleeting place, waterborne, place in which things happen and evaporate at the same time. A world of fleeting appearances is a haunted world. It is a world into which Smith seems to have wandered without believability, as if, were he to blink it would turn out he is dreaming. Smith has no doubt the world is there before him, that he dwells inside it; he cannot fathom its intelligibility and this causes him to float in it. Love is similarly dreamlike; it turns the world into a fleeting shadow, a mere resonance.

The filmmaker has always been obsessed with the way Edenic moments form and collapse around those absorbed within them. Adam and Eve, after all, lived in paradise while hardly knowing it. Only in retrospect did its nature become revealed to them, when all was too late. They had been expelled without any clear understanding of why. Malick is biblical, Old Testament. Smith's uncertainty about the world into which he is thrown, his sense of its not-quite-believability is something close to a feeling that it is a gift, a magical incantation. It is also a sign of its fragility, its liability to expulsion.

These characteristics are established through cinema, and also reflections of cinematic magic, which is also a new world in which characters dwell in a strange state of temporality for the briefest moment before the river of light disappears and the film is over. A collapse of the Edenic out of the unlikely conditions of its formation is Malick's signature theme, a theme extending to the nature of cinema itself. The theme is already present in his first film *Badlands*, where the most unlikely place on earth becomes the place of happiness and the young pair of killers have little understanding of what they are doing, to *Days of Heaven*, where the Victorian house of the farmer in the lush sun-soaked, wheat-shimmering Texas Panhandle becomes for a time the place of heaven, until the scheming and grift which has allowed the moment to form leads to an apocalypse of locust and fire.

In a Malick film characters become their own authors, articles of their own voice-over, even while they are experiencing the things they will later set in the past tense. To be is also to understand, and that means being is a problem, since understanding is always at issue, always struggling, perhaps doomed. This technique of experience also told from within at the moment of its occurrence estranges a character from the sublimity of the place in which he or she dwells. Persons are touched by an aura they hardly understand, are unable to see a rush of saturated light even when it is under their nose. Or conversely, they feel too much and with too much fragility to grasp anything. They are often young people hardly old enough to love. In *Days of Heaven* the young migrant labourers wander through the radiant light of the Texas Panhandle without a clue. The voice-over in that film is of a child remembering (telling), but also, one feels, a voice that was already telling in the present, and in a way so comically misplaced, so out of sync with what is happening, that it renders her almost metaphysically befuddled. Metaphysically yes, for she exists in a stretch of heaven and does not know it. The sublimity of landscape in which she dwells hits us over the head but hardly touches her, and her precise quality of experience eludes us – probably it is inchoate, opaque. Life slides through her fingers like light she cannot grasp, making her lack our burden. We are shattered by a sublimity that appears to *us* but not to her, passing over her, and all other characters in this film, like shadow. Our burden of knowing confirms our absence from what is happening, for we are metaphysically unable to intervene. Softened by the funniness, the quiet zaniness, empty vistas of the Dakota Badlands, by lyrically framed Victorian homes set against wheat-coloured prairies, by empty vistas of rough road pulverized by sky: the aura of nature is ours, not theirs. This is a metaphor for the position of the viewer per se: she exists in presence to things on screen that are closer, while impossibly further, than the characters themselves. Life touches them while they cannot see it; we are overwhelmed by that which touches us, in which we cannot intervene. This can make one permanently rueful.

Smith's story *was* taken from his diaries (which may, as it happens, have been made up). By having him think these diarized thoughts written down later but also in the present tense, Malick blurs narrative and consciousness. This blurring is a mirror of unsustainable perfection. It was Jean-Paul Sartre in his philosophical novella *Nausea* who showed you cannot live life and write it down at the same time. Not even in cinema. Such makings of presence are already its exit. For the philosophically minded (including Sartre) this is pure Heidegger: an imaginative riff on his concept of being 'thrown into being' and forced into an understanding of human time through time lost and gained, projected and remembered. These things are made real in film by the former translator of Heidegger,[24] Terrence Malick, whose genius is to understand that the conditions of film, the viewer's displacement from what is shown, and the blurring of past and present on the film screen, are precisely those of Smith: conditions of the Edenic, the fleeting, of an absorption that is unsustainable, of an almost automatic immersion into strangeness which is simultaneously the intensity of memory's haunted place. Time is, in Heidegger's sense, ecstatic.

And so Malick is himself that hybrid: philosopher aesthetician, filmmaker. He has recruited what philosophy already taught about being and time, and remade it in the light of a medium where certain intensities can emerge that could never do in philosophy. But the connection is crucial for philosophical criticism, in that it reveals how film also has found one of its great themes in the nature of human embodiment, not embodiment of the flesh, as in Titian, but within time, or multiple time frames, if you will. In this, film draws close to modernist literature; where, as David Foster Wallace has put it often, he lives every day between eating lunch and his dead grandmother, who remains spectral, if not active within life, speaking from his portrait in the headmaster's office; as Albus Dumbledore in the final volume of the Harry Potter series communicates with the brave and tragic Severus Snape.

Malick is a philosopher turned filmmaker, a philosopher still in film. His work raises the question of truth in art, of philosophical and other truth residing within it. It is to the truth in art that I turn in the conclusion to this book. Before venturing there, the reader is invited to think about what philosophical issues have arisen in more recent media than film, issues pertinent to U2 or U-Tube, architecture or web-based art. Perhaps there is none clearly formulated as yet. Perhaps it is up to you to venture the formulation. Philosophical aesthetics is grand if it produces an answer, but perhaps more grand if it ventures the right question. What then is the question to ask about TV, internet, new music, new art made between media, whatever?

CHAPTER 6

CONCLUSION: ART AND TRUTH

TWO AESTHETIC PERSPECTIVES: ART AS KNOWLEDGE AND ART AS TRANSCENDENCE

We have witnessed a split in the way aesthetics has approached art. On the one hand there is the view, inherited from Aristotle's study of tragic drama, that art has value because it offers knowledge: for Aristotle, philosophical knowledge. The knowledge art offers is for Aristotle more philosophical than historical because it is a kind of recognition: recognition of what can happen to human beings 'according to the laws of probability or necessity'. Tragic drama reveals how character and the events of life can spiral into disaster through the intrusion of fate.

Hegel pursues this view of art as the bearer of philosophical knowledge: knowledge that comes in the form of recognition. Through the inner antenna of the artist, art becomes a cipher for the forces of history, collecting them into a grand gesture, and through the development of a medium, catapulting them into an idealized picture of the age. This is a view with a long legacy in aesthetics.

An equally prominent legacy states the opposite. This is the position from which aesthetics was born in the eighteenth century. At its purest, it is the formalist vision of art, identified with Kant, which believes art is not different (aesthetically) from nature. The aesthetic judgement (the judgement of taste) treats both the same, since it is a judgement that is non-conceptual, and one made apart from all purposes associated with the object (art or nature). The experience of the beautiful is one of form, of sensual immersion, of the sublime. Taste is imaginative, formalizing, pleasurable, overwhelming. Hume's concept of taste is more widely construed, but of this ilk.

The beautiful is a consumerist stance, a way of enjoying this as opposed to that, be it a fine wine or a freshly sautéed truffle.

To the view that the experience of art is a free play of the imagination signifying nothing, whose end is in itself, many, following Kant, attach a large-scale picture of the symbolic value of this. For Kant, the formalist imagination is one which allows morality to be symbolized. For others, the state, the nation, the future of the revolution. These significations are attached to art – or so the story is told and so it is hoped the public will believe – and when attached to art, the story makes art *exemplary*. Art often is exemplary (as we shall see below) which means that a public's perception of the depth in its formal gesture is intrinsic to the process of experiencing it, and making meaning of it. Nevertheless the Kantian view starts from a formally composed object (the work of art) whose purpose is to occasion the play of sense and imagination rather than yielding knowledge.

The first view approaches art as a form of human recognition. The value of art is different in kind from the value of nature. Art lacks value if it fails to offer recognition. Since nature is not a form of representation, it need not satisfy this demand. The second view treats art with nature as an object of enjoyment and imagination, regardless of what comes of it. Art is a splash in the swimming pool on a hot summer's day, a special holiday taken in the South of France where you ride bicycles down country roads canopied by chestnut trees. It is an orange sunset watched while sitting on a sandy beach, purple umbrella behind, hand of lover in one's own.

For the second view recognition may follow indirectly, through the symbolic value of this formal and non-conceptual experience. Kant thinks the beautiful is our way of 'acknowledging' our inner moral sense. However, this only happens because art yields no knowledge, neither philosophical nor otherwise. The view remains sharply different from Aristotle's.

How does one negotiate between these general approaches to art? Is it a matter of either/or? Of both/and? Is each sometimes true and sometimes inaccurate, depending on context? What is this thing called art that seems to sustain both sides of the equation, even though they flatly contradict one another?

Things are more complicated on the knowledge front in at least two ways. First, twentieth-century art theory, literary criticism, theory of architecture, and musicology have all converged on the critical thought that if art offers recognition, it equally offers *misrecognition*.

Art is a mode of knowing, but this also means a signal of everything ideological in an age, a cipher for its prejudices, forms of arrogance, grandiosity, delusion. If art is an expression of human aspiration the aspiration has often been one of domination, control, repression, and art has played its role in those human disfigurements. When Marlow says all Europe contributed to the making of Kurtz, that colonialist emperor of atrocity in *Heart of Darkness* (Conrad), he means what he says. Church and state, art and philosophy have all contributed to the aura of authority and prestige which Kurtz brings to the Congo in that novel. Through the forms of culture Kurtz is cast into a mode of self-idolatry, a self-worshipping god expecting to do remarkable things among the natives who, should they not care to bow down and worship him, will be treated as beneath disgust, like so many African ants.

Through its most noble images of human spirit and devotion, art generates idolatry. This is virtually guaranteed by the utopian vision of Hegel. Art expresses the aspirations of the age in idealized form, a form which seems to smooth over all inconsistencies and rationalize all chaos. Through narrative, through a good, compelling story, life is harmonized.

Later theorists of the aesthetic, most notably French psychoanalyst Jacques Lacan,[1] will understand the misrecognitions generated through art in terms of the human desire for fantasy. In art we are given what we seek: a mirror through which we may see ourselves in the form of a more glorified other, casting ourselves as infinitely beautiful, perfect, and in a suspended moment of timelessness which, like the loving gaze of the mother received by a tiny child, allows no space for the contemplation of its passing. Art does not humble us; it sculpts us into perfectly chiselled gods and goddesses. Our lives are rendered more exciting through identification with the heroines and heroes in books, transfigured through the spiralling churches of the Baroque, turned into icons through the silver screen. It is not for nothing that while Freud wrote about painting and Lacan about literature, the theory of art in terms of the mirror stage has found its subject in film. For it is through that portal into a suspended and perfected past lived endlessly in the present, before which we sit like an absorbed and enraptured child, that our bodies and souls take on the physiognomic intensities and perfections of the actors and actresses on screen, as if their endlessly spontaneous movements recalibrated our own.

There is an entire generation of film criticism beginning with Laura Mulvey[2] and continued by Slavoj Zizek,[3] which connects the Lacanian themes of mirror and misrecognition to film viewing and indeed, the content of films. Here we are, sitting in a dark theatre, watching Grace Kelly illuminate herself by turning on three lights as she repeats the three parts to her name – Liza, Carol, Freemont, in response to Jimmy Stewart's question: Who are you? Her answer seems to be given not simply through the name but through the lighting. Answer: she is this person you see, you being not so much Stewart but everyone in the audience watching this creature of fleshy eroticism and silver emulsion become what she is: a figure of black and white, light and darkness. This becoming is for us, and through it we remake ourselves in the fantasy of being her, and possessing her. She is ours; we are hers. Never mind that Hitchcock has already played out this theme one minute before in this, his masterpiece, *Rear Window*, for as Lisa bent over to kiss the sleeping Jeff (Stewart), Hitchcock filmed it so that she seemed to break out of the screen in 3-D and kiss us. Only at the last minute does he tilt the camera back to its normal angle so we see the kiss delivered to Jeff, on screen, away from us. The fear, and overstimulation, of her seeming to break out of screen is carried forward into the conversation they have, and her answer to his question by lighting herself. She lights herself because she is uncontainable, free, her spontaneity being something no one else could have generated but herself. And yet she remains a 'bug under glass', as she herself puts it halfway through the film, a being contained on screen for us. Film creates a position of voyeurism (which is also what this film is about). The star is there for us, a female being who lingers in the allure of her silver emulsified cage for our voracious possession, smiling at each and every one of us like it is we she has been waiting for all along, yet indifferent, transcendent, a being whom we can never truly grasp.

This being of the star there for us, to be devoured by our vision, and yet forever to remain apart from us, her aura transcendent, her place in a netherworld or galaxy of the stars makes us crazy: overstimulated, omnipotent, and yet permanently incapacitated, like all voyeurs, immobilized in a chair in a dark place (like Jimmy Stewart with his broken leg) staring through the cinema portal (out the window) fetishizing that which we cannot possess – and so claiming entitlement over it (that is, her, the star). The concept of the fetish, the shoe or hat or undergarment we squirrel away and keep in our bottom drawer as a way of grasping what we are truly terrified to have (the real thing, the real act, sex and love) becomes a natural for describing the act of looking in some, if not all, its manifestations in cinema. Mulvey and the generation following have fixed on these concepts as a way of trying to fathom the aesthetics of an experience which is one of possession and emptiness at the same time, identification and incapacitation, believing she is mine and knowing she will always elude my grasp. That pleasure and pain are mixed makes the spectator into someone as screwed up as the protagonist he is watching, a central fact of cinema Hitchcock did not fail to know and exploit.

When Jimmy Stewart begins *Rear Window* in one cast (broken leg, stuck his neck out too far) and ends the film in two, spending most of the narrative sitting in his wheelchair staring out the window through bigger and bigger lenses (he's a photographer), inventing a story of murder and mayhem across his apartment complex (which turns out to be true, although he could not have known this), he is (I have suggested, and others before me) a virtual incarnation of the film viewer, especially since the most beautiful woman in the world, Grace Kelly, wants nothing more than to kiss him, and he wants nothing more than to stare out the window, no doubt as a form of protection against her erotic encroachments, the thing he desires and cannot accept. Photography is for him (and this film for us?) itself a kind of defence against reality, which in this film (as in all Hitchcock films) cannot be staved off, and rears its terrifying head through the front door of Stewart's apartment in the form of the hulking, murderous Raymond Burr, who finally realizes who has caused the police to run after him and is ready to kill.

This Hitchcock film gives us through the sleight of hand of the director, the materials to understand its own capacities for yielding misrecognition. It is reflective, one might say, philosophical, but not in the way philosophy is, writing its propositions into narrative, and logical form. It is a work which captures our minds through bringing us to a certain kind of place, through the manipulations we feel by its framing, its mode of incorporating us into Stewart's world and having us share his passion, voyeurism, and ensuing predicament. Through screenplay and camera angle, use of star and magic of medium, the film provides the materials for its own understanding, and stimulates another medium of understanding: philosophy so called, as the kind of writing it is, the kind of writing, if you will, I am doing here and now. To call the film philosophical is to say it provides an angle on misrecognition through its use of the medium, thus revealing that medium for its psychological and human values. The film leaves a lot out (which is why feminist film criticism has made a racket out of praising and blaming it at the same time, as if it wishes to have its cake – its star – and eat it – her too). But so does most philosophy.

Put another way we love this film for two reasons: it allows us to understand ourselves and it allows us to flee into fantasy.

Certain films are philosophical because they explore the conditions of their own medium, and their relations to audiences, just at the same time as they create these conditions! Hitchcock and feminist theory have been partners in the exposé of the subject, although not always happily. For Hitchcock studies voyeurism but also brings it about. This is called having your cake and eating it too.

Hitchcock's great question is: on a Saturday afternoon when the sky is blue and everyone else is outside skating, or inside baking brownies, why do you choose to pay ten dollars, sit in a dark room and watch a blonde called Janet Leigh get brutally stabbed in the shower of a motel room by one Anthony Perkins, Norman Bates? What is it about the medium that makes this pleasurable, what is it about you that you take pleasure in such a thing. It is Hume's question about tragic drama, psychoanalytically deepened to include issues of sadism, aggression, murderous thought, and so on. Hitchcock's films, and Mulvey's theory, are about this.

Through the rapt position of the voyeur, film creates and sustains conditions of male domination. Through its idealizations of human persona, it creates conditions of cult and ideology, of nationalism for a mass audience and fascist self-mythologizing. This does not always happen, but it is a tendency, or liability, of the medium, among its 'great possibilities'. To understand the possibilities of a medium is to understand its liabilities of deformation. This is to understand the darkness, sadism, desire for conformity and ideality in the human souls who care to experience it, and what they want from it. Since the study of the medium is central to aesthetics, critical theory is part of aesthetics, widely construed. Again we return to a simple theme: aesthetics has been born out of philosophy in the eighteenth century but is in fact an enterprise that must take place, and be understood as taking place, across the arts and humanities generally.

This allows us to end with a question. What does it mean for phi-losophy to call film (or another art) philosophical? What are the best words to use in trying to make this kind of claim about film, about any art, as clear as one can? One does not want to say film is in exactly the same business philosophy is in. This would diminish its inventive manner of yielding reflection, and reflection different in kind from any that philosophy as a kind of writing can easily offer. For it is through identification with Stewart, an attitude posed by Hitchcock's camera in relation to screenplay, that knowledge is occasioned about what cinema is. This transaction could well fail, because it starts in the solar plexus, the gut, and moves towards the head through that. The film does not didactically lecture us about voyeurism, it produces this position for us, and manipulates us into thinking about it by disturbing us. There is lecturing in the film, yes, but this lecturing is not philosophical. What is philosophical is the way the film uses us, and its camera, to place us in a position from which we must begin to think. Is Hegel's notion that art is philoso-phy posed in the manner of 'sensuous embodiment' sufficient to capture all the complexities of what Hitchcock is (and is not) doing? What are better words to use?

I OWE YOU THE TRUTH IN PAINTING AND I WILL TELL IT TO YOU

Let us address this question by making things more complicated. Hegel says art reveals knowledge 'implicitly', that in art, truth appears in the form of sensuous embodiment. But what does this mean, except to say there is a thing called truth which philosophy can state more clearly than art? In fact the role of truth in art, in this or that medium, is far more complicated than Hegel could have imagined, and also far more medium-specific. The most dazzling complication of this topic comes from the work of Jacques Derrida on Cézanne.[4] In a first section to his seminar turned book, *The Truth in Painting*, [5] Derrida takes up a well-known remark of Cézanne's to his friend and fellow painter, Emile Bernard: Derrida writes: '*The Truth in Painting* is signed Cézanne . . . Resounding in the title of a book, it sounds, then, like a due . . . the truth in painting was always something owed. Cézanne had promised to pay up: "I owe you the truth in painting, and I will tell it to you" (to Emile Bernard, 23 October 1905).'[6] In a masterful reading of this sentence, Derrida proposes four ways this remark in the letter can be understood.

First, to owe the truth in painting may mean to take truths presented in cloudy (what Hegel calls 'implicit') form in Cézanne's pictures and explicate these truths. Telling the truth would be taking what is unclear in painting and making it clear in words. Derrida does not make reference to Hegel; I am paraphrasing him by putting the point in this way. But the point has to do with truth being taken out of an opaque medium so that it may, once and for all, be spoken clearly ('I will *tell* it to you').

Second, to owe the truth in painting and tell it may be to tell it in painting, not outside, through the subject of a picture. Truth about religion is 'told', in painting, depictively, for a Renaissance Italian population praying in the Cathedral many of whom could not read. The word 'telling' is a stand-in for representing or depicting. There are, after all, many ways of telling. Note parenthetically: since Cézanne offers little allegory in his paintings, despising it. And since his subjects are almost entirely landscapes and still portraits, it is doubtful this is what he had in mind. Nevertheless, it is what another painter – a Sienese mystic from the early Renaissance – might have meant, had that painter written similar words.

Third, telling the truth in painting could mean a general account of the pictorial medium: of that which is proper to it, its proper subjects, materials, possibilities. This too could happen inside painting or outside it, through writing. Indeed (Derrida does not discuss this), one painting could be called on to tell the truth about another, as for example Danto believes Warhol is called upon (by history) to speak to the proper aspirations of modernist painting in general. One way the artist Marcel Duchamp has been read is this: Duchamp gave up painting in order to pursue a game in and around painting that revealed its nature, exposed its eroticism, in general pulled its pants down. Duchamp did this through his inventive sculptural installations and his large glass, just as he revealed the 'truth' in sculpture (or exposed it as the unseemly, red hot thing it is) through his 'readymades', most strikingly, his *Urinal*. A reading of postmodern literature takes it to be about literature, and not in an explanatory way but rather through its fragmentations of plot, its games played around point of view (truth), its ironizing of authorial omnipotence and the grand protagonist, into whose socks should fit the whole of humanity. Conrad's *Heart of Darkness* is about the delusory nature of narrative. Kurtz's self-narrative is a form of idolatry, capable of justifying (generating) atrocity. Marlow remains faithful to him 'to the grave' and 'beyond the grave', a sign that in spite of his disillusioned desire to tell it like it is, he chronically lies, and lies for Kurtz, even now, in this moment of confession. The truth of literature, the way that the medium of writing may show us how human beings construct judgements about the world and each other – is a matter of judgement projected from within a form of life – a family drama, a chronic shortage of money, a status of humiliation as the poor relation or upstart from the lower classes, a state of shrivelled love – and how these scenarios yield point of view and point of view yields story. Literature is a world in which character, story, judgement, are each independent, meaning each can send the other for an unexpected knock, and yet hardly too independent. Rather, they are like the objects in a decorated home: arranged to fit together in better or worse ways, depending upon the interior decorator. Then there is the placement of the narrator (if there is one). Is the narrator a mere cipher for the story or does he or she constantly extemporize, judge, provide social context? Does this require justification, or is a fictional world one where individuals may rule in the telling? Is the narrator revealed as a being with quirks and perhaps an axe or two to grind? These questions about literature and its modes of conveying truth may be approached within literature as well as outside it – as Hitchcock does about film.

Fourth, to owe the truth in painting might be to owe general truths *about* it, considered as a subject. Painting gives truth, and this is the truth about the truth, spoken rather than painted, one presumes. This might slide into offering general truths about art, into the birth of aesthetics. Or it might be the kind of enterprise Aristotle offers in telling why tragic drama has a more philosophical kind of 'truth' than history.

The really interesting question is whether any or all of these kinds of truth may be told through *paint itself* (in the pictures) or through another painting, or a game around it which remains within the sphere of art. Or must one use words, the words of a letter, an essay, a philosophical text? For something needs to be paid back, a debt restituted, and this suggests that Cézanne has not yet paid it, in his paintings anyway. Can he do so now, by painting differently? Or is it a matter now, late in life, of turning to words and telling Bernard what he has been doing all these years, what the truth he has been seeking is all about.

Cézanne seems to be saying: I paint, but here, in this letter, finally, I'm going to tell you all about it. Tell you all about it instead of doing it. I'm going to step back and explain it.

However, as Derrida asks:

> [M]ust we take a painter literally, once he starts to speak? Coming from a Cézanne, 'I will tell it to you' can be understood figuratively: he could have promised to tell the truth, in painting, to tell these four truths according to the pictorial metaphor of discourse or as a discourse silently working the space of painting. And since he promises to tell them 'in painting,' one does not even need to know of the signatory, for this hypothesis, that he is a painter . . .
>
> The signatory promises, it seems, to 'say' in painting, by painting, the truth and even, if you like, the truth in painting. 'I owe you the truth in painting' can easily be understood as 'I must render the truth to you in painting,' in the form of painting and by acting as a painter myself.[7]

And here is the ambiguity which pertains to, and is so central, in art. Truth is owed, and paid back, by telling about it. But also truth is paid back within the frame of the picture, in the form of art, since it is a particular kind of truth generic to painting, a truth told only through things relevant to that medium: perception and embodiment and form. We may improvise. Were truth not already there in painting in some distinctive, visual form, it would make little sense to philosophically explicate it. There is not one kind of truth but many, and each wants the other, is incomplete without it. One notion of truth is propositional, the kind of thing found in philosophy. The other is pictorial, the kind of thing deeply felt in a picture. Why is that also truth? Because there could be no philosophy without it, and the human viewer is convinced of it. It is what he or she explicates when picture gives way to writing. Derrida is picking up on this sense that truth must reside in both places, within and outside the work. Each kind of truth is only possible because of the other.

Then Dewey and Hegel are less far apart at least than one might have thought, since truth is found in art through its structuring of experience, and also demanded by, and found in, the reflection upon that experience (in the form of words, philosophical words). Perhaps this is what Hegel means when he says that art expresses truth in the form of sensuous embodiment. One feels it, senses it within, experiences it in the work, but also needs to step back and explain what the experience was all about. Both moments of this process are required to bring truth to art, to find the truth within art. Aesthetics and experience are joined at the hip. Each is part of the other, completes it if you will.

The idea that truth in art only, finally, emerges when one steps beyond the depths of the work (what it compels of recognition) and seeks to commute it to words, will be felt by many to be nutty. Barnett Newman famously chided: aesthetics is to art as ornithology is to birds. Total irrelevance, is what he means. And yet Newman wrote furiously about his work, wrote about everything from Jewish mysticism to colour theory and referred it back to painting. Perhaps he also felt that he owed (someone?) the truth in painting and was damned well going to tell it! – even if he had already half done so within his art. If art were not already deep, uniquely so, there would be no calling forth of philosophy, no need to put it in words. Words detach one from the power of the experience, but also complete it. Nothing is quite satisfying except the movement between these forms of truth, endlessly purveyed.

If works of art occasion truth, they do so not by stepping outside themselves and lecturing us in the manner of philosophers speaking about their meaning during a commercial break in their proceedings. They occasion truth by setting up the materials and forms of their medium in a way that places us in the position of finding ourselves wondering about something that has happened to us. Through their twists of viewer identification and belief, they foreground the visionary, and do so about themselves, but also about the world they are of.

An example is wanted: the South African artwork, made at the moment of political transition, which I discussed in Chapter 4. That work, made at the moment of transition from Apartheid to democracy, when the path was uncertain and the prospect dazzling, provides for the South African viewer an experience which is strange, unnerving, exhilarating. That viewer already has to know things. The viewer has to know about the way the various cultures of South Africa have been, during Apartheid, defined by their cultural symbols which were understood as forms of apartness. The viewer has to understand the immensity of condescension towards African cultural forms built into Eurocentric culture. The viewer has to understand, because he or she has lived it, the strangulation of life cauterized from the intrusions of other cultures, the fear, contempt, estrangement associated with other forms – and the lingering, silent fascination. It was only in 1987 that the first exhibition of black South African art took place in the Johannesburg Art Gallery (under the auspices of then Director Steven Sack[8]), only in the late 1980s that galleries started selling serious black art and simultaneously, scholars began to revise old colonial forms of scholarship which lumped traditional black art into pre-given categories of craft, religion, spirit culture and so on, as a way of finding the source of animation in a host of hitherto unknown and un-interrogated cultural objects. At stake was the rewriting of the very concept of art, since such objects blur western-generated, modern distinctions between art, craft, magical object and so on. The discovery of complex intention and design in things earlier passed off as 'quaint' would be known to some of the artists making the work in this show.

Any South African would have instinctively understood the message in gestures merging formerly separated cultural forms. Understood it as an act of refusal, an act of prospect, an act of re-association, as if they too were being called upon to remake their lives and treat others differently. This attack on identity, or openness to its potential change, would have sent some white South Africans into spirals of anger, others into delight – especially since it is easy to imagine change when one stands in a gallery, less easy when it hits one's home, bank account, workplace, school. The very experience of the work would have, for this first and intended audience of fellow South Africans, carried a message that was understood in the gut: but also an experience of shock, astonishment, fascination, confusion. A particular history had given rise to particular conditions of modern art, not easily transportable to the contemporary circuits of art exhibition, because so very much directed within culture at a moment of change. Just as Manet directed his attacks and invocations to the specifically French bourgeoisie, so these artists were making novelty for their place and time.

The truth was in the art: in the experience of decisiveness, resoluteness, spontaneity, and in the message told directly to the gut. This is a case of truth in painting (and sculpture, installation, ceramic, etc.). The satisfaction, the aesthetic pleasure in this work (in the experience of it by those not sent into paroxysms of rage) came from vision and execution. The satisfaction came from the fact that the works weren't simply talking but doing something, making a new world in miniature that seemed to radiate joy. The truth was in the doing, the pleasure taken in objects which exemplified everything noble and exciting about the times, and in an idealized way.

The philosopher Martin Heidegger would have called this 'truth set to work', meaning a project that in virtue of its execution carries the force of truth. In this, truth is in the work, in the experience of it with its emotional liberation and image of the winds of change. I should like to call what the South Africans did for their fellow South Africans something a little different from Heidegger. I will call it 'experience which carries the force of exemplification'. The viewer feels he or she is experiencing something done, which contains a message, and the message is one of exemplification. What is happening in this field of action called the work of art may happen more generally to you, to all of us, here, in life. We too are a field of action, a battleground of history, and for us too, this may be done. The 'this' is the work of art itself, with its harmonies and juxtapositions of form. Hegel's idea that with the work of art social aspiration is expressed in idealized form happens in just this way: through the work of art's status as exemplar.

It is the experience of the work as complete, but also an action, a gesture, a process of taking you somewhere, which yields this exemplary status. And so Dewey, with his emphasis on art as experience, and Kant, with his emphasis on the role of the exemplar, do in fact have a place in the competing picture of art as a giver of truth. Dewey unduly stressed the process through which the thing was made as paramount to the completed object. It is rather that the completed object yields/generates its own process of viewer positioning, and this allows the viewer to unpack it as an act of making (by the artist) which exemplifies something important, like new social relations. From that promissory note, further reflection called philosophy, performed in writing as I am doing now and did in Chapter 4, may then arise.

Telling truth in painting (or sculpture, or whatever) is providing an experience of material and form whose terms of formalization are taken by the viewer (and one assumes, intended by the artist) to have the status of an *exemplar*. The exemplar is 'good news for modern man' (or both good and bad, depending if you are Hitchcock and what you are revealing is an example of voyeurism). The role of art in many modern cultures carries this Christian basis of exemplarity (given the globalization of modernism, one can also find it in the avant-gardes of India, Japan and China). It is the concept of Christ, the moral agent, whose life tells the truth because of its exemplary nature: it is good news for modern man. The good news is not simply what Christ says (his sermons) but what he does (his acts) and what happens to him (what he endures). As Christ is a symbol, his life exemplary, so in the Kantian picture of aesthetics the judgement of the beautiful is exemplary. This is because for Kant the pleasure which leads to that judgement is taken as a symbol of the morally good. When works become exemplars they call forth this kind of judgement, and then a disputation about wherein the truth consists. Similarly when works exemplify bad things – ideology or omnipotence, illusion or degeneration – they too become exemplary, requiring critical discussion of their 'truths'. What Hitchcock shows is that works go both ways at once, requiring both voices.

Truth in art starts in the human gut and works upwards towards the brain. It is a matter of the way the work pressures you into a certain form of experience (Hitchcock, the South African work). One takes that position to be exemplary and to occasion reflection on its meaning. And so the kind of truth occasioned by the object – its sense of being exemplary – transposes itself into another medium which clarifies it, and takes it further. For a work of art to stand as an exemplar is for the audience – South Africans in that example – to understand or glimpse something of its stakes. This intimation of the stakes of the work, of what it is preaching for modern South Africa, is intimately related to the satisfaction one feels (or dissatisfaction!) upon experiencing the work. But it is not yet, necessarily, to be clear about what these stakes are. The art carries the promise of change but the explanation of what this promise is, and how it fits into a larger picture, eludes it. Art is after all not an essay but an object.

Now comes the further work of explicating the truth in the art (the truth in painting). This extra work is the paying back of a debt (Derrida) because the art object provides a sense of profound alteration in society without making it clear. We must now make it clear. The point of the art object is to affect people, to move them with its ideal image of what they might be about. This moving of people (and the satisfaction involved) is like religion, with its prayer and singing, its sense of community and its feeling of exaltation in the presence of 'God'. For this reason Hegel thought art and religion alike as forms of absolute spirit. Now truth in art slides into a related enterprise: truth about its stakes. This is the enterprise of deepening the experience of the art object itself by providing a narrative, a story about its importance, purpose, use of the medium, its historical place. Doris Lessing often said that every artist deeply wants that critic with whom they are at one, meaning the critic who is so deeply within the artist's work that he or she can bring out its message in a way that makes it seem like it was always there. 'That is what I meant, yes, that is what I really wanted to do.' Criticism, the task of the humanities – including philosophical criticism, about a body of work in relation to philosophy – takes the work and provides a story about its truth. The work is, contra Arthur Danto, not yet propositional. Not quite a statement yet, even if yes, it carries a message. For it is above all a doing, whose assemblage of elements into a formal unity is what the critic wants to 'unpack', meaning, to tell a story about, which provides meaning and significance of a kind not present within the work. Having felt the exemplary status of the work, the critic is left with working out what this news is exactly. Here is where thought, that is, reflection, is solicited. This happens not in painting but in a letter to Emile Bernard, in the writings of Barnett Newman, in the history of aesthetics.

You bring from the experience of a work a satisfaction that comes from it. You just have to work out the why and the wherefore! That is where the judgement comes in. That is where it is completed anyway. The judgement is in one sense Kantian: it is the satisfaction itself. In another it is the act of working out the terms of the satisfaction by providing a reading of the truth in the work. This is in effect making truth of its promise, doing something further than is in it, following through the glimpse in the form of letter, essay, public discourse, critical tract. We say that what we write is 'in the work' but only in this dialectical sense that the work occasions our reading of it through the force of its exemplary status, through its vision and promise, through its constructing for you a mode of experience in which such ideas are called to mind, at the time or later.

Any follower of Derrida will distrust these words, 'inside' and 'outside' the work. For reflection also happens during the experience of the work, not simply upon further reflection based in memory and imagination of it. By the time you leave the gallery where this work is shown (the then Trent Read Gallery in Johannesburg, now sadly defunct, the building occupied by an advertising agency) you may have formulated all your critical, philosophical thoughts. As probably Danto did in the five seconds or five days after leaving the

Eleanor Stable Gallery in 1964, from whence uttered his reading of Warhol, his bringing of Warhol to truth, his bringing out of the truth in Warhol. As he saw it, for one can be wrong. There is finally not a lot of evidence to decide this apart from another's experience of the work and sense of whether the words (Danto's) ring true or not. His theory of Warhol is to be decided by reference to the work (to one's experience of it, reading of it) and to his philosophical forms of argument (what you believe about his view of theory, and so on). Danto may well have decided everything in a flash, like artists do. Perhaps Hegel did? Other times the process of reflection and explication of what the truth as experience in painting amounted to comes much later, retrospectively, allowing one to re-imagine experience. As in: Now I realize what I was so taken with in Rome when I first visited as a child! Now I realize what I was so taken with when I first saw that body of art work in South Africa. I knew it meant something, I was unable to understand what at the time.

We may now return to the contradiction with which this concluding chapter opened, about the way art has been approached in aesthetics: on the one hand as a giver of knowledge, on the other a mystic enterprise whose very point consists in its non-conceptual nature. The story I've just told about truth in South African art is meant to suggest that some integration of these viewpoints is required for the understanding of art practice. There is a place for Dewey, and even Kant, in the understanding of the way truth is occasioned by art. Reflection upon art builds on the sense that the work is an exemplar, and an exemplar in virtue of having accomplished something. The sense of accomplishment comes from the depth of experience, and is intimately connected to the satisfaction (or dissatisfaction) one has in that experience. Reflection is demanded by these terms of experience, since one needs to explain what is being exemplified, why it is important, how it connects to art, philosophy and so on. Art is not non-conceptual, but it is less than propositional, if by propositional you mean the kind of story philosophical criticism tells about the work. And so Cézanne can owe the truth in painting even if he has already given it. He owes it *because* he has already given it in the form of a visual promise. What is in the work is what demands a story, and were there not already a kind of truth in the work, no story would be forthcoming. Telling is owed because of *what has already been told*, that is, shown in the forms, details, experience of the work.

Another way to approach this is through Kant. Kant takes formal experience and invests it with exemplary force. Through the free play of our imaginations we are getting in touch, symbolically, meaning indirectly, with our moral selves. Kant's reading of the beautiful per se, as a categorical approach, fails. Some art does this, sometimes, in certain kinds of ways. Some doesn't. But it is a way of reading a big picture or vision through a formal experience and that reading is not irrelevant to the way philosophy reads vision from art and understands it as truth. Kant reads symbolization from aesthetic experience and considers that experience an acknowledgement of something metaphysical about human beings: their moral capacities. How art itself stimulates these visions is the topic Hegel then brings to the fore. It is through the genius that somehow cultural aspiration gets stimulated through the use of a medium, which philosophical aesthetics can then read in its own terms, meaning, take further. At this point, the work of art has done its job of posing truth and philosophy does something else.

But when does philosophy go too far in its readings of Warhol, or South Africa, or Hitchcock, or art considered as a category of thing (as Kant reads it)? Is beauty always the symbol of the morally good or only sometimes? And if so, when and how often, and under whose gaze? How do we decide these matters in the absence of a true judge? By reference to the artist's intentions? Then how are an artist's intentions determined, by what he writes in a letter to Emile Bernard? And what does that letter say exactly? Derrida's genius is to complicate intention in a way that makes it relevant to the understanding of the object but hardly definitive of it. So we are left with the question: when does philosophical aesthetics, in its attempt to attach a big truth to a work of art (much less to art as a category of thing) go too far?

Since no single arbiter can answer such a matter, nor jury, nor club nor art world, nor any other enlightened group, nor expert culture, it is a matter of ongoing public discussion. The reason philosophical aesthetics is not an enterprise categorically distinct from Arts and Letters generally is that the decision is the joint verdict of Arts and Letters. Many critics, speaking from experience and ideology, point of view and intellectual style, will weigh in. The results are, as often as not, indecisive. Truth is central to art, insofar as art, at least in one voice and at least as often as not, aims to be exemplary and raise reflection upon itself and the world. But how much, how far and in what way: these things remain often uncertain. Art thus enters the fray of life, the community of conversation, and lives. Art is in the same boat with morals and politics in this regard. It is a matter of ongoing public debate, of interpretative practices.

The good news is that we should be so lucky to have such debate around truth 'in' art happen at all in the public sphere, in these days of talk show and network news where the arts struggle hysterically to get an appointment, an in, given their exclusion by all except select insider groups. The point of truth occasioned by art is to migrate into the public sphere. Billy Wilder said the mark of a good film is when people can't wait to go have coffee and cake and start talking about it. Were that to become a conversation of public life the point of the work shall be fulfilled, he said, which is not simply entertainment (he was a master of it) but putting life on its head so we may and must think it over. As often as not this dream of art fails. What we owe the art object remains an unpaid debt.

MORE THAN ONE KIND OF TRUTH

Let us state the obvious. There is more than one kind of truth that art may occasion or assert. Derrida points to four different things that could be meant by 'the truth in painting', and one should not think exemplification is the only way a work of art can be taken to be 'true' or 'delivering the truth about something'. Works offer truth through their modes of depiction, whether or not the story or picture depicted calls for the generality of 'an exemplar'. Recently Ian McEwan has written a novel about newlyweds from the middle classes of England, in the early 1960s, 'in a time when a conversation about sexual difficulties was plainly impossible'[9] – this in the opening sentence, setting place, time, theme. It is a story of his radiantly awkward hope and her horror at the act the pair, virgins both, will perform on this, their wedding night. She, a musician of talent, finds sex abhorrent. She struggles to complete what should have been an act of joy in a state of minutely described and highly controlled panic or quiet desperation. She loves him, desires this marriage but simply finds the thing repulsive, a violation. McEwan is a master of miniature in his detailing of her every feeling, reluctance, fantasy, as she herself initiates the physical act against her own will and in its dutiful tide, as we watch her seal her own fate against the tides and eddies of an act she cannot have a way of understanding and a mind (her own) she cannot have the tools to fathom (and therefore, respect). She is like many women in this, women who enter a social bond in a place and time (then, the middle classes) without clear ability to clear their own minds, turning finally to drink or despair, gardening or some other hobby, looking to their children as relief. In this the book aims to be exemplary (up to a point), and its deft movement from close range (the author details story as if positioned just above his and her shoulders) to mid-range (where comments are made of the form – this was a time when . . .). But it is also a book which, like so many novels, resists generality in the interests of this character, this woman, this place and time, this person of flesh, blood and individual quirk. Our involvement with it has to do with its interest in individuals, not (simply) exemplars, or the telling of an exemplary story. This commitment to knowing (through inventing) others, meaning other individuals rather than other exemplars of human aspiration or some other generality, is a defining feature of the novel, among its reasons for being. The novelty in the story, the ability to imagine a world has to do with this.

Film shares the feature: it harps on individual defining physiognomy (Jimmy Stewart's anxious twitch, Greta Garbo's liquid, imploring eyes), animating individual characters, not simply (or perhaps much at all) 'the age and its big Hegelian desires' whatever these might or might not be. One believes McEwan's every instinct about how this woman would react, about her very English (yes, there is exemplarity) attempt to stand it, stiff upper lip as his tongue is in her mouth, about her inner panic, her refusal to 'give in' to whatever is 'wrong' with her, lacking, unable. Everything, it seems, wrong with her, everything, it seems, lacking. One wants to say, McEwan has trued his characters, written with a convincing eye for their truth. This is not always the case. In *Saturday*, his novel about a single day in the life of a London surgeon, a day when, parenthetically, terror has struck London, there are certain plot problems I (and not only I) find highly unconvincing/unbelievable. The main character is a neurosurgeon and on meeting a thug whose car he's bashed, this surgeon immediately diagnoses a complex illness in the thug, without telling him. I don't believe it is very plausible, and there are other things, equally implausible, which follow from this. This means fiction creates its own laws of character but these persuade only if we've a sense of their appropriateness.[10] 'Permission granted', John Cage says, 'but not to do anything you want'. Here the rules are yours to make up, but must also convince as trued to life. This concept of being trued to life in depiction or storytelling is a different one from the concept of truth as exemplarity. For it is about individuals, and the desire, through art, of knowing individuals, other individuals, like ourselves but different, who populate the face of the world, here in fiction, removed from the burdens of direct encounter, studied like bugs under glass. This kind of knowing is not about generality of aspiration, but about individual stories. Which are finally singular because people live not as mere examples for all humanity but as the specific quirky characters they happen to be – each in his or her own way, according to his or her own drummer. Much of what people love about literature (and film) has to do with this quality of singularity in its formal features and also its portrayal of life.

There is also the kind of truth in art that happens through philosophy. When philosophy turns to seeking literary values, when Nietzsche writes as a storyteller or poet, Voltaire as a novelist, or Sartre, it is because they want to stress that philosophers are also particular kinds of characters, motivated by particular kinds of ends, and that these ends have caused a lot of trouble for themselves and others on account of their abstractedness from ordinary human desires, stories, values, embodiment: that which literature is so special at revealing in its fictions. Philosophy wants to restore itself to what literature can offer, renew itself (or end its ways rather than mending them) by showing that it too can live in sensuous form, in the spirit of a way of telling between truth and transcendence, that it too is a character in a drama and a bad one at that, but one who can do better by being something different. This assumption of the mantle of difference proves that philosophy is also within the modern system of the arts, in one respect at least, or sometimes. It too achieves its best self, best picture of knowledge, by turning towards art, just as literature has wanted sometimes to turn towards philosophy, or music, or drama, or painting. Truth is a game that is played within this system of the arts, which includes philosophical aesthetics, which includes philosophy in general. And so if truth in art demands philosophical recounting, failure of truth, or mad truth, in philosophy demands *artistic remaking*. The history of aesthetics goes both ways.

PERSPECTIVISM

How the diverse perspectives of aesthetics might be brought together in understanding is left to the reader of this book. Note this: however creatively these perspectives are integrated, they will always remain partly at odds. No grand synthesis is forthcoming. What is the upshot of this? What does it tell us about aesthetics?

For me, the best advice is given by Bernard Williams, in his discussion about the contradictory moral ideas we the present have inherited.[11] We have inherited ideas of utilitarianism, of duty, of following the moral law, of altruism and personal liberty, of always doing the right thing and also realizing that sometimes we have to put the quest or the cause to one side and live our lives in whatever ways their aesthetics call forth. These ideas are all important, and they often fall into contradiction. It would be wrong to deny that they don't all make sense, that each has its merits. For Williams morals are a matter of steering between these competing, and sometimes contradictory positions with the greatest integrity.

Williams is thinking a Nietzschean thought here, a thought about the importance of perspectivism, of assuming multiple perspectives on things, none of which is either proved true (in some absolute sense, excluding the others) or definitive, but brought in contextually, as a way of understanding this particular situation we are now in.

I think the legacy of aesthetics is similar. Aesthetics is a set of discourses we have inherited and the key is to make the best use of our inheritance. To preserve it, make it live in whatever ways it is best able to do. This does not mean one should believe everything, an absurd, debilitating, finally insulting remark. It means that appropriation of 'the wisdom of the ancients' as Montaigne would put it, matters as much as taking the next philosophical step in this web of approaches found throughout the Arts and Letters. Sometimes art calls for a formalist picture, as in certain kinds of abstract music, other times a picture of human aspiration and the giving of truth. More often than not it is a combination of positions which only as a whole, works. Few if any works are nothing but formalist, if only because they are gestures given by an artist to a world, and contain his or her imprint, as well as the imprint of place, time, context, institution, society. And yet form is always at issue, sometimes more centrally than other times. Certain works are didactic (Brecht), and need to be understood, judged, in that light. Taste is more central for some perspectives on art, and for some kinds of art, than other times. Sometimes we want to see where a work fits into a social whole, other times it is purely about whether it appeals to us. To relinquish on one or another of these positions would be to lessen the practice of art, and of aesthetics.

The real problem with the history of definition in aesthetics is that in each and every case, the richness of our experience of art, and aesthetics practices, is thereby lessened by the definition, which, were it accepted, would strait-jacket our experience and discourse about art in unacceptable ways. We have so many positions in aesthetics because the subject demands them: art and the experiences, conversations and institutions in which it variously happens and remains. Rather than seeking to reconcile contradictory positions into a grand, new theory about art, we should understand that first, these positions are contradictory because they took the form of restrictive definitions of the subject and only for that reason, and second, because the subject is one which admits of many different ways of approaching it, each of which has, to a greater or lesser degree, its merits in context. Art practice involves moving between a number of different points of view, like the moving camera in a film.

Each point of view is as it is because of its relation to the others. What I mean by this is that truth in art has the form it has because the arts are also entities which refuse truth, seeking transcendence and poetic untranslatability. This casts truth in a seductive aura, and can generate illusion, cult, mass politics and religion. It also allows truth to arise in idealized Hegelian form, and as the thing which philosophy must bring to light in its own ways.

One thing is therefore sure: art and aesthetics are joined at the hip insofar as art offers truth, which aesthetics then tells a story about, making a new kind of truth – and insofar as a philosophy requires remaking through art. Art and aesthetics are also joined because insofar as art resists the game of truth-giving, instead preferring to cast its gestures in a mystic space of the non-conceptual, aesthetics *protects* that space (this is what formalism is about). All these dimensions to aesthetics are critical. The reader may be given this advice: find a way to use them all.

NOTES

CHAPTER 1

1 Kelly, Michael, ed., *Encyclopedia of Aesthetics* (Oxford: New York, 1998).
2 Wittgenstein, Ludwig, *Philosophical Investigations*, tr. Elizabeth Anscombe (Macmillan: New York, 1968), #66, 67.

CHAPTER 2

1 Cf. Steiner, George, *The Death of Tragedy* (Hill and Wang Publishers: New York, 1968), and Lambropoulos, Vassilis, *The Tragic Idea* (Duckworth: London, 2006), for discussions of the history of this subject and its legacy in modern times.
2 Kelly, Michael, *Iconoclasm in Aesthetics* (Cambridge University Press: New York, 2003).
3 Aristotle, *Poetics*, tr. Stephen Halliwell, with introduction (Duckworth: London, 1998).
4 Nietzsche, Friedrich, 'The Case of Wagner', in *Basic Writings of Nietzsche*, tr. Walter Kaufmann, (Modern Library: New York, 1992).
5 See Foucault, Michel, *The Order of Things* (Vintage: New York, 1970); and *Discipline and Punish* (Vintage: New York, 1979).
6 Kivy, Peter, *The Seventh Sense* (Burt Franklin and Co: New York, 1976).
7 Guyer, Paul, 'The Origin of Modern Aesthetics: 1711–1735', in *The Blackwell Guide to Aesthetics*, ed. Peter Kivy (Blackwell: Oxford, 2004), pp. 15–44.
8 Ibid., pp. 32–5.

CHAPTER 3

1 Hume, David, 'Of Tragedy', from *Selected Essays*, ed. Stephen Copley and Andrew Edgar (Oxford, The Clarendon Press: Oxford and London, 1998) p. 127.

2 Hume, David, *Treatise of Human Nature*, ed. David and Mary Norton (Oxford University Press: Oxford and London, 2002), p. 316.
3 Hume, David, 'Of the Delicacy of Taste and Passion', *Selected Essays*, p. 11.
4 Ibid., p. 10.
5 Ibid.
6 Hume, David, 'Of the Standard of Taste', ibid., p. 136.
7 Ibid., p. 137.
8 Cohen, Ted, 'The Philosophy of Taste', in *The Blackwell Guide to Aesthetics*, ed. Peter Kivy (Blackwell: Oxford, 2004), p. 170.
9 Hume, David, 'Of the Standard of Taste', *Selected Essays*, p. 147.
10 Ibid., p. 141.
11 Goehr, Lydia, *The Imaginary Museum of Musical Works* (Oxford University Press: Oxford and London, 1994).
12 See selections by both of these philosophers in Goldblatt, David and Brown, Lee, *Aesthetics: A Reader in Philosophy of the Arts* (Prentice Hall: New Jersey, 1997).
13 Kant, Immanuel, *Critique of Judgment*, tr. J. H. Bernard (Haffner Press: New York, 1951).
14 Meyer, Leonard, *Emotion and Meaning in Music* (University of Chicago Press: Chicago and London, 1956).
15 Meyer, Leonard, *Music, the Arts and Ideas* (University of Chicago Press: Chicago and London, 1994).
16 Schiller, Friedrich, *Letters on the Aesthetic Education of Man*, tr. Elizabeth Wilkinson and L. A. Willoughby (The Clarendon Press: Oxford, 1982).
17 The significant writers in this area are Theodor Adorno, Walter Benjamin, Georg Lukacs, Bertolt Brecht, and Ernst Bloch. For a book of their debates, see Ronald Taylor, ed. and tr., *Aesthetics and Politics*, with an afterword by Fredric Jameson (New Left Books: London, 1977).

CHAPTER 4

1 Hanslick, Eduard, *On the Musically Beautiful*, tr. Geoffrey Payzant (Hackett: Indianapolis, 1986).
2 Hegel, G. W. F., *Aesthetics: Lectures on Fine Art*, tr. T. M. Knox (The Clarendon Press: Oxford, 1975), p. 31.
3 Ibid.
4 Ibid., p. 32.
5 Cf. for example White, Hayden, *The Content of the Form* (Johns Hopkins University Press: Baltimore, 1987).
6 Collingwood, R. G., *The Principles of Art* (Oxford University Press: Oxford, 1958).
7 Kivy, Peter, *The Chorded Shell: Reflections on Musical Expression* (Princeton University Press: Princeton, 1980).
8 Dewey, John, *Art as Experience* (Paragon Books: New York, 1959).
9 Ibid., p. 35.

10 Ibid., p. 36.
11 Ibid., p. 40.
12 Ibid., p. 54.
13 Steinberg, Leo, 'The Philosophical Brothel', *October 25* (MIT Press: Boston, 1983).
14 Wollheim, Richard, *Painting as an Art* (Bollingen Series, Princeton University Press: Princeton, 1987), p. 8.
15 Ibid., pp. 8–9.
16 See Kierkegaard, Soren, *Either/Or, Part I*, tr. David Swenson and Lillian Swenson (Princeton University Press: Princeton, 1944).
17 For a discussion of this opera in its vast legacy, see Goehr, Lydia and Herwitz, Daniel, eds *The Don Giovanni Moment* (Columbia University Press: New York and London, 2006).
18 Baxandall, Michael, *Painting and Experience in Fifteenth-Century Italy* (Oxford University Press: Oxford and New York, 1972).
19 Clark, T. J., *The Painting of Modern Life* (Princeton University Press: Princeton, 1984); and Clark, T. J., *Farewell to an Idea* (Yale University Press: New Haven and London, 1999).
20 Clark, T. J., *The Painting of Modern Life*; and Benjamin, Walter, *The Arcades Project*, tr. Howard Eiland and Kevin McLaughlin (Harvard University Press: Cambridge and London, 1999).
21 Clark says *Olympia* is a sign of the opaque bourgeois class itself with its own commodified visions of self and society.

CHAPTER 5

1 This comes from his unpublished PhD thesis, and many conversations over many years, for which I am grateful.
2 Greenberg, Clement, 'Avant-Garde and Kitsch', in *Art and Culture* (Beacon Press: Boston, 1961).
3 Greenberg, Clement, 'The New Sculpture', ibid.
4 For a discussion of the role of theory in avant-garde art see Herwitz, Daniel, *Making Theory/Constructing Art* (Chicago University Press: Chicago and London, 1993).
5 Ibid.
6 The locus classicus of his theory is Danto, Arthur, *The Transfiguration of the Commonplace* (Harvard University Press, Cambridge and London, 1981).
7 Danto, Arthur, *After the End of Art, Contemporary Art and the Pale of History* (Princeton University Press: Princeton, 1997), p. 165.
8 For a discussion of the role of theory in the avant-gardes, and of Danto's views in detail, see my *Making Theory/Constructing Art*.
9 Lyotard, Jean-Francois, *The Postmodern Condition: A Report on Knowledge*, tr. Geoff Bennington and Brian Massumi (University of Minnesota Press: Minneapolis and London, 1979).
10 Herwitz, Daniel, *Making Theory/Constructing Art*, especially chapters 6 and 7.

11 Panofsky, Erwin, 'Style and Medium in the Moving Pictures', 1934, rewritten 1947, reprinted in *Film Theory and Criticism*, 6th edn, eds Leo Braudy and Marshall Cohen (Oxford University Press: New York, 2004), pp. 289–302.

12 Panofsky reduced the screenplay to something that could be whatever it wanted so long as it did not dominate visual effects. This he called 'the principle of co-expressibility'. Where dialogue is in danger of dominating, something visual happens to match its importance, often a close-up. Panofsky's particular way of thinking this through does not do justice to the screenplay, which is not the 'junior partner' in a movie, kept in check visually in case it should assert itself too much. The meanings found in the screenplay are generative for everything that happens. Co-expressibility is right insofar as the movie must never become too 'talky'. However, a better model for thinking of the relationship between screenplay and camera is one of mutual generativity within a complex system. The screenplay is written – sometimes adapted from a documentary, work of history, short story, novel, play – with a visual realization in mind. Flow, rhythm, character, plot are all imagined with the screen in mind, often with particular actors, actresses and locations. Equally important, a sound film synergizes visual rhythm with sound rhythm, sound becomes central to physiognomy. The medium of sound film is not simply visual reality as such; it is also sound.

13 Ibid., p. 302.

14 See note 1 above.

15 Cavell, Stanley, *The World Viewed* (Harvard University Press: Cambridge and London, 1979).

16 Ibid., p. 23.

17 Walton, Kendall, 'Transparent Pictures', *Critical Inquiry*, II: 2, 1984, p. 251.

18 Walton, Kendall, 'On Pictures and Photographs: Objections Answered', in *Film Theory and Philosophy*, ed. Richard Allen and Murray Smith (Oxford University Press: New York and Oxford, 2003), p. 60.

19 Walton, 'Transparent Pictures', p. 253.

20 In formulating this I am hugely helped by my student, Everett Kramer.

21 Wittgenstein, *Philosophical Investigations*, #122.

22 Wollheim, *Art and Its Objects* (Cambridge University Press: Cambridge and London, 1968), pp. 110–11.

23 Wittgenstein, *Philosophical Investigations*, #610.

24 Malick translated Heidegger's *Essence of Reasons* after completing a PhD in philosophy at Berkeley.

CHAPTER 6

1 Cf. Lacan, Jacques, *Ecrits*, tr. Alan Sheriden (Norton: New York, 1977).

2 Mulvey, Laura, 'Visual Pleasure and Narrative Cinema', *Screen*, 16:3 (1975).

3 Zizek, Slavoj, *Everything You Always Wanted to Know about Lacan but Were Afraid to Ask Hitchcock* (New Left Books: New York, 1992).
4 Derrida, Jacques, *The Truth in Painting*, tr. Geoff Bennington and Ian McCleod (Chicago University Press: Chicago and London, 1987), in particular the opening section, *Passe-Partout*, pp. 1–17.
5 Derrida, Jacques, ibid., p. 3.
6 Ibid. I have changed Derrida's use of capitalized letters when he cites Cézanne's words, and also his arrangement of sentences on the page of his book.
7 Ibid., p. 8.
8 A publication ensued: See Sack, Steven; *The Neglected Tradition* (Johannesburg Art Gallery: Johanneburg, 1988
9 McEwan, Ian, *On Chesil Beach* (Nan Talese, Doubleday: New York, 2007), p. 3.
10 For an excellent discussion of such matters of fictional truth see Walton, Kendall, *Mimesis and Make Believe* (Harvard University Press: Cambridge and London, 2004).
11 Cf. Williams, Bernard, *Morality: An Introduction to Ethics* (Harper and Row: New York, 1972); and *Moral Luck* (Cambridge University Press: New York, 1981).

BIBLIOGRAPHY AND GUIDE TO FURTHER READING

INTRODUCTION AND BIRTH OF AESTHETICS

Aristotle, *Poetics*, tr. Stephen Halliwell, with introduction (Duckworth: London, 1998).

Foucault, Michel, *The Order of Things* (Vintage: New York, 1970), about the context in which modern aesthetics is born as an object of study of the human subject.

Foucault, Michel, *Discipline and Punish* (Vintage: New York, 1979).

Kelly, Michael, ed., *Encyclopedia of Aesthetics* (Oxford University Press: New York, 1998).

Kelly, Michael, *Iconoclasm in Aesthetics* (Cambridge University Press: New York, 2003).

Kivy, Peter, *The Seventh Sense* (Burt Franklin and Co.: New York, 1976).

Lambropoulos, Vassilis, *The Tragic Idea* (Duckworth: London, 2006).

Montaigne, *The Complete Essays of Montaigne*, tr. Donald Frame, (Stanford University Press: Stanford, 1943).

Nehamas, Alexander, *Nietzsche: Life as Literature* (Harvard University Press: Cambridge and London, 1985).

Nehamas, Alexander, *The Art of Living* (California University Press: Berkeley and London: 1998).

Nietzsche, Friedrich, 'The Case of Wagner', in *Basic Writings of Nietzsche*, tr. Walter Kaufmann (Modern Library: New York, 1992).

Plato, *Complete Works*, ed. John Cooper (Hackett: Indianapolis, 1997), especially *Ion*.

Steiner, George, *The Death of Tragedy* (Hill and Wang Publishers: New York, 1968).

Sartre, Jean-Paul, *Nausea*, tr. Hayden Carruth and Lloyd Alexander (New Directions: New York, 1964).

Voltaire, *Candide*, tr. John Butt (Penguin: New York, 1947).

Wittgenstein, Ludwig, *Philosophical Investigations*, tr. Elizabeth Anscombe (Macmillan: New York, 1968).

TASTE AND AESTHETIC JUDGEMENT

Dickie, Sclafani and Roblin; *Aesthetics* (St Martin's Press: London, 1989). Wide range of essays on taste, pleasure, the aesthetic attitude and other topics.

Goehr, Lydia, *The Imaginary Museum of Musical Works* (Oxford University Press: Oxford and London, 1994). A discussion of musical concepts which locates them in musical practice.

Goldblatt, David and Brown, Lee; *Aesthetics: A Reader in Philosophy of the Arts* (Prentice Hall: New Jersey, 1997). For discussions of the various arts including discussions of popular arts.

Guyer, Paul, *Kant and the Claims of Taste* (Cambridge University Press: New York, 1997).

Hume, David, *Treatise of Human Nature*, ed. David and Mary Norton (Oxford University Press: Oxford and London, 2002).

Hume, David, 'Of the Standard of Taste', 'Of Tragedy', and 'Of the Delicacy of Taste and Passion' from *Selected Essays*, ed. Stephen Copley and Andrew Edgar (The Clarendon Press: Oxford and London, 1998).

Kant, Immanuel, *Critique of Judgment*, tr. J. H. Bernard (Haffner Press: New York, 1951).

Kivy, Peter, ed., *The Blackwell Guide to Aesthetics*, (Blackwell: Oxford, 2004), especially essays by Cohen, Ted, 'The Philosophy of Taste', and Guyer, Paul, 'The Origin of Modern Aesthetics: 1711–1735'.

Meyer, Leonard, *Emotion and Meaning in Music* (University of Chicago Press: Chicago and London, 1956). A book which seeks to analyse the goal-oriented experience of musical form.

Meyer, Leonard, *Music, the Arts and Ideas* (University of Chicago Press: Chicago and London, 1994).

Rosen, Charles, *The Classical Style: Haydn, Beethoven and Mozart* (W. W. Norton and Company: New York, 1998). About music as a practice and the way style should be understood in its light.

Savile, Anthony, *The Test of Time: An Essay in Philosophical Aesthetics* (Oxford University Press: Oxford, 1985).

Schiller, Friedrich, *Letters on the Aesthetic Education of Man*, tr. Elizabeth Wilkinson and L. A. Willoughby (The Clarendon Press: Oxford, 1982).

Schaper, Eva, ed., *Pleasure, Preference, Value: Studies in Philosophical Aesthetics* (Cambridge University Press: Cambridge, 1983).

Taylor, Ronald, ed. and tr., *Aesthetics and Politics*, with an afterword by Fredric Jameson (New Left Books: London, 1977). Especially essays on aesthetics and politics by Theodor Adorno, Walter Benjamin, Georg Lukacs, Bertolt Brecht, and Ernst Bloch. About the politicization of the sublime.

ART AND EXPERIENCE

Baxandall, Michael, *Painting and Experience in Fifteenth-Century Italy* (Oxford University Press: Oxford and New York, 1972). Classic art historical book on the social nature of Renaissance aesthetics.

Benjamin, Walter, *The Arcades Project*, tr. Howard Eiland and Kevin McLaughlin (Harvard University Press: Cambridge and London, 1999). About the space of Parisian modernity in which modern art finds its home.

Bell, Clive, *Art* (Capricorn Books: New York, 1958). Looks at formalism in painting.

Clark, T. J., *The Painting of Modern Life* (Princeton University Press: Princeton, 1984). Following Benjamin, the social stakes of Parisian modern painting.

Clark, T. J., *Farewell to an Idea* (Yale University Press: New Haven and London, 1999). The importance of politics for modern art.

Collingwood, R. G., *The Principles of Art* (Oxford University Press: Oxford, 1958).

Dewey, John, *Art as Experience* (Paragon Books: New York, 1959).

Fry, Roger, *Vision and Design* (Meridian Books: New York, 1960).

Goehr, Lydia and Herwitz, Daniel, ed., *The Don Giovanni Moment* (Columbia University Press: New York and London, 2006). On the medium of opera.

Hanslick, Eduard, *On the Musically Beautiful*, tr. Geoffrey Payzant (Hackett: Indianapolis, 1986). Formalism in music.

Hegel, G. W. F., *Aesthetics: Lectures on Fine Art*, tr. T. M. Knox (The Clarendon Press: Oxford, 1975).

Judin, Hilton and Vladislavic, Ivan, *Blank: Art, Apartheid and After* (RAI: Rotterdam, 1999). Essays, writings, architecture addressed to the post-apartheid moment in South Africa.

Kierkegaard, Soren, *Either/Or; Part I*, tr. David Swenson and Lillian Swenson (Princeton University Press: Princeton, 1944). On the medium of opera.

Kivy, Peter, *The Chorded Shell: Reflections on Musical Expression* (Princeton University Press: Princeton, 1980).

Steinberg, Leo, 'The Philosophical Brothel', *October 25* (MIT Press: Boston, 1983).

White, Hayden, *The Content of the Form* (Johns Hopkins University Press: Baltimore, 1987).

Wollheim, Richard, *Painting as an Art* (Bollingen Series, Princeton University Press: Princeton, 1987).

Wollheim, Richard, *Art and Its Objects* (Cambridge University Press: Cambridge and London, 1968).

Wollheim, Richard; *Art and the Mind* (Harvard University Press: Cambridge and London, 1974).

MODERN DEFINITIONS OF ART AND THE PROBLEM OF NEW MEDIA

Benjamin, Andrew, ed., *The Lyotard Reader* (Blackwell: Oxford, 1989). Lyotard on the sublime and the avant-gardes.

Bordwell, David and Carroll, Noel, ed., *Post-Theory: Reconstructing Film Studies* (University of Wisconsin Press: Madison, 1996). For a position on film studies sceptical of film theory.

Braudy, Leo and Cohen, Marshall, ed., *Film Theory and Criticism*, 6th edn (Oxford University Press, New York and Oxford, 2004). Contains Panofsky essay and many articles on film as a medium.

Cavell, Stanley, *The World Viewed* (Harvard University Press: Cambridge and London, 1979).

Danto, Arthur, *The Transfiguration of the Commonplace* (Harvard University Press: Cambridge and London, 1981).

Danto, Arthur; *After the End of Art, Contemporary Art and the Pale of History* (Princeton University Press: Princeton, 1997).

Danto, Arthur, *Beyond the Brillo Box* (Farrar, Straus, Giroux: New York, 1992). Award winning book of art criticism by Danto.

Greenberg, Clement; 'Avant-Garde and Kitsch', 'The New Sculpture'; in *Art and Culture* (Beacon Press: Boston, 1961).

Herwitz, Daniel; *Making Theory/Constructing Art* (Chicago University Press: Chicago and London, 1993).

Herwitz, Daniel and Kelly, Michael, *Action, Art, History: Engagements with Arthur Danto* (Columbia University Press: New York, 2007).

Kracauer, Siegfried, *Theory of Film: The Redemption of Physical Reality* (Princeton University Press: Princeton, 1960). With an excellent introduction by Miriam Hansen, who also edited this volume.

Lyotard, Jean-Francois, *The Postmodern Condition: A Report on Knowledge*, tr. Geoff Bennington and Brian Massumi (University of Minnesota Press: Minneapolis and London, 1979). On the politics of the sublime in modern culture.

Nichols, Bill, ed., *Movies and Methods, Volume 1 and Volume 2* (California University Press: Berkeley, 1976). Another excellent compilation of essays and excerpts on film as a medium.

Rosen, Philip, ed., *Narrative, Apparatus, Ideology* (Columbia University Press: New York, 1986). Essays and excerpts in film theory.

Walton, Kendall, 'On Pictures and Photographs: Objections Answered', in *Film Theory and Philosophy*, ed. Richard Allen and Murray Smith (Oxford University Press: New York and Oxford, 2003). Walton's original paper on this subject was 'Transparent Pictures', *Critical Inquiry*, II: 2, 1984.

CONCLUSION: ART AND TRUTH

Derrida, Jacques, *The Truth in Painting*, tr. Geoff Bennington and Ian McCleod (Chicago University Press: Chicago and London, 1987).

Derrida, Jacques, *Acts of Literature*, tr. Derek Attridge (Routledge: New York, 1992).

Foucault, *This is Not a Pipe*, tr. James Harkness (Quantum Books: New York, 1983).

Heidegger, Martin, *Poetry, Language, Thought*, tr. Hofstadter (Harper and Row: New York, 1975), for discussions of truth put to work in art.

Lacan, Jacques, *Ecrits*, tr. Alan Sheriden (Norton: New York, 1977).

Mulvey, Laura; 'Visual Pleasure and Narrative Cinema', *Screen*, 16:3 (1975).

Walton, Kendall, *Mimesis and Make Believe* (Harvard University Press: Cambridge and London, 2004).

Williams, Bernard, *Morality: An Introduction to Ethics* (Harper and Row: New York, 1972).

Williams, Bernard, *Moral Luck* (Cambridge: New York, 1981).

Zizek, Slavoj, *Everything You Always Wanted to Know about Lacan but Were Afraid to Ask Hitchcock* (New Left Books: New York, 1992).

INDEX